Small Group Learning in Higher Education

Research and Practice

Edited by James L. Cooper & Pamela Robinson

Stillwater, Oklahoma
U.S.A.

NEW FORUMS PRESS INC.

Published in the United States of America
by New Forums Press, Inc. 1018 S. Lewis St.
Stillwater, OK 74074
www.newforums.com

Copyright © 2011 by New Forums Press, Inc.

All rights reserved. No part of this publication may be reproduced or transmitted in any form or by any means, electronic or mechanical, including photocopy, or any information storage or retrieval system, without permission in writing from the publisher.

Library of Congress Cataloging-in-Publication Data Pending

This book may be ordered in bulk quantities at discount from New Forums Press, Inc., P.O. Box 876, Stillwater, OK 74076 [Federal I.D. No. 73 1123239]. Printed in the United States of America.

ISBN 10: 1-58107-204-X
ISBN 13: 978-1-581072-04-4

Contents

A Note from Jim Cooper and Pamela Robinson v

Part I: Making the Case for Small Group Learning 1
Preparing Students for an Interdependent World: The Role of Cooperation
    and Social Interdependence Theory 3
    Karl A. Smith
Cooperative Learning: Relationships Among Theory, Research and Practice 10
    David W. Johnson and Roger T. Johnson
An Instructional Revolution for Higher Education: Rationale and Proposed Methods 19
    Spencer Kagan
Promoting Deep Learning Through Cooperative Learning 25
    Barbara J. Millis
The Case and Context for Cooperative Learning 31
    Joe Cuseo

Part II: Implementation of Small Group Techniques 41
Lectures: Their Place and Purpose 43
    Joseph Cuseo
Problems with Lecturing 44
    David W. Johnson, Roger T. Johnson and Karl A. Smith
Lecturing with Informal Cooperative-learning Groups 46
    David W. Johnson, Roger T. Johnson and Karl A. Smith
Using Assessment to Improve Cooperative Learning 47
    Thomas A. Angelo
Practice Activities and Your Textbook 50
    Susan Prescott Johnston
Trouble-Shooting 52
    Susan Prescott Johnston
Cooperative Poster Presentations 55
    Rose Ann Swartz
Teams of Four are Magic! 57
    Spencer Kagan
Increasing Thinking Through Cooperative Writing 59
    Barbara J. Millis
Using Group Investigation to Enhance Arab-Jewish Relationships 62
    Rachel Hertz-Lazarowitz

Part III: Small Group Learning Within the Disciplines 65
Cooperative Learning and American History 67
    Deborah Dentler
Cooperative Learning Structures to Foster Student Involvement 72
    Elaine M. Aschettino
How Chemistry ConcepTests Are Used 74
    Jim Cooper
ESL Students and the Cooperative College Classroom 78
    Kate Kinsella and Kathy Sherak
Learning Techniques and the Basic Writer 84
    Wendy Slobodnik

College Writing and Cooperative Learning: Implications for Writing Across the Curriculum 86
    Joseph B. Cuseo
Cooperative Learning in a Sequence of Engineering Courses: A Success Story 89
    Richard M. Felder
Jeopardy 305: A Cooperative Learning Method for Teaching History and Systems of Psychology 93
    Lisa Gray-Shelberg
Classroom-Tested Collaborative Learning Tasks 96
    Edwina Stoll, Barbara Illowsky, Jim Luotto, John Swensson, and Sally Wood
Cooperative-learning Teams to Establish "International Connections" 102
    Rose Ann Swartz

Part IV: Applications of Small Group Work and a Look to the Future 107
Five Must-Know Kagan Structures for Higher Education 109
    Spencer Kagan and Miguel Kagan
Constructive Controversy: Energizing Learning 114
    David W. Johnson and Roger T. Johnson
The Missing Link: Planning for Student Engagement 122
    Susan Johnston
Faculty Learning Communities as Catalysts for Implementing Successful Small Group Learning 130
    Cynthia G. Desrochers
Cooperative Learning and Disciple-Based Pedagogical Innovations:
    Taking Advantage of Complementarities 139
    Mark Maier, KimMarie McGoldrick and Scott Simkins
The Value of Interaction Treatments in Distance and Online Learning 150
    Rana M. Tamim, Robert M. Bernard, Eugene Borokhovski and Philip C. Abrami
Intellectual Exploration Together 158
    Donald Bligh

A Note from Jim Cooper and Pamela Robinson

This text is our second publication that draws on work that first appeared in *Cooperative Learning and College Teaching*, the newsletter that was published from 1990 to 1999. After we stepped down as Editor and Associate Editor, demand for work in research-based small group research and practice continued in higher education. To meet that need, in 2003 we co-edited a text entitled *Small Group Instruction in Higher Education: Lessons From the Past, Visions of the Future*. As with the current volume, it consisted of articles first published in the newsletter and new chapters solicited from leaders in active and small group learning in higher education. Friends and colleagues, such as Barbara Millis, Spencer Kagan, David and Roger Johnson, Mark Maier and Susan Johnston, contributed original chapters to that volume. A second edition of the 2003 book was published in 2009. It contained a new chapter in which we surveyed national leaders in teaching and learning concerning a variety of issues relating to small group learning.

Interest in small group teaching and learning has continued to grow since the 2003 volume. For that reason we decided to offer a second volume of edited work, much of which reflects this growth in research and practice. The reprinted newsletter articles in this current book are largely work of an applied nature that continues to have relevancy. The new chapters' authors include the Johnsons, Spencer Kagan, Joe Cuseo, Barbara Millis, Cynthia Desrochers, Susan Prescott Johnston, Karl Smith and Mark Maier. Much of their work has taken place both in and outside the U.S. along with chapter contributors Donald Bligh (England), and Philip Abrami (Canada). As with the 2003 book, we hope this volume will stimulate dialog and encourage innovation in higher education research, theory and practice.

Organization of Book

This book is organized into four parts. Part I consists of five new chapters that make the case for the importance of small group work. These chapters include work speaking to the needs of society for the skills fostered by small group work—skills often not developed by more traditional forms of teacher centered pedagogy that still dominates most classroom practice in higher education. Both empirical and theoretical arguments are made for using small group instruction in higher education, based on recent work in such areas as deep learning/critical thinking, social interdepence theory and brain research.

Part II addresses general implementation issues in small group instruction, including advice for good practice from many national leaders in small group instruction. The articles that appear in Part II were first printed in *Cooperative Learning and College Teaching*. It should be noted that material in Parts II and III do not contain reference sections due to an editorial policy in place when the newsletter was published.

Part III contains articles focusing on applications of small group instruction within the disciplines. They were also first published in *Cooperative Learning and College Teaching* and describe applications to such disciplines as journalism, writing, science and mathematics, history, engineering, psychology, business and English as a second language.

Part IV contains additional chapters written just for this book. They address recent work in applying small group instruction to practice—much of it developed since the 2003 book was published. Faculty learning communities, distance education, and synergies between cooperative learning and other cutting edge pedagogies are treated. The book's final chapter includes an interesting discussion of how we should explore new ideas, even those that may be partially formed. The author challenges the notion that only fully formed work should be presented at conferences and in written outlets such as journals and texts.

We elected to give authors considerable flexibility in formatting their work. Thus there are differences in the voice of the authors from article to article and chapter to chapter and in the formatting of references and other technical issues.

We feel that the collective voices of our authors make a compelling case for the power of small group learning in higher education as we face the challenges of preparing students for an increasingly interdependent world.

Part I
Making the Case for Small Group Learning

In this first portion of the book, five new chapters are presented, written specifically for this volume. The first is by Karl Smith, an engineer by training, in which he addresses not only the importance of skills fostered by cooperative learning within engineering, but also the skills needed in business and, ultimately, in an increasingly interdependent world. In the next chapter, David and Roger Johnson also focus on interdependence as a theoretical and empirical framework for using cooperative learning in our schools and universities. The Johnsons list a number of outcomes known to be linked to the use of cooperative learning, including important attitudinal and cognitive variables. They also provide the historical context for cooperative learning, including the landmark work of Lewin, Dewey and Deutsch.

Spencer Kagan's chapter, the third in Part I, builds on the importance of preparing students for the 21st century and notes how brain research and other recent developments in research and theory are consistent with the principles of good practice embodied in cooperative learning. He compares traditional forms of education and how these techniques fail to prepare our students for the challenges of the workplace.

Barbara Millis cites recent cutting edge research to support her call for cooperative learning. She focuses on deep learning and how small group instruction (in sharp contrast to traditional forms of instruction) can result in deep learning, versus the surface learning promoted in most existing teaching paradigms. Both Millis and Kagan offer examples of cooperative learning procedures designed to promote higher order thinking.

In the fifth chapter, Joe Cuseo develops the notion of moving from a teacher centered to a student centered approach to instruction, articulated by Barr and Tagg in the 1970s. He identifies seven procedural elements of effective cooperative learning and how these procedures can be used to develop powerful learning experiences for college students.

All five chapters in this section have somewhat different research and theory foci, from social interdependence to brain research to deep learning findings to student centered work. Yet, there is a reassuring convergence from these well documented scholarly traditions pointing to small group instruction as the most powerful pedagogy available to practitioners in higher education.

Preparing Students for an Interdependent World: The Role of Cooperation and Social Interdependence Theory

Karl A. Smith

State of the World

The world is changing and we are facing many global challenges, including poverty, education, health, innovation, climate change, human rights, resource availability and utilization. These concerns are not new; they have been documented for decades by organizations such as the Worldwatch Institute, whose annual publication, *State of the World* articulates our interdependence. Until recently the predominant design approach used in engineering was "cradle to grave" and most things were designed to be thrown away. The concept of "away" was described in an interesting way as the "toilet assumption" by Bennis and Slater (1968) in their book *The Temporary Society*.

There is a significant rise in international collaborations around education and especially research. The Global Colloquiums on Engineering Education is one effort to bring people together to address global issues and opportunities. Furthermore, the engineering design paradigm is slowing, changing from "cradle to grave" to "cradle to cradle." The idea of "cradle to cradle" was developed and championed by the international collaboration of Michael Braungart, a German chemist, and William McDonough, a U.S. architect (McDonough & Braungart, 2002).

The term global, popularized by writers such as Thomas Friedman, shows up in many conversations about engineering and engineering education as well as in prospective outcomes for engineering graduates. The notion of global first became clear to me and many of my generation on December 24, 1968 when Apollo 8 circumnavigated the moon. As the image of the earthrise was transmitted and showed up on TV screens around the world, CBS News Commentator Walter Cronkite said:

> I think that picture of the earthrise over the moon's horizon, that blue disk out there in space, floating alone in the darkness, the utter black of space, had the effect of impressing on all of us our loneliness out here. The fact that we seem to be the only spot where anything like humans could be living. And it, the major impression I think it made on most of us was the fact, how ridiculous it is that we have this difficulty getting along on this little lifeboat of ours floating out there in space, and the necessity of our understanding each other and of the brotherhood of humankind on this floating island of ours, made a great impression, I think, on everybody.

This was an extremely poignant and defining moment for me, although I didn't recognize and fully appreciate it at the time. You can see the Cronkite segment and read more about what was described as his A Call for Harmony on Lifeboat Earth on the American Experience program on Apollo 8 (PBS American Experience, 2008).

Recently several world leaders, such as former British Prime Minister Gordon Brown, called for global interdependence aimed at solving international problems, such as terrorism, poverty, and climate change (Lavoie, 2008). During his talk at the John F. Kennedy Presidential Library and Museum in April, 2008, Brown said "We urgently need to step out of the mindset of competing interests and instead find our common interests." Tom Boyle of British Telecom described our current era as the "age of interdependence" and he argued that Network Quotient (NQ) is more important than IQ (Cohen & Prusak, 2001). *The World is Flat* author Tom Friedman (2007) argues that we have to move to a more horizontal–connect and collaborate–value-creation model. Friedman argues that Curiosity Quotient (CQ) plus Passion Quotient (PQ) is more important than Intelligence Quotient (IQ). John Seely Brown, former Chief Scientist of Xerox and Director of its Palo Alto Research Center (PARC) argues that social/emotional intelligence (EQ) and communication intelligence (CQ) are equally as or more important than IQ (Brown & Adler, 2008; Brown, 2008). If, as these pundits claim, interdependence is the current coin of the realm, then what can we do to help prepare students for an interdependent world? What are the skills and competencies that students need and how can we ensure that they gain these skills and competencies?

Before proceeding too far down the collaboration path, let me reassure those who argue that competition is the be all and end all that I agree there is a role for competition and we have an obligation to help develop students' skills for competing. There are several occasions where competition is the norm; sports contests, of course, are the most common, but there is also proposals and hiring. My sense is that we've emphasized competition far more than cooperation and haven't helped students develop skills for cooperating. Buckminster Fuller argued that "cooperation is pragmatically necessary" and W. Edwards Deming (1993) made the following compelling case for the importance of cooperation and interdependence in his book *The New Economics for Industry, Government, Education:*

> We have grown up in a climate of competition between people, teams, departments, divisions, pupils, schools, universities. We have been taught by economists that competition will solve our problems. Actually, competition, we see now, is destructive. It would be better if everyone would work together as a system, with the aim for everybody to win. What we need is cooperation and transformation to a new style of management. Competition leads to loss. People pulling in opposite directions on a rope only exhaust themselves: they go nowhere. What we need is cooperation. Every example of cooperation is one of benefit and gains to them that cooperate. (p. 90)

The United States has been guided recently by calls for increasing competitive advantage and in this chapter I argue for increasing emphasis on global collaborative advantage and developing the knowledge, skills, and habits of mind that support developing collaborative approaches to challenges and opportunities. The idea of global collaborative advantage was framed by Lynn and Salzman (2006, 2007) and they argue, in a series of articles, that we need to prepare graduates for developing global collaborative advantage. For example, Lynn and Salzman argued in their 2006 *Issues in Science and Technology* article, Collaborative Advantage, "The United States should move away from an almost certainly futile attempt to maintain dominance and toward an approach in which leadership comes from developing and brokering mutual gains among equal partners. Such 'collaborative advantage,' as we call it, comes not from self-sufficiency or maintaining a monopoly on advanced technology, but from being a valued collaborator at various levels in the international system of technology development" (p. 76).

Among their three goals for the United States they argue that "the United States needs to develop a science and technology education system that teaches collaborative competencies rather than just technical knowledge and skills" (p. 81). Their research indicates that cross-boundary skills (working across disciplinary, organizations, cultural, and time/distance boundaries) are needed more than technical skills.

Another group of researchers providing strong support for the centrality of interdependence are those studying complexity and complex adaptive systems (Axelrod & Cohen, 2001; Miller & Page, 2007). Page (2009) claims that a "system can be considered complex if its agents meet four qualifications: diversity, connection, interdependence, and adaptation." (p. 4) and "the attributes of interdependence, connectedness, diversity, and adaptation and learning generate complexity" (p. 10). Furthermore, Page (2009) noted that "interdependence refers to whether other entities influence actions, whereas connectedness refers to how many people a person is connected to" (p. 11). Preparing students with a deeper understanding of complex systems is essential, since complex systems: (1) are often unpredictable and can produce large events as well as withstand trauma, (2) produce bottom-up emergent phenomena, and (3) produce amazing novelty (Page, 2009).

Cooperative learning and its underlying theoretical framework, social interdependence theory, can provide many insights into preparing students to work with others to synthesize common goals and then attain common purposes, which are essential for developing collaborative advantage and navigating complexity.

Cooperative Learning and Social Interdependence Theory in Engineering Education

Cooperative learning has been part of the landscape of engineering education for nearly 30 years. The conceptual cooperative learning model was introduced to the engineering education community in 1981 (Smith, Johnson, & Johnson, 1981a, 1981b) and was continually refined and elaborated for engineering educators (Felder, 1995; Prince, 2004; Smith, 1995; Smith, Sheppard, Johnson, & Johnson, 2005) and higher education faculty in general (Johnson, Johnson, & Smith, 1991; Johnson, Johnson, & Smith, 1998; Johnson, Johnson, & Smith, 2000, 2006, 2007; MacGregor, Cooper, Smith, & Robinson, 2000; Millis & Cottell, 1997; Smith, 1996, 1998; Smith, Cox, & Douglas, 2008). The influence of foundational work on cooperative learning can be seen in the University of Delaware Problem Based Learning model (Allen, Duch, & Groh, 1996 ; Duch, Groh, & Allen, 2001), the SCALE-UP model at North Carolina State (Beichner, Saul, Allain, Deardorff, & Abbot, 2000), the Technology Enhanced Active Learning (TEAL) model at MIT (Dori & Belcher, 2005; Dori, et.al, 2003) and many others.

Social interdependence theory is at the heart of the cooperative learning model. In our 1981 journal of *Engineering Education* article "Structuring Learning Goals to Meet the Goals of Engineering Education" David and Roger Johnson and I introduced social interdependence theory to the engineering education community and elaborated on the two types of social interdependence–positive and negative–posited by Deutsch (1949a, 1962b). *Positive interdependence* exists when there is a positive correlation among individuals' goal attainments; individuals perceive that they can attain their goals if, and only if, the other individuals with whom they are cooperatively linked attain their goals. *Negative interdependence* exists when there is a negative correlation among individuals' goal achievements; individuals perceive that they can obtain their goals if and only if the other individuals with who they are competitively linked fail to obtain their goals. No interdependence or individualistic efforts exist when there is no correlation among individuals' goal achievements and individuals perceive that the achievement of their goals is unrelated to the goal achievement of others.

David and Roger Johnson (2005) summarized the state of social interdependence theory and provided excellent insight into the latest thinking about social interdependence theory.

The empirical and theoretical evidence supporting cooperative learning is vast and I'll only provide a brief summary. During the past 90 years, over 350 experimental studies have been conducted in college and adult settings comparing the effectiveness of cooperative, competitive, and individualistic efforts. These studies have been conducted by a wide variety of researchers in different decades, learner populations, subject areas, and settings. More is known about the efficacy of cooperative learning than about lecturing, the fifty-minute class period, the use of instructional technology, or almost any other aspect of education. From this research you would expect that the more students work in cooperative learning groups the more they will learn, the better they will understand what they are learning, the easier it will be to remember what they learn, and the better they will feel about themselves,

the class, and their classmates. The multiple outcomes studied can be classified into three major categories: achievement/productivity, positive relationships, and psychological health. Cooperation among students typically results in (a) higher achievement and greater productivity, (b) more caring, supportive, and committed relationships, and (c) greater psychological health, social competence, and self-esteem. (Smith, Sheppard, Johnson & Johnson, 2005; Johnson, Johnson & Smith, 1998, 2007).

Details on the key research-based elements of cooperative learning–positive interdependence, individual and group accountability, face-to-face promotive interaction, teamwork skills, and group processing–as well as implementation of the three main types of cooperative learning–Informal Cooperative Learning, Formal Cooperative Learning and Cooperative Base Groups–are available in Smith, Sheppard, Johnson and Johnson (2005) and in extensive detail in Johnson, Johnson and Smith (2006).

Preparing for Participation in an Interdependent World

The AAC&U (2007) *College Learning for the New Global Century* report as well as several studies of engineering – Boeing and RPI's *The Global Engineer* (Boeing, 1997), NAE's *Engineer of 2020* (2005), Purdue Future Engineer (Jamieson, 2007), *The 21st-Century Engineer* (Galloway, 2007), *Engineering for a Changing World* (Duderstadt, 2008) and *Creating a Culture for Scholarly and Systematic Innovation in Engineering Education: Ensuring U.S. Engineering Has the Right People With the Right Talent for a Global Society* (Jamieson & Lohmann, 2009)–have begun to articulate the knowledge, skills, and habits of mind that are needed for students to perform satisfactorily in an interdependent world.

The AAC&U *College Learning for the New Global Century* study included the results of an employer survey conducted by Peter D. Hart and Associates (2006). Several of the top six outcomes reported by business respondents emphasize interdependence as show in Table 1 (see next page).

The *Desired Attributes of Global Engineer*[1] list is especially interesting and insightful considering that it was crafted more than ten years ago. Most of the de-

---

[1] A Manifesto for Global Engineering Education, Summary Report of the *Engineering Futures Conference*, January 22-23, 1997. The Boeing Company & Rensselaer Polytechnic Institute.

sired attributes (out of thirteen) emphasize interdependence:

- A multidisciplinary, systems perspective, along with a product focus
- A basic understanding of the context in which engineering is practiced, including:
  - Customer and societal needs and concerns
  - Economics and finance
  - The environment and its protection
  - The history of technology and society
- An awareness of the boundaries of their knowledge, along with an appreciation for other areas of knowledge and the interrelatedness with their own expertise
- An awareness of and strong appreciation for other cultures and their diversity, distinctiveness, and inherent value
- A strong commitment to team work, including extensive experience with and understanding of team dynamics
- Good communication skills, including written, verbal, graphic, and listening
- High ethical standards (honesty, sense of personal and social responsibility, fairness, etc.)
- An ability to think both critically and creatively, in both independent and cooperative modes
- Flexibility: the ability and willingness to adapt to rapid and/or major changes
- Curiosity and the accompanying drive to learn continuously throughout their careers
- An ability to impart knowledge to others

The Carnegie Preparation for the Professions project provides several interesting parallels to work on cooperation and civic engagement (Sullivan, 2005). In his overview of professionalism in America, Sullivan highlighted the problem of negative interdependence and advocated a shift of thinking toward making interdependence work through civic professionalism. Sullivan's proposed framework for renewing professional education is through three apprenticeships – the head, the hand, and the heart. The first apprenticeship, the head, focuses on intellectual or cognitive development. The second, the hand, focuses on the tacit knowledge and skills practiced by competent practitioners. The third, the heart, is focused on the values and attitudes shared by the professional community.

Engineering education stresses the first apprenticeship (intellectual development), places little emphasis on the second (skill development), and is silent, or not too explicit, about the third apprenticeship (the heart). The third apprenticeship, which embodies what it means to be an engineer, is the habits of mind and the modes of thinking, is crucial for preparing the 21st Century engineer. Cooperative learning is an excellent way to increase the focus on *learning to be* as acknowledged in *Educating Engineers: Designing for the Future of the Field* (Sheppard, Macatangay, Colby & Sullivan, 2008).

Brown and Adler (2008) argue for a social view of learning where understanding is socially constructed. In contrast to the Cartesian view of learning (I think therefore I am) where knowledge is viewed as substance and pedagogy is seen as knowledge transfer, the social view of learning (we participate therefore we are) not only emphasizes "learning about" the subject matter but also *learning to be* a full participant in the field. They argue that "viewing learning as a process of joining a community of practice…allows new students to engage in *learning to be* even as they are mastering the content of the field" (p. 20). Furthermore, they claim that emphasizing *learning to be* encourages the practice of what John Dewey called productive inquiry – that

Table 1. Proportion of Employers Who Say Colleges and Universities Should Place More Emphasis Than They Do Today on Selected Learning Outcomes

Selected Learning Outcomes	%
Concepts and new developments in science and technology	82
Teamwork skills and the ability to collaborate with others in diverse group settings	76
The ability to apply knowledge and skills to real-world settings through internships or other hands-on experiences	73
The ability to effectively communicate orally and in writing	73
Critical thinking and analytical reasoning skills	73
Global issues and developments and their implications for the future	72

is, seeking knowledge when it is needed for addressing a pressing question or to accomplish a task.

Redish and Smith (2008) claimed that we must look beyond content in the skill development for engineers, and argued that integrated content-assessment-pedagogy design approaches and active and cooperative learning are essential.

State of Cooperative Learning for Preparing Students for an Interdependent World

Cooperative learning is now embraced by many engineering faculty and its use is increasing by faculty at large as indicated by the UCLA Higher Education Research Institute Survey of Faculty as shown in Table 2 (DeAngelo, Hurtado, Pryor, Kelly, & Santos, 2009).

Brown (2004) has great hope for social software tools and hopes we can "transform the internet into the platform of life-long learning and social construction, so that we can understand story telling and knowledge sharing." He also emphasizes the ability to listen with humility: "This skill underlies the art of collaboration and is increasingly important as we interact with partners all over the globe. But it also underlies the art of innovation, listening not only to your customers but also to the world at large" and the ability to see "if you want to excel in innovation, especially socially responsible innovation, then learn how to look around with unbiased eyes" (Brown, 2005).

Continual learning, flexibility and adaptability are paramount among the skills that are essential for functioning in an interdependent world. Brown's emphasis on "listening with humility" is also central. Purposeful and thoughtfully structured cooperative-learning groups can provide many opportunities for students to observe, model, learn, refine and practice essential skills for functioning in an interdependent world.

In closing, I return to 1962 and President John Kennedy's Global Declaration of Interdependence and his famous "moon" speech on June 10, 1963, President Kennedy gave the commencement address at American University, in which he stated:

> If we cannot end now our differences, at least we can help make the world safe for diversity.

We did, of course, go to the moon, but we still have lots of work to do to embrace global interdependence and to "make the world safe for diversity." Harlan Cleveland (2002) argues that "the required solvent for civilization is respect for differences. The art is to *be different together*," and "Civilization will be built by cooperation and compassion, in a social climate in which people of different groups can deal with each other in ways that respect their cultural differences" (p. 91). Finally, complexity theorist, Scott Page (2007) provides detailed support for the claim, "Diverse perspectives and tools enable collections of people to find more and better solutions and contribute to overall productivity" (p. 13).

References

Allen, D. E., Duch, B. E., & Groh, S. E. 1996. The power of problem-based learning in teaching introductory science courses. In Wilkerson, LuAnn & Gijselaers, Wim H. (Eds.) Bringing problem-based learning to higher education: Theory and practice. *New Directions for Teaching and Learning*. San Francisco: Jossey-Bass.

Axelrod, R., & Cohen, M. D. 2001. *Harnessing complexity: Organizational implications of a scientific frontier.* New York: Simon & Schuster.

Beichner, R. J., Saul, J. M., Allain, R. J., Deardorff, D. L., & Abbot, D. S. 2000. Introduction to SCALE-UP: Student-Centered Activities for Large Enrollment University Physics. Paper presented at the Annual Meeting of the American Society for Engineering Education, St. Louis.

Bennis, W.G. & Slater, P.E. 1968. *The temporary society.* New York: Harper & Row.

Boeing. 1997. A Manifesto for Global Engineering Education, Summary Report of the *Engineering Futures Conference*, January 22-23, 1997. The Boeing Company & Rensselaer Polytechnic Institute.

Table 2. The American College Teacher: National Norms for 2007-2008

Methods Used in "All" or "Most" Classes	All Faculty 2005 - %	All Faculty 2008 - %	Assistant– 2008 - %
Cooperative Learning	48	59	66
Group Projects	33	36	61
Grading on a curve	19	17	14
Term/research papers	35	44	47

Brown, John Seely. 2004. Commencement Speech. Claremont Graduate University. May 15, 2004. http://www.johnseelybrown.com/CGU.pdf (accessed 9-9-08)

Brown, John Seely. 2005. Commencement Speech. University of Michigan. May 30, 2005. http://www.johnseelybrown.com/UM05.pdf (accessed 9-9-08).

Brown, John Seely. 2008. Learning 2.0: The big picture. http://www.johnseelybrown.com/learning2.pdf (accessed 9-10-08)

Brown, John Seely & Adler, Richard P. 2008. Minds on fire: Open education, the long tail, and learning 2.0. *Educause Review*, 43(1), 17-32.

Cleveland, H. 2002. *Nobody in charge: Essays on the future of leadership*, Jossey-Bass.

Cohen, Don & Prusak, Laurence. 2001. *In good company: How social capital makes organizations work*. Cambridge, MA: Harvard Business School Press.

DeAngelo, L., Hurtado, S., Pryor, J.H., Kelly, K.R., & Santos, J.L. 2009. *The American college teacher: National norms for the 2007-2008 HERI faculty survey*. Los Angeles: Higher Education Research Institute, UCLA.

Deutsch, M. 1949a. A theory of cooperation and competition. *Human Relations*, 2, 129-152.

Deutsch, M. 1949b. An experimental study of the effects of cooperation and competition upon group process. *Human Relations*, 2, 199-231.

Deutsch, M. 1962. Cooperation and trust: Some theoretical notes. In M.R. Jones (Ed.), *Nebraska symposium on motivation* (pp. 275-319). Lincoln: University of Nebraska Press.

Dori, Y. J., & Belcher, J. 2005. How Does Technology-Enabled Active Learning Affect Undergraduate Students' Understanding of Electromagnetism Concepts? *The Journal of the Learning Sciences*, 14(2), 243-279.

Dori, Y. J., Belcher, J., Bessette, M., Danzinger, M., McKinney, A., & Hult, E. 2003. Technology for Active Learning. *Materials Today*, 6(12), 44-49.

Duch, B. J., Groh, S. E., & Allen, D. E. 2001. *The Power of Problem-Based Learning: A Practical "How To" for Teaching Undergraduate Courses in Any Discipline*. Sterling Virginia: Stylus Publishing.

Duderstadt, J. 2008. *Engineering for a Changing World A Roadmap to the Future of Engineering Practice, Research, and Education*. Ann Arbor, MI: The Millennium Project. http://milproj.dc.umich.edu/

Fairweather, J. "Linking Evidence and Promising Practices in Science, Technology, Engineering, and Mathematics (STEM) Undergraduate Education: A Status Report." Commissioned Paper for the Board of Science Education Workshop, Evidence on Promising Practices in Undergraduate Science, Technology, Engineering, and Mathematics (STEM) Education. Retrieved December 12, 2008, from http://www7.nationalacademies.org/bose/PP_Commissioned_Papers.html

Fairweather, J., & Paulson, K. 2008. The Evolution of Scientific Fields in American Universities: Disciplinary Differences, Institutional Isomorphism. In J. Valimaa and O. Ylijoki (eds.). *Cultural perspectives in higher education* (pp, 197-212). Dordrecht: Springer.

Felder, R. M. 1995. A Longitudinal Study of Engineering Student Performance and Retention. IV. Instructional Methods and Student Responses to Them. *Journal of Engineering Education*, 84(4), 361-367.

Friedman, Thomas. 2007. *The World is Flat, Release 3.0*. New York: Picador.

Galloway, P. D. 2007. *The 21st-Century Engineer: A Proposal for Engineering Education Reform*. American Society for Civil Engineering.

Jamieson, L. 2007. Experiencing engineering. Main Plenary. ASEE Annual Conference, Honolulu, Hawaii. http://www.asee.org/conferences/annual/2007/Highlights.cfm#main (accessed December 7, 2007).

Jamieson, L.H. & Lohmann, J.R. 2009. *Creating a Culture for Scholarly and Systematic Innovation in Engineering Education: Ensuring U.S. engineering has the right people with the right talent for a global society*. Washington, DC: American Society for Engineering Education.

Johnson, D. W., & Johnson, R. T. 2005. New developments in social interdependence theory. *Genetic, Social and General Psychology Monographs*, 131(4), 285-360.

Johnson, D. W., Johnson, R. T., & Smith, K. A. 1991. *Cooperative Learning: Increasing College Faculty Instructional Productivity*. ASHE-ERIC Reports on Education, 30(4).

Johnson, D. W., Johnson, R. T., & Smith, K. A. 1998. Cooperative Learning Returns to College: What Evidence is there that it Works? *Change*, 30(4), 26-35.

Johnson, D. W., Johnson, R. T., & Smith, K. A. 2006. *Active Learning: Cooperation in the College Classroom* (3rd ed.). Edina, MN: Interaction Book Company.

Johnson, D. W., Johnson, R. T., & Smith, K. A. 2007. The State Of Cooperative Learning In Postsecondary And Professional Settings. *Educational Psychology Review*, 19(1), 15-29.

Kuh, G., Kinzie, J., Buckley, J., Bridges, B., & Kayek, J. 2007. *Piecing together the student success puzzle: Research, propositions, and recommendations*. Washington, D.C.: Association for the Study of Higher Education.

Kuh, G., Kinzie, J., Schuh, J., & Witt, E. 2005. *Student success in college: Creating conditions that matter*. Washington, D.C.: Association for the Study of Higher Education.

Lynn, L., & Salzman, H. 2006. Collaborative Advantage: New Horizons for a Flat World. *Issues in Science and Technology*, Winter 22(2), 74-82. www.nsf.gov/attachments/105652/public/**Collaborative-Advantage**-1205.pdf (accessed 9-9-08)

Lynn, L., & Salzman, H. 2007. The Real Global Technology Challenge. *Change: The Magazine of Higher Learning*, 39(4), 8-13.

MacGregor, J., Cooper, J., Smith, K, & Robinson, P. (Eds.) 2000. Strategies for Energizing Large Classes: From Small Groups to Learning Communities. *New Directions for Teaching and Learning, 81*. San Francisco: Jossey-Bass.

Miller, J., & Page, S. E. 2007. *Complex adaptive systems: An Introduction to Computational Models of Social Life*. Princeton, NJ: Princeton University Press.

McDonough, W. & Braungart, M. 2002. *Cradle to cradle: Remaking the way we make things*. New York: North Point Press.

Millis, B. J., & Cottell, P. G. 1997. *Cooperative Learning for Higher Education Faculty*. Phoenix: Oryx Press

National Academy of Engineering. 2005. *Educating the engineer of 2020: Adapting engineering education to the new century.* Washington, DC: The National Academies Press.

Page, S. E. (2007). *The difference: How the power of diversity creates better groups, teams, schools, and societies.* Princeton, NJ: Princeton University Press.

Pascarella, E., & Terenzini, P. (2005). *How college affects students: A third decade of research.* San Francisco: Jossey-Bass.

PBS American Experience. (2008). Apollo 8. http://www.pbs.org/wgbh/amex/moon/peopleevents/e_earthrise.html (accessed 9-9-08)

Peter D. Hart Research Associates. 2006. *Report of Findings Based on Focus Groups among Business Executives.* Washington, DC: Peter D. Hart Research Associates.

Prince, M. 2004. Does Active Learning Work? A Review of the Research. *Journal of Engineering Education, 93* (3), 223-231.

Redish, E. F., & K. A., S. K. 2008. Looking Beyond Content: Skill Development for Engineers. *Journal of Engineering Education* Special Issue, 97(2), 295-307.

Sheppard, S. D., Macatangay, K., Colby, A. & Sullivan, William M. 2008. *Educating Engineers: Designing for the Future of the Field.* San Francisco: Jossey-Bass.

Smith, K. A. 1995. Cooperative Learning: Effective Teamwork for Engineering Classrooms. IEEE Education Society/ASEE Electrical Engineering Division Newsletter, March, pp. 1-6.

Smith, K. A., Cooperative learning: Making "groupwork" work. 1996. In C. Bonwell & T. Sutherlund, Eds., Active learning: Lessons from practice and emerging issues. *New Directions for Teaching and Learning 67*, pp. 71-82, San Francisco: Jossey-Bass.

Smith, K. A. 1998. Grading Cooperative Projects. In B. Anderson & B.W. Speck, Eds., Changing the Way We Grade Student Performance: Classroom Assessment and the New Learning Paradigm. New Directions for Teaching and Learning (pp. 78, 59-67). San Francisco: Jossey-Bass.

Smith, K. A., Cox, M., & Douglas, T. C. 2009. Supportive Teaching and Learning Strategies in STEM Education. In Baldwin, R. (Ed.), Improving the Climate for Undergraduate Teaching and Learning in STEM Fields, *New Directions for Teaching and Learning, no. 117.* San Francisco: Jossey-Bass.

Smith, K. A., Johnson, D. W., & Johnson, R. T. 1981a. The use of cooperative learning groups in engineering education. In L.P. Grayson and J.M. Biedenbach (Eds.), *Proceedings Eleventh Annual Frontiers in Education Conference,* Rapid City, SD, Washington: IEEE/ASEE, pp. 26 32.

Smith, K. A., Johnson, D. W., & Johnson, R. T. 1981b. Structuring Learning Goals to Meet the Goals of Engineering Education. *Journal of Engineering Education,* 72(3), 221-226.

Smith, K. A., Sheppard, S. D., Johnson, D. W., & Johnson, R. T. 2005. Pedagogies of Engagement: Classroom-Based Practices. *Journal of Engineering Education* Special Issue on the State of the Art and Practice of Engineering Education Research, 94(1), 87-102.

Sullivan, W. M. 2005. *Work and integrity: The crisis and promise of professionalism in America,* 2nd edition. Stanford, CA: The Carnegie Foundation for the Advancement of Teaching.

Cooperative Learning: Relationships Among Theory, Research and Practice

David W. Johnson and Roger T. Johnson

Cooperative learning is unique for at least three reasons. First, it is the instructional method of choice because of its power to affect, in multiple ways, student performance, development, socialization, and well-being. It is also the instructional method of choice because it is derived from social interdependence theory, which is validated by hundreds of research studies. Second, cooperative learning provides a constructive context for building and maintaining constructive relationships among students, between students and faculty, and socialization into the school, community, and society in general. It also provides the context for socialization into communities of practice as students are prepared for their careers. The cooperative context determines the norms guiding classroom and school behavior and inherently teaches attitudes, values, and behavioral patterns that enhance learning and healthy cognitive and social development. Third, cooperative learning reflects an organizational structure known as "the cooperative institution," based on teamwork and the mutual commitment of all organizational members to achieve common goals. Although each of these issues is discussed, this chapter will focus primarily on cooperative learning as an instructional method and the underlying interrelationships among theory, research, and practice. Social interdependence theory will be reviewed, the research validating the theory will be summarized, and the nature of cooperative learning procedures derived from the theory will be discussed.

Theory, Research and Practice

The interrelationships among theory, research, and practice have provided a foundation for cooperative learning and probably insures that: (a) effective instructional strategies will never be discussed without including cooperative learning, and (b) cooperative learning will probably never go away (Johnson, 2003; Johnson & Johnson, 2005). Its rich history of theory, research, and actual use in the classroom makes cooperative learning one of the most distinguished of all instructional practices. Theory, research, and practice all interact and enhance each other. Theory both guides and summarizes research. Research validates or disconfirms theory, thereby leading to its refinement and modification. Practice is ideally guided by validated theory, and applications of the theory reveal inadequacies that lead to refining of the theory, conducting new research studies, and modifying the application. Cooperative learning is a classic example of this process.

Social Interdependence Theory

There are at least three general theoretical perspectives that have guided research on cooperation: cognitive-developmental, behavioral, and social interdependence. The *cognitive developmental perspective* is largely based on the theories of Piaget and Vygotsky. The work of Piaget and related theorists is based on the premise that when individuals cooperate on the environment, socio-cognitive conflict occurs that creates cognitive disequilibrium, which in turn stimulates perspective-taking ability and cognitive development. The work of Vygotsky and related theorists is based on the premise that knowledge is social, constructed from cooperative efforts to learn, understand, and solve problems. The *behavioral perspective* focuses on the impact of group reinforcers on learning. Skinner focused on group contingencies, Bandura focused on imitation, and Homans, as well as Thibaut and Kelley, focused on the balance of rewards and costs in social exchange among interdependent individuals. Although the cognitive-developmental and behavioral theoretical orientations have their followings, by far the most important theory dealing with cooperation is social interdependence theory.

Social interdependence exists when the outcomes of individuals are affected by their own and others' actions (Johnson, 2003; Johnson & Johnson, 1989, 2005a). Person A's actions affect Person B's goal accomplishment and vice versa. Social interdependence may be differentiated from social dependence, independence, and helplessness. *Social dependence* exists when the goal achievement of Person A is affected by Person

B's actions, but the reverse is not true. *Social independence* exists when the goal achievement of Person A is unaffected by Person B's actions and vice versa. *Social helplessness* exists when neither the person nor others can influence goal achievement.

Theorizing on social interdependence began in the early 1900s, when one of the founders of the Gestalt School of Psychology, Kurt Koffka, proposed that groups were dynamic wholes in which the interdependence among members could vary. In the 1920s and 1930s, Kurt Lewin extended Koffka's notions by stating that: (a) the essence of a group is the interdependence among members (created by common goals) which results in the group being a "dynamic whole" so that a change in the state of any member or subgroup changes the state of any other member or subgroup, and (b) an intrinsic state of tension within group members motivates movement toward the accomplishment of the desired common goals. Lewin's students and colleagues, such as Ovisankian, Lissner, Mahler, and Lewis, contributed further research indicating that it is the drive for goal accomplishment that motivates cooperative and competitive behavior.

Morton Deutsch, one of Lewin's graduate students, extended Lewin's reasoning about social interdependence in the late 1940s by formulating a theory of cooperation and competition based on an analysis of how the tension systems of different people may be interrelated (Deutsch, 1949, 1962). He conceptualized two types of social interdependence—positive and negative. *Positive interdependence* exists when there is a positive correlation among individuals' goal attainments; individuals perceive that they can attain their goals if and only if the other individuals with whom they are cooperatively linked attain their goals. Positive interdependence results in promotive interaction (i.e., individuals encouraging and facilitating each other's efforts to complete tasks in order to reach the group's goals). *Negative interdependence* exists when there is a negative correlation among individuals' goal achievements; individuals perceive that they can obtain their goals if and only if the other individuals with whom they are competitively linked fail to obtain their goals. Negative interdependence results in oppositional interaction (i.e., individuals discouraging and obstructing each other's efforts to complete tasks in order to reach their goals). *No interdependence* exists when there is no correlation among individuals' goal achievements; individuals perceive that the achievement of their goals is unrelated to the goal achievement of others. The basic premise of social interdependence theory is that how participants' goals are structured determines the ways they interact and the interaction pattern determines the outcomes of the situation.

Deutsch (1949, 1962) posited that positive interdependence creates the psychological processes of substitutability (i.e., the degree to which actions of one person substitute for the actions of another person), positive cathexis (i.e., the investment of positive psychological energy in objects outside of oneself, such as friends, family, and work), and inducibility (i.e., the openness to being influenced by and to influencing others). Negative interdependence tends to create non-substitutability, negative cathexis, and resistance to influence. No interdependence may be characterized by the absence of these three psychological processes.

Five Basic Elements

Deutsch (1949, 1962) focused on three variables—interdependence, interaction pattern, and outcomes. The basic premise of social interdependence theory is that how goals are structured determines how group members interact, and those interaction patterns determine outcomes. Additional research on and implementation of cooperation expanded the theory to focus on five variables that mediate the effectiveness of cooperation: positive interdependence, individual accountability, promotive interaction, the appropriate use of social skills, and group processing (Johnson & Johnson, 1989, 2005).

Interdependence

Positive and negative interdependence were defined by Lewin and Deutsch as resulting from mutual goals. Other researchers soon added other types of interdependence. Positive and negative interdependence have been structured through complementary roles, group contingencies, dividing information (or other resources) into separate pieces, divisions of labor (i.e., task interdependence), mutual identity, environmental spaces, and simulations involving fantasy situations (Johnson & Johnson, 1989, 2005). These ways of structuring interdependence may be subsumed into three categories: outcome, means, and boundary. Outcome interdependence includes goals and rewards. Goals can be real or fantasized (such as surviving being wrecked on the moon). Means interdependence includes resource, role, and task interdependence. The boundaries existing among individuals and groups can define who is interdependent with whom. The boundaries may be created by an outside enemy (i.e., negative interdependence with another group), a mutual identity (which binds members together as an entity), and environmental factors (such as a specific work area). These types of interdependence are overlapping and not independent from each other.

Individual Accountability and Personal Responsibility

Positive interdependence is posited to create "responsibility forces" that add the concept of "ought" to group members' motivation—one ought to do one's part, pull one's weight, contribute, and satisfy peer norms (Deutsch, 1949, 1962; Johnson & Johnson, 1989, 2005). Responsibility forces are increased when there is group and individual accountability. *Group accountability* exists when the overall performance of the group is assessed and the results are given back to all group members to compare against a standard of performance. *Individual accountability* exists when the performance of each individual member is assessed, the results are given back to the individual and the group to compare against a standard of performance. The lack of individual accountability may reduce feelings of personal responsibility. If, however, there is high individual accountability and it is clear how much effort each member is contributing, if redundant efforts are avoided, if every member is responsible for the final outcome, and if the group is cohesive, then the group members feel responsible for contributing their best efforts.

Promotive Interaction

Promotive interaction occurs as individuals encourage and facilitate each other's efforts to accomplish the group's goals. Compared with oppositional and no interaction, promotive interaction is characterized by individuals: (a) acting in trusting and trustworthy ways; (b) exchanging needed resources, such as information and materials; (c) processing information more efficiently and effectively; (d) providing efficient and effective help to groupmates; (e) being motivated to strive for mutual benefit; (f) advocating exerting effort to achieve mutual goals; (g) having a moderate level of arousal characterized by low anxiety and stress; (h) influencing each other's efforts to achieve the group's goals; and (i) providing groupmates with feedback in order to improve their subsequent performance on assigned tasks and responsibilities.

Oppositional interaction occurs as individuals discourage, block, and obstruct each other's efforts to achieve their goals; individuals focus both on being productive and on preventing any other person from being more productive than they are. *No interaction* occurs when individuals work independently without any interchange with each other; individuals focus only on being productive and ignore as irrelevant the efforts of others.

Appropriate Use of Social Skills

Effective cooperation is based on skilled teamwork as well as taskwork. Students, therefore, must be taught the interpersonal and small group skills needed for high quality cooperation and be motivated to use them. To coordinate efforts to achieve mutual goals, participants must: (a) get to know and trust each other, (b) communicate accurately and unambiguously, (c) accept and support each other, and (d) resolve conflicts constructively (Johnson, 2009; Johnson & Johnson, 2009). Interpersonal and small group skills form the basic nexus among individuals, and if individuals are to work together productively and cope with the stresses and strains of doing so, they must have a modicum of these skills.

Group Processing

Group processing occurs when group members: (a) reflect on which member actions were helpful and unhelpful, and (b) make decisions about what actions to continue or change. The purpose of group processing is to clarify and improve the effectiveness with which members carry out the processes necessary to achieve the group's goals.

Enhancing Variables: Trust and Conflict

During the 1950s, 1960s and 1970s Deutsch (1962, 1973) researched two aspects of the internal dynamics of cooperative groups: trust and conflict. His research demonstrated that the greater the trust among group members, the more effective their cooperative efforts tended to be. Conflict within cooperative groups, when managed constructively, enhances the effectiveness of cooperative efforts. There are two types of conflict that occur frequently and regularly within cooperative groups—controversy and conflicts of interests (Johnson & Johnson, 2005b, 2007). The research demonstrates that the more constructively conflicts among group members are managed, the more effective their cooperative efforts will be. Controversies are resolved by following the constructive controversy procedure. Conflicts of interests are resolved constructively through the use of integrative negotiations.

Conditions for Constructive, Competitive and Individualistic Efforts

Competition tends to be more constructive when winning is relatively unimportant, all participants have a reasonable chance to win, and there are clear and specific rules, procedures, and criteria for winning that are perceived to be fair. Individualistic efforts may be most appropriate when: (a) cooperation is too costly, difficult, or cumbersome due to the unavailability of skilled potential cooperators or the resources needed for cooperation to take place; (b) the goal must be perceived as important, relevant, and worthwhile; (c) participants expect to be successful in achieving their goals; (d) unitary, nondivisible, simple tasks need to be completed; and (e) the directions for completing the task are clear and specific so participants do not need further clarification on how to proceed and how to evaluate their work (Johnson & Johnson, 1989, 2005a).

Validating Research

Amount and Characteristics of Research

Although theory both guides and summarizes research, research is conducted to validate or disconfirm theory, thereby leading to its refinement. The study of cooperative, competitive, and individualistic efforts is commonly recognized as one of the oldest fields of research in social psychology (Johnson & Johnson, 1989). In the late 1800's Triplett in the United States, Turner in England, and Mayer in Germany conducted a series of studies on the factors associated with competitive performance. Since then over 1,200 studies have been conducted on the relative merits of cooperative, competitive, and individualistic efforts and the conditions under which each is appropriate. This is one of the largest bodies of research within psychology and education and it provides sufficient empirical research to test social interdependence theory's propositions.

Many of the research studies have high internal validity, being carefully conducted by skilled investigators under highly controlled laboratory (31 percent) and field (65 percent) settings. When rated on the variables of random assignment to conditions, clarity of control conditions, control of the experimenter effect, control of the curriculum effect (same materials used in all conditions), and verification of the successful implementation of the independent variable, 51 percent of the studies met these criteria.

The research on social interdependence has an external validity and a generalizability rarely found in the social sciences. The more variations in places, people, and procedures the research can withstand and still yield the same findings, the more externally valid the conclusions. The research has been conducted over twelve decades by many different researchers with markedly different theoretical and practical orientations working in different settings. A wide variety of research tasks, ways of structuring social interdependence, and measures of the dependent variables have been used. Participants in the studies varied from age three to post-college adults and came from different economic classes and cultural backgrounds. The studies were conducted with varying durations, lasting from one session to 100 sessions or more. Research on social interdependence has been conducted among numerous cultures in North America (with Caucasian, Black-American, Native-American, and Hispanic populations) and in countries in North, Central, and South America, Europe, the Middle East, Asia, the Pacific Rim, and Africa. The research on social interdependence includes both theoretical and demonstration studies conducted in educational, business, and social service organizations. The diversity of these studies gives social interdependence theory wide generalizability and considerable external validity.

Promotive, oppositional, and no interaction have differential effects on the outcomes of the situation (see Johnson & Johnson, 1989, 1999, 2005). The research has focused on numerous outcomes, which may be subsumed within the broad and interrelated categories of achievement, quality of relationships, and psychological health (Johnson, 2003; Johnson & Johnson, 1989, 2005a). Figure 1 shows the relationships among the outcomes.

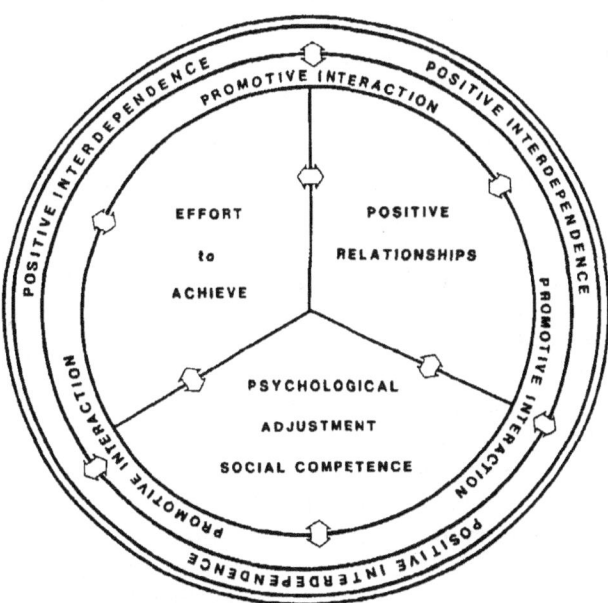

Figure 1. Outcomes of Cooperative Learning

Source: Johnson, D. W., & Johnson, R. (1989). *Cooperation and competition: Theory and research*. Edina, MN: Interaction Book Company. Reprinted with permission.

Effort to Achieve

The research indicates that cooperation promotes greater effort to achieve than competitive or individualistic efforts. Effort exerted to achieve includes such variables as achievement and productivity, long-term retention, on-task behavior, use of higher-level reasoning strategies, generation of new ideas and solutions, transfer of what is learned within one situation to another, intrinsic motivation, achievement motivation, continuing motivation to learn, and positive attitudes toward learning and school. Overall, cooperation tends to promote higher achievement than competitive or individualistic efforts (effect-sizes = 0.67 and 0.64 respectively). Cooperators spent considerably more time on task than did competitors (effect size = 0.76) or students working individualistically (effect size = 1.17). Cooperative experiences, compared with competitive and individualistic ones, have been found to promote more positive attitudes toward the task and the experience of working on the task (effect-sizes = 0.57 and 0.42 respectively).

Quality of Relationships

Quality of relationships includes such variables as interpersonal attraction, liking, cohesion, esprit-de-corps, and social support. The more positive the relationships among students and between students and faculty, the lower the absenteeism and dropout rates and the greater the commitment to group goals, feelings of personal responsibility to the group, willingness to take on difficult tasks, motivation and persistence in working toward goal achievement, satisfaction and morale, willingness to endure pain and frustration on behalf of the group, willingness to defend the group against external criticism or attack, willingness to listen to and be influenced by colleagues, commitment to each other's professional growth and success, and productivity (Johnson & Johnson, 2009).

There are over 175 studies that have investigated the relative impact of cooperative, competitive, and individualistic efforts on quality of relationships and another 106 studies on social support (Johnson, 2003; Johnson & Johnson, 1989, 2005a). Cooperation generally promotes greater interpersonal attraction among individuals than does competitive or individualistic efforts (effect sizes = 0.67 and 0.60 respectively). Cooperative experiences tend to promote greater social support than does competitive (effect-size = 0.62) or individualistic (effect-size = 0.70) efforts. Stronger effects are found for peer support than for superior (instructor) support. The high-quality studies tend to have even more powerful effects.

Psychological Health

Ashley Montagu (1966) was fond of saying that with few exceptions the solitary animal in any species is an abnormal creature. Similarly, Karen Horney (1937) stated that the neurotic individual is someone who is inappropriately competitive and, therefore, unable to cooperate with others. Montagu and Horney recognized that the essence of psychological health is the ability to develop and maintain cooperative relationships. More specifically, *psychological health* is the ability (cognitive capacities, motivational orientations, and social skills) to build, maintain, and appropriately modify interdependent relationships with others to succeed in achieving goals (Johnson, 2003; Johnson & Johnson, 1989, 2005a). People who are unable to do so often: (a) become depressed, anxious, frustrated, and lonely; (b) tend to feel afraid, inadequate, helpless, hopeless, and isolated; and (c) rigidly cling to unproductive and ineffective ways of coping with adversity.

With our students and colleagues, we have conducted a series of studies relating cooperative, competitive, and individualistic efforts and attitudes to various indices of psychological health (see Johnson, 2003; Johnson & Johnson, 1989, 2005a). The samples studied included college students, middle-class junior-high students, middle-class high school seniors, high-school age juvenile prisoners, adult prisoners, Olympic ice-hockey players, adult step-couples, and business executives in China. The diversity of the samples studied and the variety of measures of psychological health provide considerable generalizability of the results of the studies. A strong relationship was found between cooperativeness and psychological health, a mixed picture was found with competitiveness and psychological health, and a strong relationship was found between an individualistic orientation and psychological pathology.

Finally, there is evidence that cooperation promotes more frequent use of higher level reasoning strategies than do competitive (effect size = 0.93) or individualistic (effect size = 0.97) efforts. Similarly, cooperation tends to promote more accurate perspective taking than do competitive (effect size = 0.61) or individualistic (effect size = 0.44) efforts. The more cooperative learning experiences students are involved in, the more mature their cognitive and moral decision making and the more they will tend to take other people's perspectives in account when making decisions.

Nature of Cooperative Learning

Ideally, practical procedures are derived from validated theory. The implementation of the practical procedures then reveals shortcomings of the theory, thus pointing to ways the theory needs to be revised. Based on the theoretical definition of cooperation, *cooperative learning* maybe defined as the instructional use of small groups so that students work together to maximize their own and each other's learning (Johnson, Johnson, & Holubec, 2008; Johnson, Johnson, & Smith, 2005). It may be contrasted with *competitive learning* (students work against each other to achieve an academic goal such as a grade of "A" that only one or a few students can attain) and *individualistic learning* (students work by themselves to accomplish learning goals unrelated to those of the other students). In cooperative and individualistic learning, instructors evaluate student efforts on a criteria-referenced basis while in competitive learning instructors grade students on a norm-referenced basis.

History of Cooperative Learning

Cooperative learning has been around a long time. More than 3,000 years ago a famous endorsement of cooperative learning was made in the Talmud. It was announced that to learn the contents of the Talmud a person needed three things—a copy of the Talmud, a instructor, and a learning partner (because the contents were far too difficult to understand by oneself). This endorsement of the power of cooperative learning was not the only one. In the first century, Quintilian argued that students could benefit from teaching one another. The Roman philosopher, Seneca advocated cooperative learning through such statements as, "*Qui Docet Discet*" (when you teach, you learn twice). Johann Amos Comenius (1592-1679) believed that students would benefit both by teaching and being taught by other students. In the late 1700's Joseph Lancaster and Andrew Bell made extensive use of cooperative learning groups in England and India, and the idea was brought to America when a Lancastrian school was opened in New York City in 1806. In the early 1800s, the Common School Movement in the United States emphasized cooperative learning. In the last three decades of the 19th Century, Colonel Francis Parker's methods of structuring cooperative learning dominated American education. Following Parker, in the first half of the 20th Century, John Dewey promoted the use of cooperative learning groups as part of his famous project method. In the late 1930s, however, competition began to be emphasized in schools as a way to increase achievement and in the 1960s individualistic learning became the most recommended instructional method. Cultural resistance to cooperative learning existed, based on the social Darwinism premise that students should be taught to survive in a "dog-eat-dog" world and the myth of "rugged individualism." For nearly three decades, cooperative learning was practically unknown.

In the mid 1960s, the authors began training instructors how to use cooperative learning at the University of Minnesota. *The Cooperative Learning Center* resulted from our efforts to: (a) synthesize existing knowledge concerning cooperative, competitive, and individualistic efforts; (b) extend and refine social interdependence theory focusing initially on the conditions mediating the effectiveness of cooperative, competitive, and individualistic efforts; (c) conduct a systematic program of research to test our theorizing; (d) translate the validated theory into a set of concrete strategies and procedures for using cooperation in classrooms and schools; and (e) build and maintain a network of schools and universities implementing cooperative strategies and procedures throughout North America and the world. Beginning in the 1970s many other cooperative learning procedures were developed and implemented by a wide variety of people within and outside of academia (Johnson & Johnson, 2002). The dedicated people contributing to the success of the implementation of cooperative learning in schools and universities cannot all be discussed here, but many are reflected in the chapters of this book.

Cooperative learning is now an accepted and often the preferred instructional procedure at all levels of education. Cooperative learning is presently used in schools and universities in every part of the world, in every subject area, and with every age student. It is difficult to find a text on instructional methods, a teacher's journal, or instructional materials that do not discuss cooperative learning. Our writings on cooperative learning have been translated in over 17 different languages and the work of others have been translated into many more. Cooperative learning is one of education's success stories.

Types of Cooperative Learning

There are three types of cooperative learning—formal, informal, and base groups. *Formal cooperative learning* consists of students working together, for one class period to several weeks, to achieve shared learning goals and jointly complete specific tasks and assignments (Johnson, Johnson, & Smith, 2005). In formal cooperative learning groups instructors:

1. *Make a number of preinstructional decisions.* Instructors specify the objectives for the lesson (both aca-

demic and social skills) and decide on the size of groups, the method of assigning students to groups, the roles students will be assigned, the materials needed to conduct the lesson, and the way the room will be arranged.
2. *Explain the task and the positive interdependence.* An instructor clearly defines the assignment, teaches the required concepts and strategies, specifies the positive interdependence and individual accountability, gives the criteria for success, and explains the expected social skills to be used.
3. *Monitor and intervene:* Instructors monitor students' learning and intervene within the groups to provide task assistance or to increase students' interpersonal and group skills.
4. *Assess and process:* Instructors assess students' learning and structure students' processing of how well their groups functioned.

Informal cooperative learning consists of having students work together to achieve a joint learning goal in temporary, ad-hoc groups that last from a few minutes to one class period (Johnson, Johnson, & Smith, 2005). During a lecture, demonstration, or film, informal cooperative learning can be used to focus student attention on the material to be learned, set a mood conducive to learning, help set expectations as to what will be covered in a class session, ensure that students cognitively process and rehearse the material being taught, summarize what was learned and cue the next session, and provide closure to an instructional session. The procedure involves three-to-five minute focused discussions before and after the lecture or demonstration (to set expectations and provide closure) and two-to-three minute pair discussions interspersed every fifteen minutes or so throughout the lecture or demonstration (to ensure active cognitive processing of the material being presented).

Cooperative base groups are long-term, heterogeneous cooperative learning groups with stable membership whose primary responsibilities are to provide support, encouragement, and assistance to make academic progress and develop cognitively and socially in healthy ways as well as holding each other accountable for striving to learn (Johnson, Johnson, & Smith, 2005). Typically, cooperative base groups: (a) are heterogeneous in membership; (b) meet regularly (for example, daily or biweekly); and (c) last for the duration of the semester, year, or until all members are graduated. Base groups, typically consist of three to four members, meet at the beginning and end of each class session (or week) to complete academic tasks, such as checking members' homework, routine tasks such as taking attendance, and personal support tasks such as listening sympathetically to personal problems or providing guidance for writing a paper.

These three types of cooperative learning form a gestalt for teaching. A typical class session may begin with a base group meeting, followed by a short lecture in which informal cooperative learning is used. A formal cooperative learning lesson is then conducted and near the end of the class session another short lecture may be delivered with the use of informal cooperative learning. The class ends with a base group meeting.

Cooperative Context

The use of cooperative learning creates a context for classroom and school life. The *context* is the circumstances or events that form the environment within which something exists or takes place. For example, the behavior of members of one society towards another often cannot be understood until it is viewed in its historical context. Not only does behavior have to be viewed in its context, the context often determines the behavior that will occur. Thus, students will act differently depending on whether the context is primarily cooperative, competitive, or individualistic. A competitive context, for example, will tend to promote aggressive behavior as individuals seek to dominate or "win" over others, no or inaccurate communication, distrust, and the obstruction of each other's success. A cooperative context, on the other hand, tends to promote prosocial behavior and caring, supportive relationships, frequent and accurate communication, trust, and the promotion of each other's success.

One variable that context affects is socialization into the conventions, values, attitudes, roles, competencies, and ways of perceiving the world that are shared by family, community, society, and culture (Johnson & Johnson, 2009). There is general socialization which integrates individuals into their community and society. There is also specific socialization as individuals become members of communities of practice (such as physicians, lawyers, accountants, professors). Socialization takes place through group memberships (i.e., family, church, school) and interpersonal relationships (i.e., parents, friends, instructors, colleagues). When relationships are caring and supportive, socialization, positive identification, and internalization tend to occur. In cooperative endeavors individuals are assigned roles with specified responsibilities and patterns of behavior. Socialization is not a passive process. Individuals actively choose which attitudes, values, and behavioral patterns they wish to internalize and adopt within the context in which socialization is taking place. Perhaps one of the most important and least recognized contributions of cooperative learning is providing a constructive context in which students will learn and be socialized.

Organizational Structure: Cooperative Schools and Colleges

Social interdependence theory underlies the nature of social organizations, including colleges and universities. Just as positive interdependence can be structured in small groups in classrooms, it can also be structured at all levels of the school (Johnson & Johnson, 1994). *Classroom interdependence* may be created through such procedures as class goals, rewards or celebrations, roles (such as establishing a classroom government), or dividing resources (having the class publish a newsletter in which each cooperative group contributes one article). *Interclass interdependence* may be created through organizing several classes into a "neighborhood" and having them engage in joint projects. *School interdependence* may be structured through displaying the school's goals, organizing faculty into colleagial teaching teams and study groups, using cooperative groups during faculty meetings, and conducting all-school projects, methods of making these entities into learning communities. Learning communities are among the most popular and successful forms of social organizations among both K-12 and college settings in fostering student success. Projects with parents, such as creating a "strategic plan" or raising money, create *school-parent interdependence*. Finally, *school-community interdependence* may be created by mutual projects, such as having neighborhood members play in the school band or having students and neighborhood members jointly clean up a park. Although these procedures have been successfully implemented at the k-12 level, many of these techniques may be adapted for use in higher education.

Changing methods of teaching is much easier when the changes are congruent with the organizational structure of the institution. Cooperative learning forms the basis for schools and colleges to change from a mass-production competitive/individualistic organizational structure to a high-performance, cooperative team-based organizational structure (see Johnson & Johnson, 1994). The new organizational structure is generally known as "the cooperative school." The use of cooperation to structure faculty and staff work involves (a) colleagial teaching teams, (b) ad hoc decision-making groups within the school , (c) task forces to address chronic problems, and (d) faculty meetings.

In a cooperative school, students work primarily in learning groups, instructors, staff, and administrators work in cooperative teams. The organizational structure of the classrooms, schools and colleges are then congruent. Each level of cooperative teams supports and enhances the other levels.

Conclusions and Summary

The strength of cooperative learning lies in the relationships among theory, research, and practice. The combination of social interdependence theory, hundreds of validating research studies, and actual use in the classroom makes cooperative learning one of the most research-based and powerful of all instructional practices (Johnson and Johnson, 1989; 2002). In addition, it provides a constructive context for life in classrooms and in higher education institutions, and an organizational structure that enhances the effectiveness of education at all levels.

References

Deutsch, M. (1949). A theory of cooperation and competition. *Human Relations*, 2, 129-152.

Deutsch, M. (1962). Cooperation and trust: Some theoretical notes. In M. Jones (Ed.), *Nebraska symposium on motivation*, (pp. 275-319). Lincoln, NE: University of Nebraska Press.

Deutsch, M. (1973). *The resolution of conflict.* New Haven, CT: Yale University Press.

Horney, K. (1937). *The neurotic personality of our time.* New York: Norton.

Johnson, D. W. (2003). Social interdependence: The interrelationships among theory, research, and practice. *American Psychologist, 58*(11), 931-945.

Johnson, D. W. (2009). *Reaching out: Interpersonal effectiveness and self-actualization* (10ʰ Ed.). Boston: Allyn & Bacon.

Johnson, D. W., & Johnson, F. (2009). *Joining together: Group theory and research* (10th Ed.). Boston: Allyn & Bacon.

Johnson, D. W., & Johnson, R. (1989). *Cooperation and competition: Theory and research.* Edina, MN: Interaction Book Company.

Johnson, D. W., & Johnson, R. (1994). *Leading the cooperative school* (2nd ed.). Edina, MN: Interaction Book Company.

Johnson, D. W., & Johnson, R. (2002). Cooperative learning methods: A meta-analysis. *Journal of Research in Education, 12*(1), 5-14.

Johnson, D. W., & Johnson, R. (2005a). New developments in social interdependence theory. *Genetic, Social, and General Psychology Monographs, 131*(4), 285-358.

Johnson, D. W., & Johnson, R. (2005b). *Teaching students to be peacemakers* (4th ed.). Edina, MN: Interaction Book Company.

Johnson, D. W., & Johnson, R. (2007). *Creative controversy: Intellectual challenge in the classroom* (4th ed.). Edina, MN: Interaction Book Company.

Johnson, D. W., Johnson, R., & Holubec, E. (2008). *Cooperation in the classroom* (7th ed.). Edina, MN: Interaction Book Company.

Johnson, D. W., Johnson, R., & Smith, K.. (2008). *Active learning: Cooperation in the college classroom* (3rd ed.). Edina, MN: Interaction Book Company.

Montagu, A. (1966). *On being human.* New York: Hawthorn.

An Instructional Revolution for Higher Education: Rationale and Proposed Methods

Spencer Kagan

Need for an Instructional Revolution

As the world around changed, colleges and universities did not. At least they have not changed in the most important way they need to—how instructors teach. The lecture class of today strongly resembles the lecture class of centuries ago. Even the discussion group uses age-old instructional practices: The discussion group leader calls on one student at a time to respond to the leader's question or to express an opinion. Instructional practices have remained remarkably resistant to change. This is true worldwide. I have now trained teachers and observed classes in over twenty countries. Wherever I go, whether it is in higher education or K-12 schools, whether it is into schools in industrialized cities in wealthy countries, or in rural towns and villages in poor countries, instructional strategies are remarkably similar.

There is a need to radically transform how we teach. The need springs from two sources: 1) An explosion of research reveals how brains best learn, and we need to align how we teach with those findings—to teach scientifically; and 2) We need to prepare our students for a world that less and less resembles the world of the past—an interdependent world and workplace with an accelerating change rate, a world being transformed rapidly by technological advances.

Need for Brain-Friendly Instruction

Advances in active brain imaging, micro imaging, electrode probing, neurochemistry, and computational power have combined to create a profound transformation in our understanding of brain structure and function. Much of this new understanding is directly relevant to improving instruction. It is now meaningful to talk about "brain-friendly" instruction. That is, instruction aligned with how brains best learn. A more complete presentation of this topic is presented elsewhere (Kagan, 2003, 2006). To cite a few examples:

- There is little brain activity as students listen to a lecture, but a great deal of brain activity when students interact over the content (Carter, 1998).
- Students attend little to routine stimuli, but their brains light up when presented with novel and unpredictable stimuli (Hawkins, 2004).
- Major muscle movement results in an increased flow of nutrients to the brain (Ratey & Hagerman, 2008).
- The principle of retrograde memory enhancement is now well established: Any stimulus associated with emotion is better remembered (McGaugh, 2003).
- Frequent processing is essential for retention: Input not followed by processing is retained for a brief time in working memory and then lost. For longer term memory the content must be related to prior knowledge, discussed, analyzed, categorized, evaluated, and/or associated with a mnemonic (Cowan, 2005).
- A threat-free, supportive learning environment allows the prefrontal cortex to function more fully, supporting thinking and learning connections (LeDoux, 1996; Pert & Chopra, 1997).
- The brain is not an empty vessel waiting to be filled; from birth it is constantly making and testing predictions, revising and re-revising its picture of the world, constructing meaning (Gopnik, Meltzoff & Kuhl, 1999).

Given these advances in the understanding of how brains attend to, process, retain, and recall information, we cannot help but conclude that traditional instructional practices do not align with how brains best learn. Further, new cooperative, interactive instructional strategies are far better designed to accelerate learning. Thus the brain research supports the need for an instructional revolution.

Need for 21st Century Skills

The need for an instructional revolution is supported by the need to teach in ways that provide our students with 21st century skills. The world is rapidly changing; how our students will work and live will little resemble how we have worked and lived in the past. Skills that predicted success in the past will not be sufficient for success in the transformed workplace of the future.

Traditional Function of Schools. In the early days of industrialization, formal education had three major functions: 1) Teaching knowledge and skills, 2) Socializing obedience, and 3) Sorting. Many students were headed for assembly line jobs where obedience and conformity were highly valued. Preparation for those jobs placed little or no premium on thinking or creativity. Given that, schools placed a great deal of emphasis on following directions, obedience, and performing rote tasks repeatedly on one's own. It was important also to sort students—who would go on to design and own the factories and who would go on to punch a time clock? Separating the winners from losers was a traditional function of schools; our over-emphasis on competition and grading is a remnant from that era. The information base was not rapidly changing; our over-emphasis on teaching facts is also a remnant from that era.

Traditional View of the Learner. Traditionally, we viewed learners as empty vessels; our job as instructors was to fill them with the knowledge and skills they would need for success. When most people worked on farms, basic numeracy and literacy was sufficient. Rather than an emphasis on learner centered construction of knowledge, the emphasis was on acquisition of facts and basic skills. When preparing students for a predictable world in which success was determined by acquiring predetermined knowledge and skills, there was little concern about the development of learning to learn, thinking out of the box, and interpersonal skills. Our over-emphasis today on the lecture format is a remnant from the view of the learner as the empty vessel to be filled with a set of predetermined knowledge and skills.

21st Century Function of Schools and View of the Learner. To prepare students for the world in which they will live and work, our mission as educators is radically transformed. We have an unprecedented task: For the first time in human history we must prepare our students to work and live in a world we can only dimly imagine. Instructors in the past had the luxury of preparing their students for a world not too different from their own. If they provided their students with the knowledge and skills that served them well, they could be confident their students would be well prepared. Because of the accelerating change rate in contemporary society, we no longer have that luxury. The ability to function as a competent engineer is "lost within approximately 3 years after graduation....he becomes obsolete without further education and training" (Wear, 2004). Further, because of the accelerating information explosion, that three year post-graduation grace period is shrinking each year!

> In times of change, learners inherit the earth, while the learned find themselves beautifully equipped to deal with a world that no longer exists.
> —Eric Hoffer

Information Saved a Year

INFORMATION SAVED A YEAR=
5 exabytes (5,000,000,000,000,000,000 bytes)

HOW MUCH IS 5 EXABYTES?

The library of congress has 19 million books and additional print collections. 5 Exabytes = Half a million new libraries the size of the library of congress!

In other words, 5 Exabytes =
**A Stack of books 30 feet high
—for every person on earth!**

Source: Verity, J. "The Information Revolution." ***Business Week,*** May 18, 1994, 3372: 10-18.

We must prepare our students for the accelerating information explosion. The total amount of information stored in all forms doubles each year, and that doubling rate is accelerating! Today we can go on Amazon and "look inside a book" finding a phrase we are looking for and reading the page before and after that phrase. Google has plans to scan ALL books so they are available to be searched at a click. Getting our students to memorize one more fact is like trying to stop a flood with a single leaky sandbag.

If we are to prepare our students for the world of the future, providing content knowledge and skills is just part of our task. We must prepare them with thinking skills to process new information, and a love of learning to become a lifetime learner.

Unlike the farmer who could work successfully alone, today the successful worker is a team member. Complexity and interdependence are the defining characteristics of the modern workplace—no one person can build a computer. Three fourths of all organizations have employees working on teams, and that percentage is increasing. Teams work to coordinate efforts with other teams. With complexity comes interdependence, and with interdependence comes the need to prepare our students with teamwork skills — interpersonal skills to function successfully in the interdependent work world of the future. If we are to meet the challenge of aligning today's classroom experience with the world in which our students will be living and working, we need to move toward interactive structures in our lectures and discussion groups. In that way we will be preparing our students with skills for success.

Employers are very clear. They are redefining employability skills. What is top of their list? Not technical skills. Employers know those will change. They are demanding communication skills, interpersonal skills, and teamwork skills.

Because the demographics in the United States and across Europe are transforming at a very rapid rate (soon white, Euro-Americans will be in a minority in the United States), to be prepared to function well in the workplace of the future, students also need to acquire diversity skills. That is, students today need to learn to work well with others of different cultures, races, and ethnic backgrounds. Race relations improve dramatically when students work in integrated teams; they become polarized when students work in competitive or individualistic settings (Kagan, 2006b).

Teams in the Workplace

Organization Size	Employees in Teams
100-499	71%
500-999	75%
1,000-2,499	84%
2,500-9,999	83%
10,000+	86%
All Sizes	73%

Source: Training Magazine (1994)

Skills Desired by Employers
Rated on scale of 1 to 5:
1=Least important; 5=Extremely important.

Oral Communication	4.7
Interpersonal Skills	4.6
Teamwork Skills	4.5
Flexibility	4.3
Analytical	4.3
Written Communication	4.3
Proficiency in Field	4.1
Leadership	4.1
Computer Knowledge	3.9

Source: National Assoc. of Colleges and Employees (1995).

Traditional vs. Modern Views of Education

	Traditional	Modern
View of Curriculum	Fixed Information, Skills	Rapidly Changing, Expanding
Source of Curriculum	Instructor & Text	Instructor & Text Plus Internet, Multimedia
Time for Learning	Formal Education	Formal Education Plus Lifelong Learning
Essential Curriculum	Knowledge & Skills	Knowledge & Skills Plus Thinking, Creativity, Diversity Skills, Interpersonal Skills
View of Learner	Empty Vessel	Constructor of Knowledge
Desired Social Orientation	Independent & Competitive	Interdependent & Cooperative
Instructional Strategies	Lecture, Q&A, Solo Practice	Lecture, Frequent, Varied Pair and Team Cooperative Interaction Structures

Tools for the Instructional Revolution

We have a new understanding of how students best learn, as well as a new understanding of what they need to learn if they are to be successful. We cannot face these challenges successfully if we cling to ways of teaching adapted to empty vessel, fixed knowledge views. We need to adapt the ways we teach to our understanding of how students best learn and to our understanding of what they most need to learn.

For almost forty years we have been experimenting with perfecting and training instructors in alternative instructional strategies called Kagan Structures. Structures are ways to organize the interaction of students with the instructor, the academic content, and/or each other. Not all structures consistently produce positive results. Kagan Structures, in contrast, are designed to ensure cooperative interaction and participation of all students. Kagan Structures are designed to align both with how brains best learn and with the need to foster students' 21st century skills. While teaching any content, Kagan Structures engage all brains in creative thinking, in a context of cooperative interdependence — a context that fosters the skills for success in the workplace of the future. Kagan Structures do not require a change in our curriculum; they require only a change in how we deliver that curriculum.

Kagan Structures are now used at all grades, from kindergarten classrooms to college and university lecture halls in over twenty countries. When the structures are used, they transform the level of student engagement and accelerate achievement. The data supporting that claim is detailed elsewhere (Kagan & Kagan, 2009). Although we have developed over 200 structures, what follows is a description of three Kagan Structures that are easy to use in higher education.

Traditional Structures vs. Kagan Structures

RallyRobin vs. Q&A

Traditionally, when attempting to increase student engagement or check for understanding, instructors have relied on a structure called Instructor-Student Question-Answer or, for short, simply Q&A. This Q&A structure is commonly used during small lectures, labs, and discussion groups. In this familiar way of structuring the interaction, the instructor first asks a question, those students who wish to answer then raise their hands, the instructor calls on one, that student answers, and finally the instructor responds to the answer, usually with praise, a correction, or an amplification.

One of many alternative ways to structure student interaction at the moment we wish to increase engagement or check for understanding is a Kagan Structure called RallyRobin. The instructor first asks a question, but rather than calling on volunteers to answer, the instructor then tells students to turn to a partner and take turns sharing answers. For example, the instructor might say, "Turn to a partner and take turns naming possible long-term consequences of the economic stimulus package." Because Kagan Structures are content free, depending on the academic content of the course, the students might be instructed to RallyRobin inert elements, literary techniques used in a poem, possible causes of a war, or the steps in calculating a correlation of a group of paired numbers. Any structure can be used to generate an infinite number of activities; the instructor simply "plugs in" the curriculum appropriate to the lesson.

Advantages of RallyRobin. The traditional Q&A structure is sequential; that is, the instructor calls on students one after another. Kagan Structures involve simultaneous interaction: Rather than calling on one student after another, during RallyRobin one student in each pair is talking at once. At each moment, in a class of 30, traditional Q&A has 1/30th or a little over 3% of the class actively engaged at any one moment; in contrast, RallyRobin produces 50% active engagement. In the same amount of time an instructor using the traditional structure can call on and respond to at most three students, each sharing one answer, the instructor using RallyRobin gives an opportunity to every student to share several answers. In the traditional approach, only the high achievers or the outgoing students raise a hand; in RallyRobin all students respond.

Lack of active engagement is perhaps the single biggest problem with traditional instructional strategies from upper elementary through university. In 1984, John Goodlad reported on the largest study of schooling conducted to that date (Goodlad, 1984). The basic finding: general reliance on traditional instructor talk and occasional calling on students one at a time; over 90% of classes lacked intense student engagement. More recently, Pianta and colleagues observed over 2,500 classrooms and found almost identical results: Over 90% of class time is spent with instructors talking and students passively listening or working alone, and over 90% of classrooms lacked intense engagement (Pianta, Belsky, Houts, & Morrison, 2007).

Because all students are simultaneously engaged during the Kagan Structures, instruction aligns with the stimulus level to which modern students have become accustomed. When I was a student half a century ago, there were no DVDs, CDs, MTVs, Reality TV, Web Cams, iPods, PSPs, XBoxs, Wiis, or web based forms of information and interaction. The professor was the most exciting thing in my environment. Today, the interest level a lecturer can provide pales in comparison to all the other sources of stimulation to which students are constantly exposed. To have students work alone, for many students today, in their words, is "just plain boring." In contrast, interactive structures provide rich stimulation and are more aligned with the stimulus level to which today's students have become accustomed. In essence, we are in competition with media, and our best tool in this competitive game is to create a stimulating learning environment. And there is no stimulus more engaging for most students than other students.

RallyRobin, like the other Kagan Structures, is superior with regard to authentic assessment as well. With the traditional structure we hear only from the high achievers, giving us an illusion that the level of comprehension in the group is far higher than it is. With RallyRobin the instructor can move through the discussion group and listen in to a larger, more representative sample of the group.

Compared to traditional Q&A, RallyRobin results in educational outcomes better aligned with 21st century skills and brain-friendly instruction:

21st Century Skills

- Students are thinking of and evaluating many possible answers, not just one.
- Students are taking turns, showing mutual respect, listening to each other, learning collaborative skills.
- Students work in heterogeneous pairs, acquiring diversity skills.
- Students are more active, and because they enjoy class and learning more they are more likely to become lifelong learners.

Brain-Friendly Instruction

- More brains are engaged and the brains that are engaged are more actively engaged.
- More students are verbalizing so retention is increased.
- All students process the content so content is transferred from short- to long-term memory.
- More emotion is evoked so retrograde memory enhancement increases retention.
- The structure is an episode so episodic memory increases retention.
- Students are actively constructing meaning rather than passively listening to a lecture or listening to one student answer the instructor's question.

RallyRobin vs. Pair Discussion. Some instructors think they are doing good cooperative learning when they are not. Rather than structuring the interaction so students take turns talking, they use a structure we call Pair Discussion. They simply say, "Turn to a partner and talk it over." During Pair Discussion, in many pairs the high achiever or more outgoing student does most or even all of the talking while the mind of the lower achieving or shy student begins to wander. We all have had the experience of being in a Pair Discussion and have our mind wander while our partner goes on and on about something that is not of particular interest to us. Pair Discussion does not consistently lead to all brains engaged, and does not consistently lead to the other gains outlined above. RallyRobin is verbal ping-pong or tennis; it is quick moving back-and-forth interaction that does not allow one partner to dominate or pontificate. The meta-communication: We are all of equal status, and our contributions are equally valued.

Timed Pair Share vs. Q&A. RallyRobin is a great structure for responding to a question that has many short answers: Students take turns adding items to an oral list. If, however, we want an in-depth response from each student, Timed Pair Share is preferable. In Timed Pair Share each student in turn shares with a partner for a predetermined amount of time. For example, the instructor might have students express their opinion on whether cloning humans is ever desirable; how they might modify a law; the thinking process they went through as they solved a math problem, or their personal reaction to a painting, photograph, poem, or piece of music. To ensure the acquisition of active listening skills, after each partner shares, listeners' responses may include, "What I learned as you shared was..." Or "Your most interesting point was..."

Advantages of Timed Pair Share. Like RallyRobin, Timed Pair Share is a simultaneous structure so in a very short time every student has the opportunity to share. Let's say we want to give every student in a discussion group or lecture a minute to share their ideas. In a class of only thirty students, it would take well over an hour to reach our goal if we call on students one at a time! During Instructor-Student Question-Answer, the instructor talks twice for each time a student talks, first asking the question and then responding to the answer. The instructor talks about 60% of the time. Naturally, as thoughtful instructors we would never spend a full hour doing Q&A. But in fact we do! We may average only ten minutes each hour for Q&A, doing, for example, five minutes of Q&A a third of the way through a presentation and then doing another five minutes of Q&A two thirds of the way through the presentation. After six hour-long classes we have used up a valuable hour for Q&A. How have students spent their time during that hour? They verbalized their ideas for a minute and spent the rest of that hour looking at the back of the head of a student talking to the instructor! In fact, however, because not all students volunteer to respond, some students don't get even a minute an hour of active brain engagement. Traditional Q&A is not aligned with how brains best learn: It creates disengagement and boredom. To reach our same goal of giving every student a minute to verbalize their thinking, using a Timed Pair Share, it does not take an hour — it takes us only a little over two minutes: Once we ask the question, in two minutes students have expressed their ideas for a minute each. In two minutes with Timed Pair Share we create as much active brain engagement as the traditional instructor creates in an hour.

Timed Pair Share, like RallyRobin is carefully

aligned with the requirements for brain-friendly instruction and for development of 21st century skills. There is emphasis on active listening so every brain is fully engaged. Timed Pair Share is quite in contrast to one student in the class sharing, responding to the instructor, while many or most of the other students tune out. All brains are engaged and the emphasis on active listening ensures that students are acquiring collaborative communication skills that predict success in the 21st century workplace.

Sage-N-Scribe vs. Solo Practice. In many classes we teach a skill that students need to practice to obtain mastery. Traditionally we have assigned problems or worksheets or have had students practice the skill in a lab or at a workstation. Often these assignments are done alone. A Kagan Structure designed to help students obtain mastery of a skill is Sage-N-Scribe. Students work in pairs to practice a series of problems or procedures. On the first problem one student (the Sage) tells the other (the Scribe) the steps of the procedure as the Scribe performs the procedure. The Scribe is instructed not to write down or perform a step if she is not certain it is correct, either offering a correction opportunity, or if both are uncertain, seeking help. The Scribe praises the Sage upon completion. The students then switch roles for successive problems.

Advantages of Sage-N-Scribe. Among the advantages of Sage-N-Scribe over Solo Practice are: 1) immediate reinforcement and correction opportunities, 2) peer tutoring and encouragement, 3) students keeping each other on task, 4) 100% active engagement because one is talking while the other is performing, and 5) less need for instructors or discussion group leaders to correct papers. As they interact, students are acquiring collaborative teamwork skills that transfer well to the interdependent workplace. Further, because one student is writing while the other is directing, all brains are engaged at once. The praising creates emotion, releasing the power of retrograde memory enhancement.

When students interact in cooperative structures like Sage-N-Scribe, peer norms among students change radically. In the traditional approach, students work in isolation or in implicit competition. Who will get the limited supply of the best grades? Students experience themselves — and in fact are — isolated or in competition with each other. With Sage-N-Scribe and other Kagan Structures students feel themselves to be on the same side; the structures create a community of learners eager to help each other. Thus Sage-N-Scribe more closely simulates the collaborative workplace team for which students need to be prepared. In the modern workplace, employees do not all work independently on identical tasks, later to be informed who did the best and who did not pass. As in the modern workplace, there is interaction and cooperation.

Call for Action

What we teach has changed. Sources of information have changed. The jobs for which we must prepare our students have changed. The world is rapidly changing. It is time we change the way we teach. Traditional instructional strategies prepare our students for the world that was. Interactive structures prepare our students for the world that will be. We are on the verge of an instructional revolution. Only by joining that revolution can we best prepare our students for the world of the future.

References

Carter, R. (1998). *Mapping the Mind*. Berkeley, CA: University of California Press.

Cowan, N. (2005). *Working Memory Capacity*. New York, NY: Psychology Press.

Goodlad, J. (1984). *A Place Called School*. New York, NY: McGraw-Hill Book Company.

Gopnik, A., A. Meltzoff & P. Kuhl. (1999). *The Scientist in the Crib: What Early Learning Tells Us About the Mind*. New York, NY: Harper-Collins.

Hawkins, J. (2004). *On Intelligence*. New York, NY: Times Books.

Kagan, S. (2003). "Cooperative Learning Structures for Brain-Compatible Instruction." In Cooper, J., P. Robinson & D. Ball. *Small Group Instruction in Higher Education: Lessons From the Past, Visions of the Future*. Stillwater, OK: New Forums Press.

Kagan, S. (2006a). "Pedagogy." In Feinstein, S. (ed.). *The Praeger Handbook of Learning and the Brain, Volume 2: M-Z*. Westport, CT: Greenwood Publishing Group, Inc.

Kagan, S. (2006b) "Cooperative Learning, The Power to Transform Race Relations." *Teaching Tolerance*, 2006, 53.

Kagan, S. & M. Kagan (2009). *Kagan Cooperative Learning*. San Clemente, CA: Kagan Publishing.

McGaugh, J. (2003). *Memory and Emotion: The Making of Lasting Memories*. New York, NY: Columbia University Press.

Pert, C. & D. Chopra (1997). *Molecules of Emotion: Why You Feel the Way You Feel*. New York, NY: Scribner.

Pianta, R., J. Belsky, R. Houts & F. Morrison (2007). "Opportunities to Learn in America's Elementary Classrooms." *Science*.

Training Magazine, October 1994. Based on 1,194 companies.

Ratey, J. & E. Hagerman (2008). *Spark: The Revolutionary New Science of Exercise and the Brain*. New York, NY: Little, Brown and Company.

Wear, J. (2004). "Section IV: Education and Training." In Dyro, J. (ed.). *Clinical Engineering Handbook*. Burlington, MA: Elsevier Academic Press.

Promoting Deep Learning Through Cooperative Learning

Barbara J. Millis

How many times have we, as well-meaning teachers, cheerfully charged our students to "Read chapter eight. It contains really important information that I'll be covering on Wednesday." When Wednesday arrives, we enter class armed with our well-thought-out discussion questions, carefully calculated to elicit responses showing higher order thinking. We lob the first question toward the student audience like a carefully wrapped gift and wait for the frenzy of discussion to erupt. Alas, all we observe is a sea of blank faces, or worse—inverted faces trying desperately not to make eye contact. With a sinking feeling we realize that few, if any, students even read chapter eight. So, what can we do?

As a first step, we can stop blaming our students. They lead busy lives: why should they invest their time reading material that we promised to "cover." They are expecting us to carefully outline chapter eight in a well-rehearsed lecture. That is pretty much "business as usual" in many classes, particularly those with burgeoning enrollments. Even if our students respect us and intend to read chapter eight if a free hour surfaces, they know they have the safety of numbers should we decide to be punitive, abusive, or reproachful. So, what is the alternative?

The alternative is to take a lesson from the literature on deep learning and recognize that as Laird, Shoup, Kuh, and Schwartz (2008) point out, "... faculty members, as the designers and facilitators of learning activities and tasks, play a key role in shaping students' approaches to learning" (p. 471). Bain and Zimmerman (2009), in fact, define "great teachers as those people with considerable success in fostering deep approaches and results among their students" (p. 2). The assessment practices that faculty adopt can be particularly effective in encouraging students to take a deep approach. But other contextual factors such as course design are also within faculty control.

What is Deep Learning?

Looking at reading strategies, Marton and Saljo (1976) did the original ground-breaking work on deep and surface approaches to learning. They found that students took two radically different approaches to preparing for a test over specific material. The so-called deep learners read for understanding and overall meaning; surface learners, in contrast, focused on individual facts and memorization. Diamond, Koernig, and Iqbal (2008) give a complex, synthesized definition of deep learning:

> Deep learning is described by Marton and Saljo (1976) as including both process and outcome. The process involves 'engaging in elaborative processing to find additional meanings . . . [and] achieve a deeper understanding of the material' (Bacon & Stewart, 2006, p. 183). . . . A key outcome of deep learning is the ability to apply concepts acquired in one context to a variety of new situations. (p. 118)

Faculty members who do all the work for students are typically not teaching for deep learning. McKay and Kember (1997) label as "spoonfeeding" the reliance on "information transmission" (p. 56). Leamnson (2002) notes:

> What is often called 'deep learning,' the kind that demands both understanding and remembering of relationships, causes, effects and implications for new or different situations simply *cannot be made easy*. Such learning depends on students actually *restructuring* their brains and that demands effort. (p. 7)

Many researchers (e.g., Biggs, 1987, 1988, 1989, 2003; Entwistle, 1981; Ramsden, 2003) have since added to the deep learning research. Clearly, deep learning is related to critical thinking because both concepts focus on critical analysis and forging connections between new knowledge and prior knowledge. They both lead to a genuine understanding that promotes long-term retention of the learned material and the ability to retrieve it and apply it to new problems in unfamiliar concepts (the idea of "transfer" which is so important for real-life applications).

Surface learning, on the other hand, focuses on the uncritical acceptance of knowledge with an emphasis on memorization of unquestioned, unrelated facts. Retention is fleeting and there is little long-term retention and less understanding. Faculty committed to content coverage, particularly those in the so-called hard science, technology, engineering and mathematics disciplines, often overload students despite the fact that a heavy work load is related to surface learning. A study by Kreber (2003) found, for example, that Heavy Workload was the strongest predictor of a surface approach.

The two approaches are summarized in a table created by Atherton, 2009 (See Table 1).

Some researchers have added a third dimension to this research by discussing an achieving or strategic approach, which is an approach to learning calculated to maximize success while doing the least amount of work. However, scholars such as Richardson (1994) and Zeegers (2002) have pointed out that strategic intentions can lead to either deep or surface approaches, making the third approach unnecessary.

Why Focus on Deep Approaches?

Just as Miss America contestants routinely assured Bert Parks they wished for world peace, typical faculty members, when questioned about their dreams for the perfect course, comment, "I want my students to learn to think critically." As Johnson (1995) suggests, "It seems that critical thinking is on almost every educator's list of priorities" (p. 37). When Ramsden (1992) reviewed several studies focused on crucial learning goals, he too discovered that faculty "describe content-related versions ... of the general principles of 'critical thinking' and understanding" (p. 21).

Furthermore, as Kreber (2003) points out: "Deep-level learning, typically understood as learning characterised [sic] by a motivation to seek meaning, understand underlying principles and identify relationships between ideas or concepts, has been shown to be an important prerequisite for self-directed learning" (p. 58) as defined by Candy, 1991.

A study focused on the impact of various disciplines and deep learning approaches (Laird et. al., 2008) also examined "the relationships between deep learning approaches and three student learning outcomes: student self-reported gains in personal and intellectual development, satisfaction with college, and self-reported grades" (p. 474). Although the study found that deep learning approaches had a weak correlation to grades, the other two outcomes — outcomes virtually all faculty would regard as desirable — were positively correlated to deep learning.

So, there are many reasons — critical thinking, lifelong learning, personal and intellectual development, and satisfaction with college — for faculty to switch to a deep learning model. The problem is that they often lack both role models and a logical frame work for organizing learning. Fortunately, by synthesizing and applying the research on both deep learning and cooperative learning, a framework emerges.

Teaching for Deep Learning

In an overview of the international research on deep learning, Rhem (1995) provided insights into the four characteristics of deep learning, which are echoed by McKay and Kember (1997). These characteristics are:
1. A well-structured knowledge base with a focus on concepts, integration of knowledge, and a cumulative experience.
2. An appropriate motivational level, with an emphasis on intrinsic motivation and a sense of "ownership" of the material.
3. Learner activity associated with active, not passive learning.
4. Interaction with others, including student-teacher interactions and student-student interactions.

Table 1. Summary of Deep and Surface Learning.

Deep	Surface
Focus is on "what is signified"	Focus is on the "signs" (or on the learning as a signifier of something else)
Relates previous knowledge to new knowledge	Focus on unrelated parts of the task
Relates knowledge from different courses	Information for assessment is simply memorised
Relates theoretical ideas to everyday experience	Facts and concepts are associated unreflectively
Relates and distinguishes evidence and argument	Principles are not distinguished from examples
Organizes and structures content into coherent whole	Task is treated as an external imposition
Emphasis is internal, from within the student	Emphasis is external, from demands of assessment

Cooperative learning—structured group work—plays a crucial role in the final two characteristics. Some good resources for cooperative learning are Johnson, Johnson, and Smith (1991); Millis and Cottell (1998); Millis (2002); Cooper, Robinson, and Ball (2003); and Millis (2010).

The "secret" to teaching for deep learning lies in sequencing assignments and activities. In face-to-face classes, for example, the sequence would emphasize getting students into the well-structured knowledge base through motivating out-of-class assignments (homework) and then "going deeper" with the learned material through cooperative learning methods (active learning and student-student interactions). To be useful, the homework assignment must be visible; thus, asking students to read chapters with no written output cannot guarantee deep learning. The written output can take a variety of forms. It can be as simple as a graphic organizer (McTighe, 1992), such as a Pro-Con-Caveat chart where each student lists, as a homework assignment, the arguments in favor of a certain decision and against the decision with caveats placed in a third column. Teachers could ask students to explore the pros, cons, and caveats of building a hospital in a certain neighborhood in their city. The assignment would be motivating for most students because it involves a real-life problem relevant to themselves. Below is an example of a Pro-Con-Caveat Grid (See Figure 1).

In other cases, the homework assignment might be fairly complex, such as having students prepare a two-page double-entry journal (DEJ) on an assigned reading. On the left-hand side of the journal (a Word table with two columns), the students provide an outline of the author's main points. Opposite each point, the students write their responses, making links to material learned in other classes, to class readings, or to their own experiences. To avoid overloading students, faculty members can limit either the length of the DEJ or the number of key points. This type of assignment becomes motivating for two reasons: (1) when students know their homework will be reviewed by peers, they are more likely to come to class prepared, as Nelson (2004) notes, and (2) because of the positive impact of the self-referent effect (Rogers, Kuipir, & Kirker, 1977; Symons & Johnson, 1997). On the next page is an abbreviated example of a DEJ (See Figure 2).

Rather than having a teacher then stuff this homework into a yawning briefcase for later teacher-generated one-on-one feedback, a deep learning approach would ensure that the other two characteristics came into play by using cooperative learning approaches. The students would do something with their homework in pairs or in small groups where everyone is actively engaged.

In the case of the Pro-Con-Caveat grid, the faculty member could have students in heterogeneous groups of four review all four grids and create a synthesis with the best ideas of all four students. To complete this task, they will be working at the highest levels of Bloom's (1956) original taxonomy by making judgments (evaluation) and synthesizing. The deliberate heterogeneity of teams or pairs helps build the skills needed for critical thinking. Critical thinking depends on identifying and challenging assumptions and subsequently exploring and conceptualizing alternatives (Brookfield, 1987). These challenges will rarely occur when students select their own group members because then students typically think alike. Group heterogeneity also helps students build the skills needed to work with others in the workplace and in the community.

When students are in groups where

Pro-Con-Caveat Grid
by
Barbara J. Millis

Should Parking on Campus be Pro-Rated Based on Position Title?

Pro	Con	Caveats
This system would be much fairer because an administrative assistant and a faculty member parking in the same designated area, such as the parking garages, would not pay the same amount. Often the people who are carrying the heaviest burdens end up parking the furthest away. This would give people in lower pay grades a better opportunity to afford closer parking.	A pro-rated system would be very complex to administer because each designated parking area would have to have various levels of fees. Parking fees constitute a major source of revenue for the university, so efforts to reduce overall costs could negatively impact the budget. Some faculty and administrators would resist any changes that might increase their parking fees.	A feasibility study would be needed. The university would need to be able to prevent people from giving their parking passes to others.

Figure 1. Pro-Con-Caveat Grid

group members can be easily identified, faculty can then build in individual accountability by using a Numbered Heads Together/Structured Problem-solving approach (Kagan & Kagan, 1994; Millis & Cottell, 1998). The faculty member can call on students randomly—not students pre-identified in advance as spokespersons or reporters—a practice that makes everyone accountable. This practice also encourages peer coaching because no one knows who will be called on, and it allows shyer students—who typically never respond—to feel more comfortable presenting a group, not a personal, response to the problem. This approach can be effective even in large classes. Using decks of playing cards and multiple set of file folders, faculty can assign students to permanent groups of four. Each student has a unique identity even within a large class when folders are color-coded so that the first 52 students are in 13 groups with say, red folders; the next 52 have blue folders, etc. Within the sets of folders, students have unique identities based on their suits within a given number, e.g., Three of Hearts, Jack of Clubs. To determine the spokespersons randomly, the teacher merely announces the color of the folder and draws a card (blue folders: Queen of Hearts) and that person gives the group report.

The folders are a wonderful class management tool as well. Faculty can use them to collect and return homework, for example. If faculty use rotating group roles, typically recorder/scribe, discussion leader/facilitator, and reporter/spokesperson—except when employing Numbered Heads Together/Structured Problem-solving approach when the reporter/spokesperson role could fall to anyone—then a fourth role could be the folder monitor. That person is responsible each week for picking up the team folder, recording attendance, distributing homework—often folded over or stapled to insure privacy—and collecting the homework after the in-class cooperative activity. There is no longer a need for faculty to alphabetize homework and painstakingly return it. The grade book can match the students' team assignments, which can change at the mid-term point in smaller classes, but typically remain in place all semester in larger classes. Anything needed in class is also placed in advance in the folders, saving distribution time.

The DEJ sequencing is even more complex than the one just described using a Pro-Con-Caveat grid/graphic organizer. A DEJ prepared out-of-class gets students into the knowledge base and as already noted, also motivates them.

What becomes of the out-of-class homework assignment is critically important. The sequencing is very important to build for deep learning. Teachers can pair students randomly and have them read and comment on each other's DEJ. (Unprepared students do not pair: they work on their DEJs at the back of the room.) The paired conversations should lead to both learning and honest conversations. The original article—or notes from a guest lecturer's presentation—should be available for easy reference as students read each others' DEJs. But the reflective responses, too, should prompt authentic "connections." In a nursing class, for example, a student would likely not ignore a highly personal comment from his partner and offer an appropriate response: "Your Uncle Joey died of AIDS? I am so sorry."

An Abbreviated Version of a Double Entry Journal with Two Key Points

Double Entry Journal on the "Introduction" of *Made to Stick: Why Some Ideas Survive and Others Die*, by
Chip Heath and Dan Health
by
Barbara J. Millis

Authors' Key Points	My Response to the Key Points
The premise behind this book is, "How do you design an idea that sticks?"	I find this premise both intriguing and practical. It's intriguing because all of us remember commercials, jingles, or urban legends, such as the hook in the car door. Why!? I also want practical answers to this question for several reasons. I need to market faculty development at a research institution—a "hard sell." How do I make the concept of investing in teaching an appealing idea? I also want to convince people through workshops that the ideas I share with them, such as deep learning, can strengthen student learning if properly adapted. What can I do to help them remember key research and "best practices"? How can I motivate them to apply the "best practices" I model?
The authors summarize the answer to the question above through an acronym, SUCCESS: a Simple Unexpected Concrete Credentialed Emotional Story.	I am motivated to continue reading! I want to learn more about each of the six principles. I am particularly intrigued by the "power of story."

Figure 2. Abbreviated Version of a Double Entry Journal

The learning is further sequenced when the teacher provides feedback beyond the peer feedback offered through the paired discussion. Bransford, Brown, and Cocking (2000) emphasize that "students need feedback about the degree to which they know when, where, and how to use the knowledge they are learning" (p. 59). Teachers can return DEJs with their own brief comments focused on the accuracy of the key points and the relevance and depth of the reflective responses. (Although marked, DEJs need not receive a labor-intensive letter grade: a pass/fail grade motivates students without adding significantly to the grading load. A "pass" counting 10 points toward a criterion referenced point-based final grade, for example, allows the teacher to comment quickly and personally, rather than justifying a grade based on the nuances between an A- and a B+.)

Feedback can also be provided through yet another stage in the sequence: whole-class feedback on DEJs. The teacher can share exemplary student DEJ examples ostensibly to "coach" students to write better DEJs in the future. But, as part of a sequence, this final stage also promotes learning through "repetition without rote."

Two biologists help us understand the basics of learning and why sequencing is so important: Zull (2002) identifies the art of teaching as "creating conditions that lead to change in a learner's brain" (p. 5) and Leamnson (1999) defines learning as "stabilizing, through repeated use, certain appropriate and desirable synapses in the brain" (p. 5). Reading the assigned article or hearing the guest lecture is exposure one. Then, crafting the DEJ draws the student back into the material — with personally relevant responses — for repetition two. The paired discussion in class provides a third repetition. As a fourth repetition, students are likely to review their DEJ when the teacher returns them with comments. A fifth repetition occurs when teachers coach students on preparing an ideal DEJ by presenting exemplary examples as an in-class follow-up.

A Final Example of Deep Learning: Cooperative Debates

A literature teacher assigning *Antigone,* could have students, prior to the individual reading, form four debate teams examining two key questions relevant to the play: "Pro/Con: Should Antigone have buried her brother?" and "Pro/Con: Should Creon be impeached for poor leadership?"

The debate teams are formed randomly by having students draw slips of paper. This approach enables students to interact with classmates they may not know well. It also prevents the high achieving students from forming self-selected teams that would skew the debate results.

Because students have a particular focus — the debate question they need to support — they typically are motivated to read *Antigone* outside-of-class with care. They gather support for their teams' stances, receiving in-class time to compare their notes and work on preparing the best possible arguments (active learning/interactions).

Teachers need to tell students up-front that they will be using Numbered Heads/Structured Problem Solving (Kagan & Kagan, 1994; Millis & Cottell, 1998), so teams will not know in advance who their spokespersons will be. Thus, the teams have a genuine reason to be certain that all members are prepared to provide the best possible arguments, resulting in peer coaching and genuine learning. The randomly chosen spokespersons have a set amount of time, based on the length of the class period, to present their teams' cases. After the initial opposing arguments, the teams have time in class to prepare rebuttals. To avoid frustration, teachers can allow teams to select the students who will present the rebuttals. Rubrics help the observing students (the half of the class assigned to the other debate topic) to vote for the team that made the most convincing arguments. The second set of paired teams then follow the same procedure for their debate on the second question.

Almost all disciplines lend themselves to debate topics: (a) Computer science: Blackboard or Moodle course management platforms? (b) History: Should the US have dropped a second atomic bomb on Nagasaki? (c) Biology: To clone or not to clone? (d) Economics: Should the US adopt a flat rate income tax?

Conclusion

Deep learning and cooperative learning are natural partners. The framework of deep learning — motivating out-of-class assignments to get students into the knowledge base followed by in-class active learning and student-student interactions (cooperative learning) — get students to sequentially build on their learning. The robust research base for both cooperative learning and deep learning will enable creative teachers to engage students in the highest levels of learning.

References

Atherton, J. S. (2009) *Learning and Teaching; Deep and Surface learning* [On-line] UK: Retrieved February 28, 2010 from http://www.learningandteaching.info/learning/deepsurf.htm.

Bacon, D., & Stewart, K. (2006). How fast do students forget what they learn in consumer behavior? A longitudinal study. *Journal of Marketing Education, 28,* 181-192.

Bain, K & Zimmerman, J. (Spring 2009). Understanding great teaching. *Peer Review: Emerging Trends and Key Debates in Undergraduate Education,* 1(2), 9-12.

Biggs, J. B. (1987). Student approaches to learning and studying. Melbourne: Australian Council for Educational Research.

Biggs, J. B. (1988). Approaches to learning and to essay writing. In R. R. Schmeck (Ed.), Learning strategies and learning styles (pp. 185-228). New York, NY: Plenum.

Biggs, J. B. (1989). Approaches to the enhancement of tertiary teaching. *Higher Education Research and Development,* 8, 7-25.

Biggs, J. B. (2003). Teaching for quality learning at university. Buckingham: Open University Press.

Bloom, B. S. (1956). *Taxonomy of educational objectives (Cognitive domain).* New York: Longman.

Bransford, J. D., Brown, A. L., & Cocking, R. R. (Eds.). (2000). *How people learn: Brain, mind, experience, and school.* Commission on Behavioral and Social Sciences and Education National Research Council. Washington, DC: National Academy Press.

Brookfield, S. D. (1987). *Developing critical thinkers: Challenging adults to explore alternative ways of thinking and acting.* San Francisco: Jossey-Bass.

Candy, P. (1991). *Self-direction for lifelong learning.* San Francisco: Jossey-Bass.

Cooper, J. L., Robinson, P, & Ball, D. (Eds). (2003). *Small group instruction in higher education: Lessons from the past, visions of the future.* Stillwater, OK: New Forums Press.

Diamond, N., Koernig, S. K. & Iqbal, Z. (May 20, 2008). Uniting active and deep learning to teach problem-solving skills: Strategic tools and the learning spiral. *Journal of Marketing Education* 2008; 30(2), 116-129. DOI: 10.1177/0273475308317707

Entwistle. N. J. (1981). *Styles of integrated learning and teaching: An integrated outline of educational psychology for students, teachers, and lecturers.* Hoboken, NJ: John Wiley & Sons.

Entwistle, N. J., & Ramsden, P. (1983). *Understanding student learning.* London: Croom Helm.

Johnson, G. R. (1995). *First Steps to Excellence in College Teaching.* Madison, WI: Magna Publication.

Johnson, D.W., Johnson, R.T., & Smith, K.A. (1991). *Cooperative learning: Increasing college faculty instructional productivity.* ASHE-ERIC Higher Education Report No. 4. Washington, DC: The George Washington University School of Education and Human Development.

Kagan, S. & Kagan, M. (1994). *Kagan cooperative learning.* San Juan Capistrano, CA: Kagan Publishing and Professional Development.

Kreber, C. (2003.) The relationship between students' course perception and their approaches to studying in undergrauduate science courses: A Canadian experience. *Higher Education Research and Development,* 22(1), 57–75. DOI: 10.1080/0729436032000058623

Laird, T. F. N, Shoup, R. Kuh, G. D. & Schwarz, M. J. (2008). The effects of disciplines on deep approaches to student learning and college outcomes. *Research in Higher Education,* 49, pp. 469–494.

Leamnson, R. (1999). *Thinking about teaching and learning: Developing habits of learning with first year college and university students.* Sterling, VA: Stylus Press.

Leamnson, R. (2002). Learning (Your First Job). Retrieved January 18, 2010 from http://www.ctl.uga.edu/Learning/.

Marton, F., & Saljo, R. (1976). On qualitative differences in learning: I. Outcome and process. *British Journal of Educational Psychology, 46,* 4–1.

McKay, J. & Kember, D. (1997). Spoon Feeding Leads to Regurgitation: A better diet can result in more digestible learning outcomes, *Higher Education Research & Development,* 16(1), 55–67. DOI: 10.1080/0729436970160105

McTighe, J. (1992). Graphic organizers: Collaborative links to better thinking. In N. Davidson & T. Worsham (Eds.), *Enhancing thinking through cooperative learning* (pp 182-197). New York: Teachers College Press.

Millis, B. J. (October 2002) Enhancing learning—and More!—through cooperative learning. IDEA Paper #38. Kansas State University: IDEA Center. Retrieved March 1, 2010 from http://www.idea.ksu.edu/papers/Idea_Paper_38.pdf.

Millis, B. J. (Ed.). (2010). Cooperative *Learning in Higher Education: Across the Disciplines, Across the Academy.* Sterling, VA: Stylus Press.

Millis, B. J. & Cottell, P. G. (1998). *Cooperative learning for higher education faculty.* American Council on Education, Oryx Press.

Nelson, C. (21 November, 2004). "Responding to diversity: Three pedagogical changes that can make a real difference in ANY college classroom. Workshop at the 24th annual Lilly Conference on College Teaching. Miami University of Ohio.

Ramsden, P. (1992). *Learning to teach in higher education.* London: Routledge.

Ramsden, P. (2003). *Learning to teach in higher education.* London: Routledge.

Rhem, J. (1995). Close-Up: Going deep. *The National Teaching & Learning Forum,* 5(1), 4.

Richardson, J.T.E. (1994). Cultural specicity of approaches to studying in higher education: A literature survey. *Higher Education,* 27, 449-468.

Rogers, T.B., Kuiper, N.A., & Kirker, W.S. (1977). Self-reference and the encoding of personal information. *Journal of Personality and Social Psychology,* 35, 677-688.

Symons, C. S. & Johnson, B. T. (May 1997). The self-reference effect in memory: A meta-analysis. *Psychological Bulletin,* 121(3), 371-394.

Zeegers, P. (2002) A Revision of the Biggs' Study Process Questionnaire (R-SPQ), *HigherEducation Research & Development,* 21(1), 73-92.

DOI: 10.1080/07294360220124666

Zull, J. E. (2002). *The art of changing the brain: Enriching teaching by exploring the biology of learning.* Sterling, VA: Stylus Press.

The Case and Context for Cooperative Learning

Joe Cuseo

Cooperative learning shares features with other instructional alternatives to the lecture method that have been loosely referred as engaging pedagogy, active learning, group learning, and collaborative learning. The objective of this chapter is to make a case for these learner-centered alternatives to the lecture method and articulate how cooperative learning relates to, but differs from, this larger family of instructional alternatives to the lecture method.

In the mid-1990s, clarion calls were sounded for improving the quality of undergraduate education that solicited a paradigm shift — away from the traditional focus on the teacher and the teaching process — to a new learning paradigm that focused on the *learner* and the *learning* process (American College Personnel Association, 1994; Angelo, 1997; Barr & Tagg, 1995). This was a new starting point for improving the teaching-learning process, one that centered on what the learner is doing, rather than what the teacher is doing (and covering) in class. In the new learner-centered paradigm, the defining features and goals of effective college teaching are facilitating the learning *process* and assessing learning *outcomes*.

Implications of the new learning paradigm for college professors include the following shifts in educational philosophy and instructional practice.

1. Instruction shifts from teacher-centered and content-driven to *learner*-centered and *learning process*-driven.

   Instructional methods may be conceptualized as ranging along a continuum from *teacher*-centered to *learner*-centered. Extreme, teacher-centered teaching is best illustrated by the straight (uninterrupted) lecture, in which the professor does all the talking and is the center of attention and control of the learning process. In contrast, learner-centered instruction involves less didactic discourse or "talk time" on the part of the instructor and shifts more class time, control and responsibility for learning to the students.

2. The student's role changes from being a passive receptacle and recipient of teacher-delivered information to being an *engaged learner* and *active agent* in the learning process.

   Instead of instructors delivering information-loaded lectures for the sole purpose of transmitting knowledge, learner-centered instruction goes beyond the learning of content to include the learning of *process*—i.e., educating students in the process of *learning how to learn* and developing *lifelong learning* skills (e.g., critical thinking, problem solving, and communication skills).

3. The instructor's role expands from being a professor who professes and disseminates "truths" to being a *facilitator* or *mediator* of the learning process. In this expanded role, the instructor engages in three key educational tasks:
   (a) educational *design* — creating learning tasks and classroom conditions that are conducive to active student involvement;
   (b) educational *coach* — facilitating, coordinating, and orchestrating learning from the sidelines while students assume the role of active players in the learning process;
   (c) educational *assessor* — evaluating the effectiveness of learning by collecting data on learning outcomes and using this data as feedback to improve the learning process.

Thus, in the learner-centered paradigm, students spend less time being "instructed" (lectured to or talked at) and more time engaging in learning activities that ask them to actually *do* something — other than rote recording of lecture notes (O'Neill & McMahon, 2005).

The Case for Learner-Centered Alternatives to the Lecture Method

Among the primary forces propelling the paradigm shift toward learner-centered pedagogy are the limitations of the lecture method. Lest we forget, the dominant pedagogical strategy used by college professors is lecturing (Pascarella & Terenzini, 2005) and the frequency of its use has been remarkably consistent over several decades (Bligh, 2000; Nance & Nance,

1990). While professors may think that students are cognitively engaged when they are taking lecture notes in class, research suggests otherwise. For example, Fassinger (1996) surveyed over 1,000 students in more than 50 classes in a wide variety of academic disciplines that met during the same time period. She found that students reported being less actively involved in class than their instructors perceived them to be. Furthermore, the quality of student note-taking during lectures leaves much to be desired. For example, one study revealed that most students take notes that are written on the board (or projected on a slide); however, they record less than half of the important ideas that professors state verbally, but do not put in print (Johnstone & Su, 1994). Other research indicates that approximately one-half of students' time during lectures is spent on thinking about things unrelated to the lecture content, and up to 15% of their class time is spent "fantasizing" (Milton, Polio, & Eison, 1986). (Mercifully, the investigators neither examined the specific nature of, nor offered hypotheses about, the content of student fantasies during lectures.)

In particular, student attention and concentration tend to drop precipitously after the first 10-15 minutes of a continuous lecture (Penner, 1984; Verner and Dickinson, 1967). This drift and drop in attention occurs among all type of students, including intrinsically motivated, learning-oriented (vs. grade-oriented) undergraduates (Milton, Pollio, & Eison, 1986) and advanced students taking courses in graduate and professional school (Stuart & Rutheford, 1978). Thus, attention loss during lectures cannot be simply dismissed as a "student problem" attributable to lack of student motivation, a breakdown in self-discipline, or an outbreak of attention deficit disorder among contemporary youth. Instead, the problem lies with the lecture method itself—or, more precisely, continuous use of the lecture method for an extended amount of time. This research suggests that the ability to sustain attention to aurally-received information for a prolonged period of time is a task that the human brain it is not naturally inclined or equipped to perform. Evolutionary psychologists and neurobiologists theorize that the brain is not wired to process information emanating from a single source for an extended period of time because it would not have contributed to the survival of the human species. Our early ancestors needed to process information in short segments so they could swiftly shift their attention from the task at hand to respond immediately to a potential threat (predator) or opportunity (prey) (LaBerge, 1995; Sylwester, 1996). The human brain is better equipped to perceive and process information in short, focused timeframes (lasting no longer than 10-15 minutes) followed by opportunities to act on the information it has processed (Jensen, 1998).

Even if students were able to sustain maximum attention throughout a typical 50-minute lecture, important educational outcomes, such as higher-level thinking and attitude change, would not likely be realized. Studies show that when humans engage in prolonged performance on a repetitive mental task (such as continuous note-taking), lower centers of the brain that control automatic (mindless) behavior become involved in performing the repetitive task, with limited involvement of higher (cortical) areas of the brain normally responsible for higher-level thinking (Bligh, 2000; Mackworth, 1970). This finding reinforces the old aphorism: "During lectures, information passes from the lecturer's notes to the students' notes, but through the minds of neither."

To achieve educational outcomes beyond information acquisition, students need to be more actively engaged in the learning process (Pascarella & Terenzini, 1991; 2005). As McKeachie et al. (1986) conclude from their review of the research literature on college teaching methods, "If we want students to become more effective in meaningful learning and thinking, they need to spend more time in active, meaningful learning and thinking—not just sitting and passively receiving information" (p. 77). This is consistent with the results of an extensive literature review conducted by Donald Bligh (2000), whose conclusion provides a fitting summary statement for research on student learning outcomes associated with the lecture method: "The balance of evidence favors this conclusion: *Use lectures to teach information. Do not rely on them to promote thought, change attitudes, or behavioral skills if you can help it*" (p. 20).

This is not to imply that lecturing should be totally eliminated or eradicated at the postsecondary level. Certainly, higher education is a place where knowledgeable professors share their knowledge with undergraduates and model thinking processes for students to emulate. However, to do so for an extended period of time in one sitting is not an effective, brain compatible form of learning. For students to be cognitively engaged in the college classroom, teacher-centered pedagogy needs to be alternated or punctuated with learner-centered experiences that empower students to take a more active and responsible role in the learning process.

Learner-Centered Instructional Alternatives to the Lecture Method

There are four major types of instructional strategies that have been used to promote greater student engagement in the college classroom: (a) whole-class discussions, (b) small-group discussions, (c) collaborative learning groups, and (d) cooperative learning groups. What follows is a discussion of why and how each of these learner-centered teaching strategies can effectively complement and augment the lecture method.

Whole-Class Discussions

Strategic insertion of instructor-posed questions during lecture can stimulate higher levels of student involvement with course content and the course instructor. Infusing thought-provoking questions into instructional presentations creates a climate of intellectual inquiry that serves to model and encourage students to ask their own questions in class. However, not all instructor-posed questions are equally effective in eliciting student involvement. The types of questions that are most likely to involve students are *open-ended* questions, which call for more than one correct or acceptable answer (e.g., "What may be possible interpretations of explanations for ____?). Such questions invite multiple responses, welcome a diversity of perspectives, and promote *divergent* thinking—i.e., expansive thinking that does not converge on one (and only one) correct response (Cuseo, 2005).

Small-Group Discussions

The major limitation of whole-class discussion is that it involves students on an individual and sequential basis, i.e., one student raises a hand and makes a contribution, followed by the instructor calling on a second student who makes a contribution, etc. In contrast to this sequential involvement of individual students, when discussion takes place in small groups (2-4 students), multiple students become involved simultaneously.

The need to augment whole-class discussion with small-group work is supported by research, which indicates that typically less than 10% of students in class account for more than 75% of all contributions made during class discussions. Students themselves are acutely aware of this phenomenon; when surveyed, almost 95% of them agreed with the statement: "In most of my classes, there are a small number of students who do most of the talking" (Karp & Yoels (1976). Small-group discussions can provide an antidote to these disturbing findings by creating a better opportunity for all students—not just the most assertive or most verbal—to become involved with the course material and with each other in the college classroom.

Collaborative Learning Groups

Collaborative learning may be defined as a small-group learning experience in which group members reach *consensus* with respect to some decision or action. Scholars in the fields of English and Literature have argued that in order to ensure that group work moves beyond interaction to collaboration, consensus must be reached by group members, (e.g., Bruffee, 1993; Wiener, 1986). The argument that consensus as the sine qua non for collaboration has its roots in the professional education of medical students who were asked to work in small groups to reach unified diagnostic decisions—which often proved superior to decisions reached individually (Abercrombie, 1960). (Fittingly, the etymological root of the word *discussion* means to "divide" or "break up"—as in the words, differentiate and disintegrate; in contrast, the etymological root of *collaboration* denotes integration or convergence—i.e., to "co-labor" or work together.) Thus, the key feature differentiating a discussion group from a collaborative learning group is that the latter does not simply generate or aggregate individual ideas; instead, its members attempt to reach a unified group decision with respect to the ideas they generate. For instance, rather than simply aggregating their ideas, a collaborative group will take it further by attempting to reach agreement on how best to categorize or prioritize their ideas.

Collaborative group work qualifies as a form of "brain compatible" learning. The human brain is likely to be wired for collaboration because working harmoniously in groups has been critical to the survival and evolution of the human species (Jensen, 1998). In fact, brain-imaging studies reveal that more activity occurs in thinking parts of the brain when people learn through social interaction than when they learn alone (Carter, 1998).

Cooperative Learning Groups

Cooperative learning (CL) may be defined as a specific form of collaborative learning, which employs structured procedures that are deliberately designed to convert group work into teamwork. Succinctly described, CL involves the use of small, *intentionally selected* groups of students who work *interdependently* on a well-defined learning task, have equal opportunity to contribute to the completion of task, and are held *individually accountable* for their contributions; the role of the instructor during CL is to serve as an unobtrusive *facilitator*, *coach*, or *consultant* to the learning groups (Cooper, 2003).

More specifically, CL attempts to strengthen the effectiveness of small-group work by attention to the following seven procedural features:

1. Positive Interdependence among Group Members (Collective Responsibility)
2. Individual Accountability (Personal Responsibility)
3. Intentional Group Formation
4. Intentional Team Building
5. Explicit Attention Paid to the Development of Students' Social Intelligence
6. Instructor Assumes the Role as Facilitator during the Group Learning Process
7. Attention to Inter-Group Interaction and Integration of Work Generated by Separate Learning Groups

What follows is a description of these key features accompanied by strategies for implementing each of them.

1. Interdependence among Group Members (Collective Responsibility)

When humans interact in an interdependent fashion, they share common goals, engage in collective effort and, as a result of their collective effort, experience mutual benefits. Arguably, positive interdependence is the quintessential feature of cooperative learning; it is the feature that effectively transforms group work ("talking heads") into bona fide *teamwork*. The following instructional strategies may be used to promote positive interdependence among students working in groups.

- The group creates a common, jointly-constructed work product.

In contrast to small-group discussions, in which students engage in informal discussion of a course-related issue, CL groups are expected to generate a *formal work product* that represents a concrete manifestation of the group's *collective effort*. For example, the CL group may complete a common, final product that takes the form of a worksheet, a list or chart of specific ideas, or an overhead transparency, that can be presented to the instructor or other groups. The objective of working toward a common, tangible outcome keeps team members "on task" and focused on the group's ultimate goal—the creation of a unified product that captures and reflects the team's concerted effort.

- Each group member assumes a complementary, interdependent role with respect to the group's final product.

A sense of personal responsibility and commitment to the team increases when each member has a *specific and indispensable role* to play in achieving the group's final goal. For instance, different group members may be assigned the following interdependent roles:

Functional roles—whereby each member is responsible for performing a particular functional duty for the group, such as: (a) group manager—keeps the group on task and ensures that all its members make contributions, (b) group recorder—keeps a written record of the group's ideas, (c) group spokesperson—orally reports the group's ideas to the instructor or other groups, (d) group processor—monitors the social interaction or interpersonal dynamics of the group process (e.g., whether individuals listen actively and disagree constructively), (e) research runner—accesses and retrieves information for the learning group, and (f) accuracy coach—attends to procedural details and troubleshoots errors.

Resource roles—each member is responsible for providing one key piece of information to be incorporated into the group's final product (e.g., information from one chapter of the text or one unit of classroom instruction).

Cognitive roles—each member contributes one component or dimension of *higher-level thinking* to the group's final product (e.g., application, analysis, synthesis, or evaluation).

Perspective roles—each member contributes an important perspective or viewpoint (e.g., ethical, historical, economic, or global).

Specialized roles such as these serve to ensure that each group member has a well-defined and well-differentiated responsibility to fulfill throughout the learning process. A further advantage of such role specialization is that the quality of each member's contribution to the final product can be readily identified and assessed by the instructor, thus ensuring individual accountability in the grading process.

- Teammates rely on each other before seeking help from the instructor.

This feature may be implemented by using the following strategies:

Redirecting students' questions back to their teams so their teammates get in the habit of relying on each other, rather than their instructor.

> Having teams seek help from other teams before seeking help from the instructor.
> Having the last team who received help, provide help to the next team who seeks help.
> Having group members consistently use team responses. For example, all teammates raise their hands if they need assistance from the instructor, teammates provide a choral response to instructor-posed questions and all teammates sign their names on the completed work product.

- Provision of individual rewards or incentives to stimulate positive interdependence.

    Positive interdependence and mutual support may be encouraged among group members by: (a) awarding extra (bonus) points that count toward individual student's course grade if each teammate's performance exceeds a certain criterion (e.g., each member achieves a score of at least 90%), or (b) having students' total grades for group work equal the sum of their individual score plus their team score (Slavin, 1990).

2. Ensuring Individual Accountability (Personal Responsibility)

    Experimental research in social psychology has documented the phenomenon of "social loafing," i.e., if the effort or output of individuals working within a group is anonymous or not clearly identifiable, it will be less than if the individuals were working alone (Williams, Harkins, & Latane, 1981). Listed below are procedures that may be used to combat social loafing and promote individual accountability in learning groups.

- Assign individual grades to students, not group grades.

    High-achieving students often report that they dislike group projects in which all group members receive the same grade because their individual effort and contribution to the group's final product often exceeds the efforts and contributions of their less motivated teammates — who receive exactly the same grade, despite the fact they exerted appreciably less effort (Fiechtner & Davis, 1991). Thus individual accountability is enhanced when students do not receive undifferentiated grades.

- Prior to discussing their ideas in small groups, give students some private reflection time to gather their thoughts individually and to record their individual ideas in writing.

    These written products can serve as evidence that each student has given thought to the group task, and they may be collected by the instructor and counted toward the student's individual grade (e.g., as points for attendance and participation).

- Have individual members keep an ongoing record of the specific contributions they make to their team (e.g., by recording them in a journal or learning log), and inform students that you will check this record and count it as part of their course grade.

- Use *random response sampling*, whereby any one person in the group is randomly selected to report the team's response, or provide a summary of the group's ideas.

- Have teams turn in their work product with individuals initialing their particular contribution(s) to it.

- Have students engage in:
    (a) *self evaluation* — each member assesses the quality of his individual effort or contribution to the group, and
    (b) *peer evaluation* — each member assesses the effort or contribution of her teammates.

3. Intentional Group Formation

    Learning teams may be formed on a *random* basis (e.g., students count off numbers consecutively from 1 to 4 and form groups with other students who have the same number), or they be formed on an *intentional* basis, i.e., teammates are selected according to some predetermined criteria that are likely to maximize or magnify the educational impact of small-group learning. In contrast to traditional approaches to small-group formation, in which students typically select their own group members or groups are randomly formed by the instructor, CL begins with intentional. For instance, teams may be deliberately formed to maximize diversity of perspectives by grouping students of different: (a) gender, (b) racial, ethnic, or cultural background, (c) chronological age — traditional age and re-entry students, (d) level of prior academic achievement — based on performance in high school or on early course exams, (e) learning style — based on learning-style inventories completed in class, or (f) personality profile — based on the Myers-Briggs Type Indicator.

    The particular criteria used to form groups, and the decision about whether to place students in heterogeneous or homogeneous groups with respect to this criteria, will vary depending on the instructor's educational objective. However, a thematic procedural principle of CL is that group formation should not be left to chance; instead, careful forethought is given to the decision about the learning group's composition in order to create an optimal social-learning environment.

4. Intentional Team Building

The following practices may be used to build solidarity and sense of team *identity* among CL groups.

- Before launching into the task, group members are given informal interaction time to develop social cohesiveness. For example: (a) students participate in warm-up activities when they first form their groups (e.g., learning each other's names and sharing information about themselves), or (b) group members engage in practices that promote team identity (e.g., a distinctive team name, symbol, photo mascot, cheer or handshake).

  The objective of these team-building activities is to create a social-emotional climate conducive to creating an esprit de corps among group members, enabling them to feel comfortable in future group activities that may require them to express their personal viewpoints, disagree with each other, and reach consensus in an open (non-defensive) fashion. Small-group learning often involves both cognitive and social risk-taking; students are more likely to take these risks in an interpersonal climate characterized by group cohesiveness, mutual trust, and emotional security. Listed below are strategies for creating such a climate.

- Have students consistently use *team language* in the classroom ("we" and "our" vs. "I" "me" or "mine").
- *Allow for continuity* of group interaction among teammates across successive class periods.

  In contrast to traditional small-group discussions or buzz groups, which usually bring students together sporadically for a relatively short period of time (e.g., a single class period or portion thereof), CL groups may be asked to meet regularly over an extended period of time (e.g., every class period for five weeks or more). This continuity of contact among group members provides opportunity for interpersonal bonding to develop among group members, and supplies CL groups the time needed to congeal into a tightly knit social network or social-support group.

5. Explicit Attention Paid to the Development of Students' Social Intelligence

Unlike the strictly cognitive objectives of most small-group work in higher education, a major objective of CL is the intentional development of students' interpersonal communication and human relations skills. Rather than simply placing students in small groups and hoping they will act like a team, CL involves intentional preparation of students for teamwork. To achieve this objective, the following procedures may be implemented.

- Provide students with explicit instruction on effective skills for communicating and relating to others prior to, and in preparation for, participation in small-group work. Instruction may include explicit strategies for:
  (a) encouraging and supporting other group members,
  (b) listening actively,
  (c) learning to disagree constructively,
  (d) resolving conflict, and
  (e) building consensus.

  Thus, rather than being left entirely to their own devices, students receive at least some orientation and preparation for handling the social and emotional demands of small-group work.

- Intentionally recognize and publicly reinforce effective interpersonal behavior displayed by students within groups.

  During CL, the instructor should be ready to identify and praise specific instances of effective interpersonal communication and collaboration exhibited by students in their learning groups. In addition to reinforcing the exemplary behavior, it also showcases it as a behavioral model for other students to emulate.

- Encourage students to reflect on and evaluate the group's social dynamics.

  Students' social intelligence is further developed by having them assess their group interaction with respect to principles of effective interpersonal communication and human relations. Students may also be asked to reflect on how the social dynamics of their group interaction affected their individual learning. For example, students may be asked how effectively they were able to: (a) verbalize their thoughts to other group members, (b) question the reasoning of other group members, and (c) express personal disagreement with their teammates.

6. Assuming the Role of Facilitator during the Group Learning Process

In CL, the instructor takes on the role of a learned peer or collegial coach while students work in groups, interacting with them in a much more personal, informal, and dialogic fashion than would be possible in the traditional lecture or whole-class discussion format. The instructor becomes a group-learning facilitator and consultant, circulat-

ing actively among the learning groups, performing such duties as:
(a) offering encouragement,
(b) reinforcing positive instances of cooperative behavior,
(c) clarifying task expectations,
(d) catalyzing dialogue, and
(e) issuing timely questions designed to promote reflection, elaboration, and higher-level thinking.

Interacting with students while they work in small groups not only facilitates the learning process, it also enables instructors to learn about their students (e.g., learn their names, ways of thinking, and styles of learning and communicating).

7. Attention to Inter-Group Interaction and Integration of Work Generated by Separate Learning Groups

Promoting communication among different learning groups and synthesizing their separate work products has three key benefits:
(a) It brings a sense of *closure* to the group-learning experience (Millis & Cottell, 1998).
(b) It stimulates *synergy* across the work generated by separate learning teams.
(c) It creates a stronger sense of class *community*, in which students perceive their class as a unified "group of groups."

Although there may be many occasions where small-group work is an end in itself and cross-group interaction is unnecessary, periodic attempts should be made to transform the separate experience of small, isolated subgroups into a larger, unified class community. The following practices are offered as strategies for making this transformation.

- After completing small-group work, one student from each learning group plays the role of plenary reporter whose job is to share the group's main ideas with the entire class. The instructor can use the chalkboard to record the main ideas reported from each group, validating their contributions, and identifying important themes or variations that emerge across groups.
- Following completion of the small-group task, one roving reporter from each team visits other groups to share her team's ideas. Remaining members of her team stay together and play the role of listener-synthesizer—actively listening to the ideas presented by successive roving reporters from other groups and integrating these ideas with those generated by their own group (Kagan, 1992).
- Following completion of the small-group task, each learning team rotates clockwise and merges with another small group to share and synthesize their separate work. This share-and-synthesize process continues until each group has paired interaction with all other learning groups in class. The last step in the process is for each team to generate a final product, which reflects an integration of their own work with the best ideas gleaned from their successive interactions with other groups.

These different procedures for promoting inter-group interaction have the following benefits: (a) they provide meaningful synthesis and closure to the group-learning experience; (b) they promote class synergy by harnessing and pooling the ideas generated by separate learning groups; and, (c) they enable students to meet and collaborate with a variety of classmates beyond their own small group. In so doing, the team building that takes place within individual learning groups is augmented by class building across all groups, and a class that was initially deconstructed into multiple, isolated subgroups is reconstructed into a single, unified community.

Conclusion

The foregoing features of CL differentiate it from other varieties of group work and all other forms of learner-centered pedagogy. When small-group work is intentionally implemented with the majority of these seven procedural elements in place, there is substantial empirical evidence that CL can have significant impact on both cognitive and affective learning outcomes (Slavin, 1990). In one meta-analysis of the effects of CL on college students' academic performance in science, math, engineering and technology—conducted by the National Institute for Science Education—it was found that CL had a robust positive effect on multiple educational outcomes, including: (a) academic achievement, (b) student retention, and (c) attitude (liking) of the subject matter (Cooper, 1997).

One particular outcome that CL has great potential to realize is appreciation of diversity. Research strongly suggests that increasing exposure or contact of majority students to students from minority racial and ethnic groups is not a sufficient condition for promoting interracial interaction and intercultural education because these students still self-segregate (Burgess & Sales, 1977; Stephan, 1978). Something more than mere exposure to minority-group members must occur in order to stimulate intercultural contact and multicultural appreciation. As Hill (1991) puts it, "Real educational progress will be made when multiculturalism becomes interculturalism" (p. 41). The capacity of CL to provide such a context for "*interculturalism*" is supported by research indicating that inter-group contact under CL conditions reduces racial prejudice and promotes formation of interracial friendships (Aronson, 1978; Blake & Mouton, 1979; McConahay, 1981; Worchel, 1979). CL has the potential to capitalize on the rising demographic wave of student diversity, empowering instructors to access and harness its educational power by intentionally forming learning teams with diverse membership, creating equal opportunity for all members to participate via well-defined roles, and promoting positive interdependence among teammates through their pursuit of a clear and common goal.

References

Abercrombie, M. L. J. (1960). *The anatomy of judgment.* New York: Hutchinson.

American College Personnel Association (1994). *The student learning imperative: Implications for student affairs.* Washington, D.C.: Author.

Angelo, T. A. (1997). The campus as learning community: Seven promising shifts and seven powerful levers. *AAHE Bulletin, 4*(9), pp, 3-6.

Aronson, E. (1978). *The jigsaw classroom.* Beverly Hills, CA: Sage.

Barr, R. B., & Tagg, J. (1995). From teaching to learning: A new paradigm for undergraduate education. *Change, 27*(6), pp. 12-25.

Blake, R., & Mouton, J. (1979). Intergroup problem solving in organizations: From theory to practice. In W. Austin & S. Worchel (Eds.), *The social psychology of intergroup relations.* Monterey, CA: Brooks/Cole.

Bligh, D. A. (2000). *What's the use of lectures.* San Francisco: Jossey-Bass.

Bruffee, K. A. (1993). *Collaborative learning: Higher education, interdependence, and the authority of knowledge.* Baltimore, Johns Hopkins Press.

Burgess, J. M. & Sales, S. (1977). Attitudinal effects of "mere exposure": A reevaluation. *Journal of Experimental Social Psychology, 7,* 461-472.

Carter, R. (1998). *Mapping the mind.* Berkeley and Los Angeles: University of California Press.

Cooper, J. L. (1997). New evidence of the power of cooperative learning. *Cooperative Learning and College Teaching, 7*(3), pp. 1-2.

Cooper, J. (2003). What is cooperative learning? In J. L. Cooper, P. Robinson, & D. Ball (Eds.), *Small group instruction in higher education: Lessons from the past, visions of the future.* Stillwater, OK: New Forums Press. (Originally published in the *Cooperative Learning and College Teaching Newsletter,* Fall, 1990).

Cuseo, J. (2005). "Questions that Promote Deeper Thinking Skills." *On Course Newsletter* (July), Monkton, MD.

Fassinger, P. A. (1996). Professors' and students' perception of why students participate in class. *Teaching Sociology, 24*(1), 25-33

Fiechtner, S. B., & Davis, E. A. (1992). Why some groups fail: A survey of students' experiences with learning groups. In A. S. Goodsell, M. Maher, & V. Tinto (Eds.), *Collaborative learning: A sourcebook for higher education* (pp. 59-67). The National Center on Postsecondary Teaching, Learning, and Assessment, The Pennsylvania State University.

Hill, P. J. (1991). Multiculturalism: The crucial philosophical and organizational issues. *Change, 23*(4), 38-47.

Jensen, E. (1998). *Teaching with the brain in mind.* Alexandria, VA: Association for Supervision and Curriculum Development.

Johnstone, A. H., & Su, W. Y. (1994). Lectures—a learning experience? *Education in Chemistry, 31*(1), 65-76, 79.

Kagan, S. (1992). *Cooperative learning.* San Juan Capistrano, CA: Resources for Teachers, Inc.

Karp, D. A., & Yoels, W. C. (1976). The college classroom: Some observations on the meanings of student participation. *Sociology and Social Research, 60,* 421-439.

LaBerge, D. (1995). *Attentional processing.* Cambridge, MA: Harvard University Press.

Mackworth, J. (1970). *Vigilance and habituation.* New York: Penguin.

McConahay, J. B. (1981). Reducing racial prejudice in desegregated schools. In W. D. Hawley (Ed.), *Effective school desegregation: Equity, quality, and feasibility* (pp. 35-53). Beverly Hills, CA : Sage.

McKeachie, W. J., Pintrich, P., Lin, Y., & Smith, D. (1986). *Teaching and learning in the college classroom: A review of the research literature.* Ann Arbor: University of Michigan, NCRIPTAL.

Millis, B. J., & Cottell, P. G., Jr. (1998). *Cooperative learning for higher education faculty.* Phoenix, AZ: American Council on Education and The Oryx Press.

Milton, O., Pollio, H. R., & Eison, J. A. (1986). *Making sense of college grades.* San Francisco: Jossey-Bass.

Nance, J. L., & Nance, C. E. (1990). Does learning occur in the classroom? *College Student Journal, 24*(4), 338-340.

O'Neill, G. & McMahon, T. (2005). Student centred learning: What does it mean for students and lecturers? In G. O'Neill, S. Moore, & B. McMullin (Eds.), *Emerging issues in the practice of university learning and teaching.* Dublin: AISHE.

Pascarella, E. T., & Terenzini, P. T. (1991). *How college affects students: Findings and insights from twenty years of research.* San Francisco: Jossey-Bass.

Pascarella, E. T., & Terenzini, P. T. (2005). *How college affects students, Volume 2: A third decade of research.* San Francisco: Jossey-Bass.

Penner, J. (1984). *Why many college teachers cannot lecture.* Springfield, IL: Charles C. Thomas.

Slavin, R. E. (1990). *Cooperative learning: Theory, research, and practice.* Englewood Cliffs, NJ: Prentice-Hall.

Stephan, W. G. (1978). School desegregation: An evaluation of predictions made in "Brown vs. Board of Education." *Psychological Bulletin, 85,* 217-238.

Stuart, J. & Rutheford, R. (1978, September). Medical student concentration during lectures. *Lancet, 23,* 514-516.

Sylwester, R. (1996). *Recent cognitive science developments pose major educational challenges* (Unpublished paper). Eugene, OR: School of Education, University of Oregon.

Verner, C., & Dickinson, G. (1967). The lecture: Analysis and review of research. *Adult Education, 17,* 85-100.

Wiener, H. S. (1986). Collaborative learning in the classroom: A guide to evaluation. *College English, 48,* 52-61.

Williams, K., Harkins, S. & Latane, B. (1981). Identifiability as a deterrent to social loafing: Two cheering experiments. *Journal of Personality and Social Psychology, 40,* 303-311.

Worchel, S. (1979). Cooperation and the reduction of intergroup conflict: Some determining factors. In W. Austin & S. Worchel (Eds.), *The social psychology of intergroup relations.* Monterey, California: Brooks/Cole.

Part II
Implementation of Small Group Techniques

Part II of this text contains articles first printed in the *Cooperative Learning and College Teaching* newsletter that address implementation of small group techniques. The first article is a short piece taken from a workshop Joe Cuseo presented that outlines when traditional lecture formats are appropriate (and when they are not). It is followed by a piece by David and Roger Johnson and Karl Smith who elaborate on research that highlights why the lecture is problematic, based on research concerning how people learn. The Johnsons and Karl then offer an article which describes methods for making the lecture more interactive by inserting informal cooperative learning structures within traditional instructional formats. The authors of these three articles make the case that there are times when the lecture is appropriate in teaching and times when more student centered approaches are better choices.

In the fourth article in Part II, Tom Angelo offers a description of work based on his landmark study of Classroom Assessment Techniques (CATs) completed in collaboration with Pat Cross. He notes that CATs can be used to provide feedback to instructors about the progress of their students, including the process and products relating to group work. These CATs have been adapted by many in the higher education community and can be seen in the ConcepTests work of physicist Eric Mazur, the Quick-thinks work of Susan Prescott Johnston and Jim Cooper and the use of clickers in many classrooms.

Tom's contribution is followed by two newsletter articles by Susan Prescott Johnson. The first describes how textbooks can serve as vehicles for engaging students in a course. Too often students fail to read the text and Susan offers techniques in which students, working alone and in pairs and teams, can engage more deeply in course content. This article is followed by one of her *Trouble-Shooting* pieces that were a staple of the newsletter. In it, she identifies ways for getting students more engaged in course work by scaffolding (using visual frameworks and demonstrations) and fostering student interaction prior to engaging them in cooperative tasks.

Rose Ann Swartz then offers a method for making testing a more engaging process. She has her students make posters relating to important elements of her course work. Poster content is presented to the entire class, followed by questions and answers. The poster format is used as an *adjunct* to traditional forms of assessment, such as papers and tests, not as a replacement for them.

Spencer Kagan wrote many articles for the newsletter and contributed to our 2003 book. In his article, *Teams of Four Are Magic!*, he makes the case for an optimal size for long-term base groups. He outlines techniques for ensuring equal participation of group members, an element of group work often neglected in traditional collaborative learning.

Another long-time contributor to the newsletter and the 2003 book is Barbara Millis. Her article appearing in this section of the book, deals with procedures for fostering critical thinking using cooperative writing. Barbara outlines a variety of procedures for fostering deeper thinking in writing tasks, including such techniques as Reciprocal Reading, Responsive Written Exchanges and Team Anthologies.

The last article in this second part of the book focuses on a procedure for fostering tolerance, if not appreciation, of diversity. It is written by Rachel Hertz-Lazarowitz, based on her work using Group Investigation in Israel. She reports that her work has helped ease tensions between Arabs and Israelis and has helped both groups understand each other as people sharing common experiences, not just as dehumanized members of a hated enemy.

Lectures: Their Place and Purpose

Joseph Cuseo

Faculty Should Use Lectures to:

1. Reorganize textbook material to best meet course goals and student needs.

2. Connect, integrate, or interweave seemingly unrelated concepts contained in separate chapters of the text.

3. Apply reading material to specific contexts/situations likely to be encountered by your students at your college and in your particular program.

4. Illustrate theoretical principles cited in reading material with concrete, contemporary examples to which your students can relate.

5. Introduce important concepts/issues or late-breaking information that is not contained in the text or assigned readings.

6. Model problem-solving strategies or critical-thinking skills with respect to the subject matter.

7. Share personal experiences/insights relating to the subject matter, your profession, or your preparation for the profession.

8. Demonstrate enthusiasm and excitement about the subject matter (e.g., lecturing on topics for which you have an intrinsic interest or personal passion).

9. Provide an opportunity for faculty to serve as role models who inspire learning and elevate students' educational or professional aspirations.

Faculty Should Not Lecture on:

1. Material that is already available and comprehensible to students in print (i.e., in the textbook or assigned readings).

2. Rote factual information that can be more effectively and efficiently presented to, and processed by, students in the form of a supplementary handout or detailed outline that can replace or accompany lectures.

3. Information/concepts that would be more effectively learned and retained by students via direct, personal experiences or social interaction (e.g., diversity awareness via volunteer projects or peer interaction vs. lectures).

Editors' Note: This is excerpted from the supplementary materials Joe used for a presentation made to faculty and staff at Delgado Community College in New Orleans, August 1998.

Problems with Lecturing

David W. Johnson, Roger T. Johnson and Karl A. Smith

While direct teaching may be appropriately used, there are also problems with direct teaching that must be kept in mind. Much of the research on lecturing has compared it with group discussion. While the conditions under which lecturing is more successful than group discussion have not been identified, a number of problems with lecturing have been found.

The first problem with lecturing is that students' attention to what the instructor is saying decreases as the lecture proceeds. Research in the 1960s by D. H. Lloyd, at the University of Reading in Berkshire, England found that student attention levels during lectures followed the pattern of: a) five minutes of settling in, b) five minutes of readily assimilating material, c) confusion and boredom with assimilation falling off rapidly and remaining low for the bulk of the lecture, and d) some revival of attention at the end of the lecture (Penner, 1984). The concentration during lectures of medical students, who presumably are highly motivated, rose sharply and peaked 10 to 15 minutes after the lecture began, and then fell steadily thereafter (Stuart & Rutherford, 1978). J. McLeish, in a research study in the 1960s, analyzed the percentage of content contained in student notes at different time intervals throughout the lecture (reported in Penner, 1984). He found that students wrote notes on 41 percent of the content presented during the first fifteen minutes, 25 percent presented in a thirty-minute time period, and only 20 percent of what had been presented during forty-five minutes.

The second problem with lecturing is that it takes an educated, intelligent person oriented toward auditory learning to benefit from listening to lectures. Verner and Cooley (1967) found that in general, very little of a lecture can be recalled except in the case of listeners with above average education and intelligence. Even under optimal conditions, when intelligent, motivated people listen to a brilliant scholar talk about an interesting topic, there can be serious problems with a lecture. Verner and Dickinson (1967, p. 90) give this example:

...ten percent of the audience displayed signs of inattention within fifteen minutes. After eighteen minutes one-third of the audience and ten percent of the platform guests were fidgeting. At thirty-five minutes everyone was inattentive; at forty-five trance was more noticeable than fidgeting; and at forty-seven minutes some were asleep and at least one was reading. A causal check twenty-four hours later revealed that the audience recalled only insignificant details, and these were generally wrong.

The third problem with lecturing is that it tends to promote only lower-level learning of factual information. Bligh (1972), after an extensive series of studies, concluded that while lecturing was as (but not more) effective as reading or other methods in transmitting information, lecturing was clearly less effective in promoting thinking or in changing attitudes. A survey of 58 studies conducted between the years of 1928 and 1967 comparing various characteristics of lectures versus discussions, found that lectures and discussions did not differ significantly on lower-level learning (such as learning facts and principles), but discussion appeared superior in developing higher-level problem-solving capabilities and positive attitudes toward the course (Costin, 1972). McKeachie and Kulik (1972) separated studies on lecturing according to whether they focused on factual learning, higher-level reasoning, attitudes or motivation. They found lecture to be superior to discussion for promoting factual learning, but discussion was found to be superior to lecture for promoting higher-level reasoning, positive attitudes and motivation to learn.

Fourth, lecturing is limited by the assumptions that all students need the same information presented orally at the same time and at the same pace, without dialogue with the presenter, and in an impersonal way. Regardless of whether students have different levels of knowledge about the subject being presented, the same information is presented to all at the same time and pace. Although students learn and comprehend at different paces, a lecture proceeds at a single pace—

the lecturer's. Even students who listen carefully and cognitively process the information presented will have questions that need to be answered, and lectures typically are one-way communication situations with large numbers of classmates inhibiting question asking (Stones, 1970). If students cannot ask questions, misconceptions, incorrect understanding, and gaps in understanding cannot be identified and corrected. Lectures can waste students' time by telling them things that they could read for themselves. Lecturing by its very nature makes learning impersonal. There is research indicating that personalized learning experiences have an impact on achievement and motivation.

The fifth problem with lecturing is that students tend not to like it. Costin's 1972 review of the literature indicates that students like the course and subject area better when they learn in discussion groups than when they learn by listening to lectures. This is important in introductory courses where disciplines often attempt to attract majors.

Finally, there are problems with lecturing as it is based on a series of assumptions about the cognitive capabilities and strategies of students. When instructors lecture they assume that all students learn auditorially, have high working memory capacity, have all the required prior knowledge, have good note-taking strategies and skills, and are not susceptible to information processing overload.

Lecturing with Informal Cooperative-learning Groups

David W. Johnson, Roger T. Johnson and Karl A. Smith

The following procedure will help you plan a lecture that keeps students more actively engaged intellectually. It entails having focused discussions before and after the lecture (i.e., bookends) and interspersing pair discussions throughout the lecture. Two important aspects of using informal cooperative-learning groups are to: (a) make the task and the instructions explicit and precise, and (b) require the groups to produce a specific product (such as a written answer). The procedure is as follows.

1. Introductory Focused Discussion: Have each student pair up with whomever is sitting nearest. You may wish to require different seating arrangements each class so that students will meet and interact with a number of other students in the class. Then give the pairs the cooperative assignment of completing the initial (advanced organizer) task. Give them only four or five minutes to do so. The discussion task is aimed at promoting advanced organizing of what the students know about the topic to be presented and establishing expectations about what the lecture will cover.

2. Intermittent Focused Discussions:

A. Lecture Segment. Deliver the first segment of the lecture. This segment should last from 10 to 15 minutes. This is about the length of time a motivated adult can concentrate on a lecture. For unmotivated adolescents, the time may be shorter.

B. Pair Discussion. Give the students a discussion task focused on the material you have just presented that may be completed within three or four minutes. Its purpose is to ensure that students are actively thinking about the material being presented. The discussion task may be to: a) give an answer to a question posed by the instructor, b) give a reaction to the theory, concepts, or information being presented, or c) relate materials to past learning so that it gets integrated into existing conceptual frameworks.

Discussion pairs respond to the task in the following way:
1. Students formulate their own answers.
2. Students share their answers with their partners.
3. Students listen carefully to their partners' answers
4. Each pair creates a new answer that is superior to each member's initial formulation through the process of association, building on each other's thoughts, and synthesizing.

Randomly choose two or three students to give 30-second summaries of their discussions. It is important that students are randomly called on to share their answers after each discussion task. Such individual accountability ensures that the pairs take the tasks seriously and check each other to ensure that both are prepared to answer.

3. Closure Focused Discussion: Give students an ending discussion task lasting four to five minutes to summarize what they have learned from the lecture. The discussion should result in students integrating what they have just learned into existing conceptual frameworks. The task may also point students toward what the homework will cover or what will be presented in the next class session.

Informal cooperative learning ensures students are actively involved in understanding what they are learning. It also provides time for instructors to gather their wits, reorganize notes, take a deep breath, and move around the class listening to what students are saying. Listening to student discussions can give instructors direction and insight into how well students understand the concepts and material being taught (who, unfortunately, may not have graduate degrees in the topic you are presenting).

Using Assessment to Improve Cooperative Learning

Thomas A. Angelo

Reading this newsletter over the past three years has convinced me that Cooperative Learning (CL) can be a powerful tool for improving student learning in higher education. I've become convinced partly by articles summarizing CL's strong foundation in theory and validation through research, and partly by articles on practice—realistic examples of what works and what doesn't. But although I am sold on the value of CL in general, I still have doubts about how, and how well it will work in my classes. After all, my students and my courses are quite unique, and what applies in general may not apply in particular. Put another way, determining that CL does work in general was a necessary, but not sufficient first step to ensure that it is used well. As a college teacher, I want to know—in terms of my classes and my students—what is likely to work best for whom, when, where, how and why.

It would be reasonable to assume that CL works, just as we've long assumed lecturing works. However, as Mark Twain once wrote, "Supposing is good, but finding out is better," and that's the heart of what I'm proposing here. As teachers committed to improving student learning each of us needs ways to find out how well CL works for the particular students in our classes. Classroom Assessment can provide us with some tools to do just that.

Classroom Assessment (CA) is one simple, straightforward method faculty can use to find out what, how much, and how well their students are learning. Faculty use simple feedback devices, referred to as Classroom Assessment Techniques (CATs), to collect data on their students' learning. Almost all CATs require students to reflect on and explain their learning, usually by writing brief, anonymous responses to simple questions or prompts. This focus on making one's own learning explicit can promote metacognition and critical thinking. For example, the Minute Paper, one of the simplest CATs, asks students some variant of the following two questions: What was the most important thing you learned in today's class? and, What question remains uppermost in your mind? In response to the Minute Paper, students write short, anonymous answers, usually during the last few minutes of class.

Whatever the CAT, once students have responded, the teacher collects the data, looks for patterns and prepares to respond in turn. After a quick, usually informal analysis of that data, faculty use information gleaned from Classroom Assessments to inform and refocus their teaching and to help students make their learning more effective. To analyze responses to the Minute Paper, for example, it's usually enough for the instructors to ask questions such as: What proportion of the class listed most or all of the most important points on my list? What did they list as important that wasn't on my list? How many and what kinds of questions did they raise? and, How can I use their responses to fine tune my efforts and theirs?

Closing the feedback loop—giving the class-as-a-whole timely, focused feedback on their responses—is vital in Classroom Assessment. Faculty need to let students know what they learned from the CAT responses, what they intend to do about it, and what they suggest the students do to improve their learning. To continue with the Minute Paper example, at the beginning of the next class session, the instructor might quickly list a handful of the most important ideas students had mentioned that he or she wanted to reinforce, then point out any significant items they had missed. Next, the instructor might briefly respond to the two or three most commonly raised questions—or to ask members of the class to tackle them. To save class time, the teacher might instead use a handout, an overhead transparency or an e-mail message, or export the response to a review session led by a graduate teaching assistant.

Most teachers use CATs to get anonymous feedback from the individual students in their classes. But many techniques can and have been adapted for use with CL groups. Let's now consider several CATs teachers can use to assess CL. For more information on and examples of the CATs mentioned below, see Angelo, T.

A. and Cross, K. P., *Classroom Assessment Techniques: A Handbook for College Teachers* (Jossey-Bass, 1993).

Assessing the *Process* of Cooperative Learning

In the Spring 1992 issue of this newsletter, Joseph Cuseo defined CL "in terms of six procedural elements, which when implemented together, distinguish it from other forms of small-group learning in higher education." Those six distinguishing procedural elements were: (1) intentional group formation, (2) continuity of group interaction, (3) interdependence among group members, (4) individual accountability, (5) explicit attention to the development of social skills, and (6) instructor as facilitator. There are CATs which faculty can adapt to assess and enhance each of these elements.

For example, to set up CL groups intentionally, teachers need information about their students as individuals and as a group. The Background Knowledge Probe, a simple, teacher-constructed questionnaire administered at the outset, can be used to assess what kinds of groupwork experiences students have read about, observed, participated in or led. Or, a brief Interest and Skills Checklist might be used for much the same purpose. Since we know that students often have preconceptions and misconceptions about CL that interfere with their learning, it might be helpful to develop a Misconception/Preconception Check consisting of two or three questions designed to uncover those beliefs and opinions.

To assess the continuity and intensity of group interaction, students could respond individually to Productive Study-Time Logs, keeping track of the quantity and rating the quality of their work in and related to the CL group for a week. They could then compare their individual logs in the group, perhaps making the comparison graphic through a diagram, and calculate group averages. The CL groups in the class could compare group averages for total amounts of time worked and subtotals at different quality rating levels. Most importantly, students could then discuss ways to make their time use more effective — as individuals and group members based on their observations and Time Logs.

Another CAT, the Groupwork Evaluation, was designed specifically to collect feedback on students' interactions, individual responsibility, and interdependence in CL groups. The teacher who developed the following form asked students to identify their responses only in terms of which CL group they were in. After collecting the forms, she tallied responses by group, correlated them with group exam scores. Not surprisingly — at least to the instructor — the groups that reported the highest average participation, preparation and effectiveness ratings also received the highest average grades. After showing her students these results, she led a discussion of their implications.

Sample Groupwork Evaluation Form

1. Overall, how effectively did your group work together on this assignment?

1	2	3	4	5
not at all	poorly	adequately	well	extremely well

2. How many of the five group members participated actively most of the time? (circle the appropriate number)

   0   1   2   3   4   5

3. How many of you were fully prepared for the groupwork most of the time? (circle the appropriate number)

   0   1   2   3   4   5

4. Give one specific example of something you learned from the group that you probably wouldn't have learned on your own.

5. Give one specific example of something the other group members learned from you that they probably wouldn't have learned without you.

6. Suggest one specific, practical change the group could make that would help improve everyone's learning.

The Groupwork Evaluation form can easily be adapted to include questions on social skills or other skills which the instructor is trying to develop. To find out how well they are doing as facilitators in CL, teachers can use the Group Instructional Feedback Technique or GIFT. This simple CAT asks working groups to respond to only three questions: (1) What specific things do I do that really help you learn from groupwork?, (2) What specific things do I do that make it more difficult for you to learn from groupwork?, and (3) What are one or two specific, practical changes that we could make which would help your group learn better?

Over the years, I've gained many more useful insights into my teaching — and made many more useful adjustments — as a result of these three simple questions than from all of my formal, end-of-semester student evaluation results combined. Nevertheless, before using any CAT which might elicit responses critical of your teaching, I always suggest faculty consider this advice: Don't ask if you don't want to know.

Assessing the *Products* of Cooperative Learning

Just as CATs can often be easily adapted to assess group rather than individual feedback on process, many of these techniques can also be adapted to assess the products of CL, instead of or in addition to the products of individual learning. Let me give one brief example of a way in which a college teacher adapted CATs to assess and improve content learning by groups.

In an Anatomy and Physiology course designed for future nurses, this biology professor stressed the importance of understanding the connections between structures, functions, and processes. To assess how well his first-year students were making these connections in relation to the digestive system, he created a Memory Matrix. The matrix consisted of three columns—labeled structure, function, and enzymes—intersected by eight rows, each representing one of the digestive organs. The organs he included were the mouth, esophagus, stomach, small and large intestines, pancreas, liver, and gall bladder. The empty matrix was a rectangle containing twenty-four boxes in which students could write answers.

A firm believer in CL, the instructor divided the class of forty into eight groups of five, then handed each group one oversized copy of the empty Memory Matrix. He gave the groups fifteen minutes to fill in the critical, missing information. A flurry of activity took place as groups scrambled to complete their matrices. When time was up, he collected the eight large sheets. During the next twenty minutes, as the students watched a videotape on enzyme functioning, the instructor quickly scanned the assessments, looking for missing, misplaced and incorrect information. He made a rough tally of correct responses on his own master sheet, then noted the patterns. He used this information to selectively review the digestive system during the last third of the class session. As a result of this CL/Classroom Assessment cycle, students in this class scored higher on the section of the exam dealing with the digestive system than on any other segment of the course content.

In the end, of course, it is not the Classroom Assessment itself, but rather the teacher's and students' responses to the assessment results that can lead to improved learning of skills and knowledge. If faculty regularly respond to the results of Classroom Assessments by explicitly modeling the thinking and groupwork skills they are hoping to develop, and by engaging learners in focused, interactive discussions about the assessments results, college students are more likely to become effective group workers and learners. At the same time, frequent use of simple CATs provides students with guided practice in self-assessment and metacognition within the context of the course and the discipline.

Practice Activities and Your Textbook

Susan Prescott Johnston

This article is intended to ease the burden of the instructor who desires to provide in-class practice activities for student learning teams. One alternative to designing original materials is to use the existing course textbook in original ways. It can be a powerful resource of ideas for team learning.

The following strategies are based on the assumption that the most important ideas and/or skills in the course have already been identified by the teacher. Each practice activity needs to be linked to a specific outcome, so that students spend valuable course time focused on content that has the highest priority. It is not necessarily intended that instructors grade each group's effort. The purpose of the team learning activity is to provide an opportunity for interactive practice so that complex material can be more readily understood prior to the traditional exam. Each of the following strategies can be designed to fit a range of time requirements. Even if the active learning time must be brief, students who are able to discuss ideas with others are more likely to understand and retain the important course content.

1. Writing captions for photos, illustrations, charts, graphs or diagrams.

Many textbooks contain useful visual information. Student teams can be asked to create original captions or add to existing ones. Students explain the pictures in terms of the important concepts just stressed in the prior lecture/discussion. Each student in a team of four might contribute one sentence to ensure participation by all members. Teammates can provide helpful feedback to each other, after each contribution, to increase understanding. If time allows, some teams can share their ideas with the whole class.

A sociology class might describe the different norms for behavior they would expect to find in the photographs of people shown in various settings. A biology class studying ecosystems could have each person on a team hypothetically remove a different element from the habitat illustration and then teammates predict a specific impact on that community. An economics class studying current trade policy could interpret a graph showing past and current U.S. import-export figures by incorporating at least four key words (concepts) assigned by the instructor.

2. Finding statements in the text that prove given inferences or generalizations.

Here the instructor creates conclusions that reflect important understandings regarding a particular key concept, process, or event. These can be printed on the chalkboard, overhead projector, or handout. The students' task is to then locate and copy the corresponding supporting sentences found in the assigned section of the text. A team of four students can divide up the assignment and then share or scan the text together. This can be a valuable strategy when difficult material is first presented, when students appear to have low self-esteem or motivation, and when second language learners need to be considered. The key is to develop statements that reflect important content and that can be substantiated by specific sentences found in the section of the text that matches the current topic.

For example, in a psychology class studying the influences of heredity and environment on behavior, the teacher might write these statements on the board: Early positive physical contact can affect the rate of human development. Some psychological disorders appear to be genetically linked. Destructive relationship patterns are often passed on from one generation to the next. Student teams would then search for evidence in the text that would support each statement.

An interesting twist to this strategy is to give the class statements that contain misinformation, faulty assumptions, or incorrect conclusions. The student teams then work to locate evidence in the text that refutes the original statement.

3. Using bold face subtitles to create summaries.

In this case, each student team is assigned a subtitle that reflects an important idea related to the current course topic. Students are asked to use their notes from class and the reading to generate a concise summary of that subtopic in their own words. Each student needs to make a contribution to the group effort. The summaries can then be shared with the whole class. This strategy can be an effective way to help students focus on and review selected content at the end of a unit of instruction.

4. Presenting the opposite point of view.

In textbooks that contain statements reflecting a position on an issue that has potential for multiple viewpoints, the instructor can select key statements and ask student teams to present the opposing position. The rationale here is that if students can logically defend an opposing point of view, they are more likely to need to understand the original idea in some depth. If the same statement is assigned to each team, the range of thinking presented during the whole class sharing will further increase understanding of the main idea that was pre-selected by the instructor.

5. Comparing answers to homework questions or problems assigned from the text.

This activity can take place as class begins so that students have an opportunity to obtain feedback on their homework. If time allows, teams can present unresolved issues to the instructor for additional explanation. With this strategy, students are able to help each other clarify their understanding of content, and the teacher gains valuable information regarding students' mastery of the material. The assumption here is that questions or problems assigned for homework correlate with priority concepts and skills that form the framework of the course.

The strategies described above are intended to provide instructors with some generic structures that can be applied to different curricular topics and texts. The intent is to create a classroom atmosphere for active learning even when time does not allow the instructor to create original custom-designed team practice activities.

Trouble-Shooting

Susan Prescott Johnston

Dear Susan:

I am frequently disappointed with my students' responses once I have assigned a group task. Some classes work in silence with no interaction taking place among group members. At other times students do begin to interact promptly, but often their discussions center on trying to figure out what it is that I have asked them to do. I'm not sure if my students lack the maturity and intellect to successfully handle groupwork, or if the problem lies more with my methodology and lack of experience. I am convinced of the potential benefits of Cooperative Learning (CL) and do not want to abandon this effective teaching strategy. Can you offer some advice that I might try in the near future?

Signed,
Waiting in Winnetka

Dear Waiting,

You are to be commended for your perseverance and willingness to try alternative ideas. My experience is that all classes are capable of successfully participating in CL activities. Because not all students have experience working with others or with tasks that require initiative, creativity, or critical thinking, the instructor must take time to sufficiently prepare a class for cooperative activities. A description of this preparation follows.

1. Show Examples Using Visual Frameworks

Students' confidence is greatly increased when they have a clear picture of what is expected. Their energy can then be positively directed toward accomplishing a specific goal instead of being dissipated into anxiety and frustration regarding the requirements of the task.

Some faculty fear that showing specific examples prior to groupwork will diminish creativity or limit depth of thinking. My own experience, as well as that of my colleagues, does not support these concerns. In fact, examples serve to stimulate and encourage students to take risks and set high standards. When showing examples, it is important to state that the group product cannot reflect the same ideas already used during the demonstration.

Providing a visual format to organize a group's ideas can also greatly increase students' motivation to begin the assignment and to produce quality work. These formats need not be intricate; the idea is to avoid having students face a totally blank sheet of paper as they begin the activity. I am always impressed how easily a simple blank chart matrix, a two-column list with headings and numbers, or an empty box to contain a drawing with lines underneath for filling in a caption can accelerate a group's productivity. These graphic organizers can be copied by students from the chalkboard, an overhead or handed out to the class.

2. Demonstrate Steps or Procedures

In addition to showing an example, the instructor may also need to demonstrate specific steps or procedures required by the activity. While an experienced teacher can easily anticipate an effective approach necessary to complete a task, most students will waste precious time simply trying to determine what needs to be done first. Much confusion can be eliminated by taking a few moments to show (or brainstorm with students) a logical sequence of steps.

The tasks that require this type of initial instructor support are those of a more complex and creative nature (i.e., creating informational flyers to alert the school to specific issues, critiquing an argument for sound reasoning, designing graphs to display data, planning a presentation, preparing for an intra-group debate, designing an experiment). Groupwork that involves more traditional responses, such as solving math problems from a text or answering comprehension questions from a worksheet may not require as much attention.

3. Discuss Strategies for Interaction

While examples and procedures give students a clear goal, they may still be unclear on how to go about reaching that goal together. It may be necessary to demonstrate patterns of interaction that students might use to guarantee the participation of all members while working on their task. Alternatives include: partners share or compare, roundtable contributions, jigsaw teaching, individual work followed by members comparing ideas or answers. It is often effective for the instructor to stand close to one group and conduct a brief oral walkthrough of the activity with that team while the whole class observes.

The class is then given the opportunity to ask any procedural questions they may still have. I usually request that only my team leaders ask for clarification; this reduces time needed for questions and also reinforces the responsibility assigned to that role.

Once students gain increased competence with the skills of groupwork, their requirements for pre-structured patterns for interaction may decrease. An instructor who has students themselves determine how they will work together must carefully monitor groupwork to ensure that all students are involved and participating.

Following are specific examples of how to provide sufficient preparation for CL activities using each of the three dimensions described above. These examples are based on the assumption that students have acquired the background knowledge required by the activity through prior readings, discussion, or lecture.

Example 1.

COURSE: Foreign Language
CONTENT: Formal vs. informal usage
GROUP TASK: Create and perform a realistic one-minute dialogue for a formal and informal scenario
EXAMPLE: Brief sample dialogues are shown on an overhead projector; one between a French ambassador and a U.S. ambassador, and the other between two art students at the Louvre. The visual organizer on which the dialogue is written takes the form of two columns labeled with each character's name, numbers one through ten under each name, and arrows between the numbers to show the direction of dialogue. Above the columns are five blank lines starting with one word labels to facilitate the pre-writing decisions that need to be made (i.e., setting, characters, etc.).
PROCEDURE: Each pair assumes responsibility for the formal or informal dialogue. They then select a setting, choose two characters, think of a topic of conversation, think of a disagreement the characters might have, think of a resolution to that conflict and finally write the dialogue.
INTERACTION STRATEGY: Each group separates into two partner pairs. Each pair writes one of the scenarios. The pairs then come together and perform the dialogues for each other.

Example 2.

COURSE: Biology
CONTENT: Graphing experimental data
GROUP TASK: Create a linear graph to show results of a longitudinal study of the effects of dietary fat on life span, artery content, and cholesterol levels of male laboratory rats.
EXAMPLE: Show data from a different study with a corresponding linear graph and ask students to identify all features and elements that were necessary to portray the information.
PROCEDURE: Ask class to generate a list of the specific steps taken by the scientist to create the graph, including: identification of dependent and independent variables, placement of intervals, and plotting the data points. Each student copies the steps to use as a personal guide during the cooperative task.
INTERACTION STRATEGY: Each student constructs his own graph, but only as each step is given by a team member. Each person needs to signal agreement before going on to the next step. Ideally, members take turns giving directions.

Example 3.

COURSE: Anthropology
CONTENT: Assimilation of cultures
GROUP TASK: From ethnographers' written accounts of the daily life of an American Indian tribe in the eighteenth and twentieth century, list ten pieces of evidence to prove that assimilation has occurred.
EXAMPLE: Lead a brief whole class discussion in which students are asked to generate the first two examples together. The visual organizer can be a simple chart titled Evidence of Assimilation with numbers one through ten listed under the title. The first two examples are written on the board or overhead projector as students contribute ideas. All students can copy these onto their own papers and then will have a model to serve as a referent as they start locating items three through ten on their own.
PROCEDURE: Students scan the first account and record (on the back of their papers) descriptors of any rituals, survival tasks, or miscellaneous activities that seem unique to this culture. They then scan the second account for a similar category of event and decide if the

specific descriptors warrant evidence of assimilation into the larger culture. If so, they then add that evidence to their list.

INTERACTION STRATEGY: Team members can each make their own lists and then take turns sharing items with each other. A final list (reflecting team consensus) is constructed that can be used for comparison with other teams when reporting to the whole class.

The most important technique I use to assist me in planning the specific details of providing structure is to anticipate all the potential pitfalls students may experience as they attempt to complete the cooperative task. I actually picture my students starting to work without any preparation from me, and I imagine all the specific and urgent questions that I will have to answer for each group as my name is called from all directions at once. At this point I am sufficiently motivated to spend a few extra minutes deciding in advance how I will introduce the groupwork for that lesson. Anticipated points of confusion for students serve as a guide for me as I plan the preparation in terms of any examples, procedures, or interactive strategies that might be necessary.

I find that this preparation is in reality not as complicated as the earlier detailed descriptors might imply. Quite often the three dimensions naturally weave together, and by thinking through one aspect, the other two fall into place. Separating them for discussion, as was done above, helps me to keep the potential pitfalls at a more conscious level.

Some teachers of college students often feel that the kind of preparation described above should not be necessary and admit that they resent having to take time to lay the necessary groundwork. I feel strongly that it is an unfortunate widely held myth that older students do not both require and appreciate structure in the form of examples, procedures, and interactive strategies. My graduate level students often express gratitude and relief that I am willing to take the time to increase the likelihood of successful groupwork. Following the few minutes it takes to prepare the class, students are usually quite eager to begin working; I attribute this enthusiasm to their increased comfort level and anticipation of a successful experience.

Students report that prior collaborative experiences in school were often negative precisely because the instructor simply turned groups loose after providing only a brief and vague verbal assignment. Advanced students shared a similar reaction during my own doctoral coursework. Our sociology professor asked us to form groups and discuss the chapter we had read for homework. The learning environment rapidly deteriorated as many students left in disgust because of the lack of structure and subsequent lack of meaning.

It is crucial that instructors resist the temptation to blame students when their initial efforts to implement CL do not meet expectations. A far more productive response is to determine by observing and questioning students which factors in the preparation might have been problematic so that immediate and/or future teaching modifications can be made. As students gain more experience interacting with peers and engaging in problem-solving tasks, they will often begin to demonstrate greater autonomy in structuring all aspects of their own group process.

Cooperative Poster Presentations

Rose Ann Swartz

While on sabbatical during the fall semester 1996, I interviewed dozens of professional men and women on how work teams were being used in their respective businesses and how these teams were being designed, implemented, maintained, and evaluated. Those interviewed included members of upper management, managers/supervisors, team leaders, and team members. What I learned is that we who are using cooperative-learning teams to facilitate learning are on the right track! Business needs men and women who can be effective team members and leaders, and who are good communicators. Now the task at hand is to construct classroom experiences that imitate what students will need as they enter the business world.

During the interviews, I was particularly impressed with the way those being interviewed explained concepts visually. It was natural for these professionals to use the whiteboard or poster board to sketch a diagram, prepare a flowchart, illustrate their organizational structure, outline team functions, etc. They seemed very comfortable making impromptu presentations and using visual aids to promote understanding. In addition, I found the visual explanations easier to understand and retain.

I wondered how I might find out what my students "know" about a concept in a way other than through traditional testing. Believing that one really needs to understand a subject in order to prepare an effective impromptu response to a question, I decided to use poster presentations as a form of quizzing my students on the concepts being learned in my organizational behavior classes. Because my students work primarily in cooperative-learning teams, I decided to "quiz" team members by having each team design a poster presentation in answer to a particular question or set of questions. Six poster presentations were given during the semester.

This is the way I incorporated poster presentations into my classes:
1. Each team was responsible for explaining an organizational behavior topic or concept that was discussed in class. Topics were selected that emphasized major "learning moments" from the chapter(s) being discussed. Depending on the complexity of the unit, teams were either assigned a single topic in advance or asked to prepare responses to all of the questions assigned. Each student was asked to reflect on the concept being addressed or, write down ideas to share with the team. As an example, the following questions were designed so that students would reflect on a unit about work teams and apply what was learned:
a. What is the value of establishing behavior and process norms? Have your team norms been challenged? If so, which ones and how? How has your team maintained its norms? How can you "enforce" your team's norms?
b. How can we analyze team interaction? Why are some teams more effective than others? What external conditions are imposed on the team? (Use your own team as an example.) How do the resources of team members contribute to a team? How can you develop cohesiveness as a team? How do you think member expectation might affect team performance?
c. Compare the Punctuated-Equilibrium Model and the Five-Stage Model of group development. How is your team progressing through the Five-Stage Model? Cite examples. What problems might surface in teams at each stage of the Five-Stage Model?
d. Read and analyze "Point/CounterPoint" on pages 367-368 of our text. Summarize both viewpoints. Indicate your personal or your team's preference and why.
2. Teams were given 10-15 minutes at the beginning of class to share their individual responses to the question(s), to decide on the major "learning moments" to use in the presentations, and to prepare their posters. Each student then selected one or two points to cover in his/her portion of the presenta-

tion. Equal participation during the presentations was required.

Time limit depends on the class size. I used this activity on seven different days during the semester, but if the class is large two class periods may be needed to allow all teams to present.

3. Colored pens/pencils, magic markers, and flipcharts were supplied for each team. Creativity was encouraged! At first students mainly used "bullets" to outline major concepts; as the semester progressed, teams started using symbols, charts, music, etc. to present their ideas. Team names/logos were also included. Students used the posters for their visual aids as they explained concepts to the class; no note cards were needed.

4. Class members were encouraged to ask questions during a short question and answer period at the end of each presentation. At the conclusion of all presentations, students were asked to evaluate each team and provide written feedback on how individual teams could improve the effectiveness of their presentations

See Figure 1 for the evaluation form which was designed by the students and used by both the instructor and teams. Although the student evaluations did not count toward course grades they did provide constructive feedback for individual teams. The points earned via my evaluations were assigned to all members of a given team and served as a quiz grade.

This strategy for visually assessing what students "know" was a refreshing change from the typical objective test. It should be noted, however, that objective and essay examinations were also part of student evaluation. The poster presentations allowed students to reflect on what was being taught, apply new knowledge, and share that information visually with other students.

The next time I use this activity, I will allow more time for questions and answers. I found students eager to ask questions and seek clarification from other team members. The Q&A provided more in-depth responses to questions and explanations of concepts than an objective test. (Often students state, "I can't take tests, but I can explain it..." This activity provided the opportunity for such students!)

By the end of the semester, students seemed more at ease in speaking before an audience and made effective presentations using their visuals. Of special benefit was the feedback provided to students—from students—on how to improve their presentations. At first I feared that an unhealthy interteam competition would develop; I found just the opposite. The feedback was excellent! And the spirit of cooperative learning was alive and well.

Figure 1. Evaluation Form

Poster Presentation Evaluation

Team _____ Topic _____ Date_____

Topic Coverage: (1-10 pts.)
    Thoroughly covered topic; added practical application and information.
Equal Participation: (1-4 pts.)   _____
    Equal time; on time.
Poster Effectiveness: (1-6 pts.)   _____
    Used as visual aid; readable.
Presentation Styles: (1-5 pts.)   _____
    Clear voices; proper use of notes; appropriate dress.
Extra Effort: (1-5 pts.)   _____
    Worked together as a TEAM; enthusiastic; creative.

                                    Total Points _____
Comments:

Teams of Four are Magic!

Spencer Kagan

At a number of recent workshops and on the Kagan web page, teachers have been questioning the best team size and team composition. There is a national trainer who is advocating cooperative-learning teams of seven, with a student strong in each of the multiple intelligences on each team. Teams of seven, though, violate the basic principles of cooperative learning, and classrooms do not break evenly with regard to the intelligences!

Let me say why I feel Teams of Four are Magic.

I continue to recommend teams of four, based on two of the four basic principles of cooperative learning. The first of the two principles is the Simultaneity Principle. The Simultaneity Principle has us ask a simple but powerful question: What percent of our students are overtly active at any one moment? Or, to phrase it another way, How much simultaneous interaction is there? The Simultaneity Principle not only tells us why cooperative learning is so much more powerful than traditional whole-class interaction, it tells us also that teams of four are the best. Here is why: If a teacher asks a question of the class and uses the whole class question-answer structure, calling on one student to answer, one of her thirty students is active at that moment, articulating her thoughts. If the teacher in the same moment asks the same question of the class, but rejects the whole-class structure, instead having her students discuss the question in teams of four, in the same timeframe at least one of every four students is actively engaged, articulating her thoughts It is this increased active participation in cooperative learning that is partially responsible for the greater gains shown among students in cooperative learning. It is far better to have a quarter of the class overtly active than just one student!

As we increase team size, we cut down active participation. In a team of seven, only one seventh of the class is verbalizing at any one moment during a group discussion, cutting the active participation almost in half compared to teams of four. Another way to demonstrate the superiority of the smaller team size is to ask how much time it takes to obtain a learning objective. Imagine that we have a very limited objective, say, that each student in the class states a personal reaction to a poem or current event, for one minute each. If students are seated in teams of seven, we reach our objective in seven minutes. The same exact outcomes for students are obtained in four minutes if students are seated in teams of four! Thus, teams of seven are about half as efficient as teams of four. Further, in teams of seven because on the average each student must wait six minutes to share for a minute, students seeking more active involvement will form subgroups and the team will lose focus. The second basic principle of cooperative learning which applies to team size is the Equality Principle. The Equality Principle has us ask a second powerful question: How equal is the participation among students? In the traditional classroom the Equality Principle is violated because highly motivated students always have their hands up, while less motivated students almost never do. The participation is very unequal.

That is why in cooperative learning we use strategies carefully crafted to equalize participation. For example, in a Timed-Pair-Share, A speaks for a minute then B speaks for a minute. Or in a RallyRobin A shares, then B shares, then A, then B, and so on. There are quite a number of these pair-based structures. For example, in Pairs Compare, one pair in the team works on a problem capable of many solutions while the other pair (out of contact with the first pair) also works on the problem. Later, the two pairs compare their solutions. In teams of three or five, these pair-based structures do not work nearly as well because the team breaks into a pair and a triad, creating unequal participation. In a Timed-Pair-Share with a team of three or five, someone is left out.

That is why I say Teams of Four are Magic!

Teams of four maximize and equalize active participation compared to any other number. The only other team size which does as well is a team of two! But a team of two does not provide enough diversity of points of view for many cooperative-learning activities. The Simultaneity Principle, however, does tell us that within our teams of four we would do well to very often have pair work. Pair work creates more active participation than square work.

Having, at least to my satisfaction, settled the question of team size, there remains the question of team composition. There is a great deal that can be said about team composition; we may select students for teams differently for different purposes. There are heterogeneous teams, random teams, multiple-intelligences teams, interest teams, topic-specific teams, homogeneous teams, sponge groups, and a variety of ways to form each.

Increasing Thinking Through Cooperative Writing

Barbara J. Millis

Virtually all educators agree that critical thinking skills need to be developed and nurtured to produce citizens capable of functioning in an increasingly complex, technological society where the knowledge base is exploding at a phenomenal rate. Increasingly, cognitive researchers are recognizing that knowledge lies not solely in someone's head, but in socially shared activities and the interactions that occur with other people in the surrounding environment. Critical thinking experts such as Brookfield (1987) and Kurfiss (1988) suggest that peer interactions can foster critical thinking because they often result in increased exposure to new ideas and alternatives and because they often offer challenges to existing beliefs and assumptions. Thus, work in groups can provide positive triggers to critical thinking.

Writing instructors, including experts such as Fulwiler (1987) and Moffett (1981), also advocate frequent, focused group work. They have long recognized the value of writing as a process, a process involving peer responses, an audience other than faculty members, and real world writing assignments. The connection between writing and thinking and their mutual, intertwined impact on the learning process have been amply discussed. Moffett (1981), for example, states, "Instead of using writing to test other subjects, we can elevate it to where it will teach other subjects, for in making sense the writer is making knowledge."

A key question for faculty—one discussed at length in the Cooperative Learning literature—is whether critical thinking skills should be taught separately (generic thinking skills) or infused with the subject matter (situated cognition connected to the environment in which thinking occurs). Similarly, Cooperative Learning advocates debate the value of teaching social skills directly as opposed to allowing them to emerge spontaneously through group activities as they are modeled and reinforced by the teacher. In both cases, I am a strong advocate of the content-centered approach because students often resist what they may regard as add-ons or busy work; they need to see the relevance of each cooperative activity. Furthermore, faculty in higher education are content-driven and time conscious. Thus, they too prefer a content-centered approach. They can do their students a great service, however, by continually emphasizing the critical elements of the skills—thinking, writing, and social—that emerge from each content-based cooperative activity and their applicability to other disciplines, personal situations, and the work place. Helping students see the connections between what they learn in college classrooms and real-world applications avoids the acquisition of what cognitive scientists call inert knowledge: information that is stored in the brain but never applied. Knowledge and skills cannot be taught in isolation. The use of cooperative groups focused on meaningful content avoids this isolation.

Many activities that promote and reinforce critical thinking and writing skills, such as journals or learning logs and peer editing groups, have been widely discussed. One of my favorite cooperative writing activities is Dyadic Essay Confrontations. The three activities described below—which I developed for literature and composition classes, but which have applicability in many disciplines—are not well-known in higher education. Jay McTighe introduced me to Reciprocal Reading during a critical thinking workshop at University of Maryland University College (UMUC). Similarly, I learned of Responsive Writing Exchanges at a writing-across-the-curriculum workshop conducted at UMUC by Toby Fulwiler. The third activity, Team Anthologies, I developed after reading a column by Morton D. Rich describing individual research anthologies in the May 1991 issue of *Inquiry: Critical Thinking Across the Disciplines*. The activities are described in order from simplest to most complex.

Reciprocal Reading

This short-term activity has two objectives: (a) to heighten students' awareness of metacognition (thinking about their own thinking), and (b) to emphasize the variety of textual interpretations that emerge with multiple viewpoints. This cooperative activity also enables faculty members to reinforce the use of sophisticated thinking strategies that experts, rather than novices, bring to complex tasks. Skillful thinkers, for instance, stop their reading to ask themselves what an author means, to conjecture about what comes next, to paraphrase difficult passages, or to reread earlier material to clarify current portions.

Students working in pairs are given two content-related one-page readings. The title and each paragraph are clearly numbered for easy referencing. In a literature class, for example, a reading selection might be the evocative prologue to Natalie Babbit's *Tuck Everlasting*, which begins "The first week of August hangs at the very top of summer, the top of the livelong year, like the highest seat of a ferris wheel when it pauses in its turning." In a history course a six-paragraph excerpt about the invention of barbed wire from William Least Heat Moon's *Blue Highways* could be used: "That a handcrank coffee mill helped kill off the Old West has not been widely appreciated."

Key steps:

(1) One student serves as a reflective reader, thinking aloud as she reads the given passage. As the student reads, her partner takes careful notes about her responses to the material.
(2) The two switch roles with the second student reading the second selection aloud and the original student serving as recorder.
(3) During a whole-class discussion students share and compare the various responses their partners had to the two selected passages (which are common to all pairs within the class). The instructor emphasizes the significance of the various reader responses in terms of literary, historical or other interpretations. In an optional fourth step the teacher can collect the written transcripts and use them to provide feedback in a subsequent class.

Teaching tips:

The teacher should model the reading process initially with another written passage so that students see the practice in action. Students must appreciate the need to say out loud all of their spontaneous thoughts, no matter how tangential. Processing this activity is critical: the teacher must help students see the relevance of the activity to their own reading and interpretations and appreciate the value of receiving multiple viewpoints for their writing.

Responsive Written Exchanges

In this activity, students reflect in writing on issues identified through sentence stems. To personalize the assignment and to engender commitment to the ideas and/or a plan of action outlined, the writing takes the form of letter exchanges between classmates. The objectives are: (a) to foster critical thinking with a written record; (b) to offer immediate, responsive feedback; (c) to encourage one-on-one communication and team building; and, (d) in some situations, to encourage commitment to a planned activity.

Key steps:

(1) The teacher prepares an activity sheet with the prompts (sentence stems) for reflection. These can be presented as individual handouts or projected on an overhead. All assignment sheets begin with a salutation (Dear X) and end with a P. S. "One personal thing about me you may not know is..."

Typical prompts might be:

(Writing class) "I plan to write my classification paper on the topic of..." "My key points are ..." "My reservations about this assignment are..."

(Accounting or Computer classes) "Unreliability in a computer accounting system can be caused by events such as..." "Accounting controls for this unreliability are..."

(Ecology, Biology, or Economics classes) "The spotted owl controversy involves the following issues." "I think the most important issue is ..."

(Psychology or Pre-Medicine) "I do/do not feel that Prozac should be frequently prescribed because..."

(Sociology) "The causes for homelessness are...." "I think we can attack the issue by..."

(2) Paired students, working simultaneously, write a personal letter to their partner based on the sentence stems.
(3) They exchange letters, read them, and write responses focused primarily on the issues, but they may also address, in their own post scripts, responses to the personal comments made by their partners.
(4) The partners again exchange letters so they can read each others' responses (No one likes to write a letter without getting a reply!). The letters can be kept by the students without teacher review, but more often they are taken up, read informally, and returned.

Teaching tips:

Students, as always, must see the relevance of this activity. Underscore the importance of written commentary, which implies commitment, as opposed to verbal exchanges that are meaningful, thought-provoking, but too often ephemeral. Consider building in a sponge or extension issue for students who write quickly. The assignment sheet can be set up with additional prompts for those completing the key sentences. This step sends a signal to students that they can't blow off the assignment by whipping through it. The activity should be a reflective exercise lasting at least twenty minutes, depending on the complexity of the sentence stems.

Team Anthologies

A longer, ongoing semester assignment requires the use of formal learning teams. The key objective with this activity is to teach research skills without having the students actually write a research paper. Too often, writing research papers is a time-consuming, product-centered effort coming too late in a semester to allow for meaningful processing and feedback. This assignment sends students to the library—either physically or electronically—to research a given topic and to evaluate and analyze the original sources. In this activity teams of four (quads) select a discipline-specific topic, one which typically might generate a term paper. They are given the task of preparing a team research anthology that contains a bibliography and annotations on the most valuable articles or chapters.

Key steps:

(1) Each team agrees on a discipline-specific topic for research.
(2) Each team member, working individually, identifies the most important sources on the topic. This bibliography is submitted independently.
(3) The team compiles a team research bibliography drawn from the work of all four members: they debate the relative merits of each entry, including its relevance, currency, and value.
(4) Each team member, working individually, prepares a reflective commentary on one of the most valuable articles or chapters. They do so using a double column format with excerpts from the original source on the left-hand side and reactions, questions, commentary, and connections with other readings on the right (the columns will not be the same length). The teacher collects these reflective commentaries with the student retaining a copy.
(5) Team members then pair, exchanging the articles they have just analyzed. Each writes a double columned reflective commentary on their partner's article, which is turned in with a copy retained.
(6) The two teammates now read one another's reflective commentaries, comparing their responses to the two articles. Together, they prepare a composite annotation summarizing the article.
(7) Steps 4, 5, and 6 are repeated several times, pairing different students within the quad, until the team has completed the desired number of annotations.
(8) Students now prepare their work for publication by adding three elements to the bibliography and annotations: a) a coversheet; b) an introduction stating the purpose of the anthology and its value for the intended audience (fellow students); and c) a conclusion giving suggested uses or applications of the annotations and recommended future research on the topic, including unanswered questions. Students might also include their own plans for future research within the discipline.
(9) The anthologies can be duplicated for each class member, depending on class size, shared through a gallery walk (the anthologies remain stationary while students rotate among them making comments on a nearby sheet of paper), or placed on reserve in the library.

Teaching tips:

This activity is deliberately structured to promote both individual accountability and positive interdependence. Individual bibliographies and reflective commentaries are submitted to the instructor, but the students work together on the team bibliography, the composite annotations, and the final anthology. Teachers must monitor each step of the activity carefully to be certain that all students understand and complete their share of the tasks. Students will need to see model anthologies. Although the research and writing can be done outside of class, students will definitely need class time to compare and discuss their responses if the activity is to have critical thinking value.

Using writing to promote critical thinking helps students examine, evaluate, verify, analyze, weigh alternatives, and consider consequences as ideas develop. Writing and thinking cannot be separated. Pulitzer Prize winner Don Murray (1978) contends: "I believe increasingly that the process of discovery, of using language to find out what you are going to say, is a key part of the writing process." It is also a key part of the thinking process.

Using Group Investigation to Enhance Arab-Jewish Relationships

Rachel Hertz-Lazarowitz

Every second year I taught a seminar at the University of Haifa (UH) entitled "Cooperation and Communication Between Arab and Jewish Students on Campus." It is an elective seminar which meets once a week for an hour and a half throughout the academic year (26-28 class sessions). Two features characterize this seminar: its ethnic mix — half Arabs and half Jews, and its pedagogy — we become a group of investigators in the area of our own coexistence on campus. This article tells the story of that seminar.

Background

The University of Haifa, on the top of beautiful Mount Carmel, is situated in the northern region of Israel, where the majority of Arabs live, and UH has the largest percentage of Arab students in the Israeli University system: 20%, roughly the percentage of Arabs in Israel itself. It is a demanding challenge for UH to integrate its Arab and Jewish students, made harder because here they are integrated for the first time, having been educated in a totally segregated system from kindergarten through high school. This is the only context in Israeli society where youngsters from these two groups encounter each other on an equal basis. Moreover, since Arabs don't serve in the Israeli army (except for the Druse), most Arab students are 18 when they enter the university, whereas Jewish students are 21 or 22, after 3-4 years of army service. Arabs differ by religion: Christian, Muslim and Druse. Most Arab students are Christians. Jewish students are also varied. Those of Middle-Eastern origin ("Sepharadim") comprise 50-60% of the Israeli Jewish population, but only 20% at UH. The majority of Jewish students is of European origin ("Ashkenazim"), and comprises 50-60% of the student body. This distribution is roughly similar within all seven Israeli universities.

This diverse national and ethnic mix is in itself a fascinating laboratory for group relations. Life at UH has a history divided between periods of tension and conflict and periods of relatively quiet coexistence. Many issues that evoke conflict are related to the macro-level: the political situation, the right of Arab students to celebrate national events or demonstrate against government decisions. But many are also related to the micro-level, such as a demand to take entrance exams in Arabic, the right to form Arab student organizations, and the money assigned for Arab student scholarships. The most painful conflict, which resulted in police involvement and blood on campus, occurred in 1985, and was studied by me in detail (Hertz-Lazarowitz, 1988). I concluded that a lack of understanding of the "other" group, misconceptions of each other's deeds and needs, and the absence of meaningful contact between Jewish and Arab students were at the heart of this conflict. It was the reality I discovered in 1985 which made me decide to create this seminar.

I was born in Haifa when Jews and Arabs lived together in relative peace, before the War of Independence. My parents were tenants of a well-known and respected Arab family. I lived in this mixed neighborhood and loved it. As a student at UH in the late sixties I studied in mixed classrooms. When I returned to UH as young faculty member in the mid-seventies, I knew the importance of creating a positive and equal learning environment for my Arab and Jewish students as a model of coexistence on campus. However, no formal academic courses were offered to study the UH experience until I introduced my seminar. The study of coexistence on the UH campus was an open field for research. The students could be the observers, the participants, the researchers, and the creators of new knowledge.

The Seminar

The first seminar was offered in 1986. I will use the class of 1991 to illustrate the structure and content of the seminar. We were 25 students and me: 12 Jewish women, 12 Arab women, and one Jewish man from a kibbutz. (This is not typical, two years earlier a third were men, both Arabs and Jews.) Among the Jewish women, four were Sepharadim and eight Ashkenazim, including two newcomers from Russia. In the Arab group, nine were Christians, two Muslims, and one Druse. The Arab students were in their early twenties, and most of the Jews were a couple of years older. One Jewish woman, a nurse, was in her late thirties, and the Jewish man, a teacher, was in his early thirties.

The beginning of the first meeting was devoted to hearing students' motives and expectations: Why did they choose to take this seminar? What did they want to experience and what did they want to avoid in this course? Most were looking for channels of communication to learn more about the other group. Many had participated in structured meetings between Arabs and Jews in high school.

Students were then asked to form mixed groups by nationality and to talk about their names. Who named them? Why were they given this name? What is the meaning of their names? This activity encouraged personal sharing and provided rich cultural understanding. One reflection that came out in every group was that it is very hard for Jewish students to remember Arab names and vice versa. The feeling that Jews and Arabs are "nameless" to each other was shared by many. They discussed the importance of knowing a person by name and made a commitment to learn each other's names in the seminar.

After processing the name activity, I took 20 minutes to present my agenda:
1. To investigate the theoretical literature on Jews and Arabs as two national groups in political conflict to enrich our understanding of the UH experience.
2. To work in and out of class in heterogeneous groups to elaborate, discuss, report, clarify and debate issues relevant to the life of Jewish and Arab students on campus.
3. To plan and carry out research topics following the model of Group Investigation as described in Sharan and Hertz-Lazarowitz (1980).
4. To be direct and open about our own experiences in the seminar.

Students were asked to keep an interactive log, where they wrote reflections after each meeting and responses to their readings. These could be kept private or shared. In addition, every meeting was summarized by a student, and these minutes typed, distributed and discussed during the first ten minutes of the following session.

After two sessions in which I presented an overview of topics and research available in this field, the students, with my assistance, composed a basic reading list and chose the following topics for Group Investigation:

1. Identify Formation. What are the processes by which the Arab and the Jew define and form their identities? How did the students define and form their own identities? Are there legitimized Arab and Jewish definitions of identity? Why do some Arab definitions threaten Jews and vice versa?
2. Intergroup Conflicts. What are the roots and history of Jewish-Arab conflict in Israel? What are other intergroup conflicts in Israel? What are the conflicts on the UH campus? What models are there for resolving these conflicts? What can we, as students, do to reduce intergroup conflicts on campus and in general?
3. Delegitimization and Dehumanization. How do these, processes develop and express themselves in our society? Do they exist on campus? How do we feel about being dehumanized or delegitimized? How can we become sensitive to these dangerous processes? Which societies, and under what conditions, create such processes? Is there any society that is immune?
4. Life on the UH Campus. How do I feel on campus as an Arab? As a Jew? What is the nature of relationships between these two groups? Does UH give an equal chance to Arabs and Jews? Why do conflicts and tensions occur on campus? Can these be avoided? What is the role of student leaders in enhancing or inhibiting coexistence? Are we doing a good job at being an integrated university?
5. The Intifada. What is its impact on Jews, Israeli Arabs, Palestinian Arabs in the West Bank and Gaza? How do the Israeli Arabs feel and do they have a role in the situation?

The class decided that each topic would be investigated by all students, each topic lasting 4-6 weeks. Students first read topic-related articles at home and responded to questions. Then they reported, discussed, and elaborated on these readings in their mixed groups in class.

The next meeting was devoted to relating the topic to the students' lives. Here a meaningful dialogue was created among students, with their own perspectives, ideas and feelings at the center.

The third meeting was devoted to planning an investigation related to the topic. For example: Students decided to interview other students on campus to find out how they defined their identity. In order to gather data on Arab/Jewish interactions on campus, students observed seating arrangements in other classes, in the cafeteria and the library, and recorded their interaction. Students analyzed university documents and regulations, recorded political and social student events as data to search for legitimization and equality. They observed student elections to define the role of activists on campus, and interviewed activists for both groups.

But more than anything I encouraged them to use their own voices and their private life stories as legitimate and significant sources of data. These investigations usually took two weeks. The meeting following those two week investigations was devoted to comparing and summarizing the data gathered by each group. Then each group planned its final presentation. Some of these were in the form of written reports, oral reports, position papers addressed to people in the university, or journal writings.

Students changed their groups for each topic, and each of them got to work with all of their classmates. The first four topics were investigated in mixed groups. The Intifada was studied in uni-national groups. The pain involved in the Intifada demanded this.

A Critical Event

During the year we experienced some critical events that presented the conflicts, prejudice, and mistrust that we held toward each other. The reality in Israel is so loaded with pain, frustration, fear and suspicion, that it enters every door in the country. Daily events of the Intifada, stone throwing, terror, blood and death were constantly in the seminar background. It challenged what we were trying to do, and faced us with harsh questions: Is there hope? What will be the end of all this? Who is right and who is wrong? Who is the victim? Can we change "little things" when there are such big issues that seem to get worse?

Once a month a meeting was devoted to group dynamics, structured activities such as "planning my future" or "imagining peace," sharing journal writing, and talking about the "here and now" experiences of being in this class. Several of the students gave me permission to share entries from their journals with readers of this article. I thank them for that. There is room for only one selection, but this journal entry reflects the many open and painful discussions students held about the roots of our own attitudes of prejudice and discrimination.

Sophi wrote: "Two weeks ago one of our roommates left the apartment, and we put an ad to find a new roommate. We had many applicants, but we turned them down for many reasons... We also had an Arab young man come, and we turned him down because he seemed 'not nice'. I thought about it a lot. I know we turned him down because he was an Arab. And here I am taking this seminar on coexistence... I was very disturbed, but I tried to justify it by saying: he really was not that nice, our parents would not approve it... But I knew I was fooling myself. I brought it up with a couple of friends and shared my distress, but they all said: 'We would do the same, why are you bothered? It is only natural that Jews don't feel like having Arab roommates...' I tried to analyze what was going on within me; I finally admitted that I was scared to live in an apartment with an Arab. I also knew my parents wouldn't approve it. I feel torn by these feelings, I feel ashamed, I feel terrible, but we continue to refuse to accept Arab roommates even when another Arab man comes, and another."

Sophi shared this experience with her group. The Arab members were furious. Fatan attacked Sophi bitterly, and said she wouldn't work with her any more. Fatan said that this event is proof that nothing can improve, that lots of hypocrisy is taking place in the class, and that we are all doomed to hatred with no hope. This event led to much self-inquiry and discussion about one's own moral thinking and acting. It did not turn into a "blame battlefield," but rather to examining the balance we need between integration and separation in order to keep our sense of uniqueness. Students examined their borders as to how much social closeness and intimacy they can take, and created a tolerance for individual differences.

In Conclusion

From the journals, the research projects and ongoing communication with my former students since 1986, I conclude that the seminars were meaningful experiences for them as well as for me. A few of the group products have been presented at national and international conferences, and submitted for publication. Furthermore, the issue of coexistence on the UH campus is much more salient these days. One sign of this is the growing number of workshops and courses offered in this area, mainly within the School of Education. As one of my students put it, "I understand now, mainly via this seminar, that nobody in my 13 years of school education took the role to cultivate and enhance positive beliefs... The education system has to take a role in this issue, and at a young age, because if not it will be a tragedy for both sides."

Part III
Small Group Learning Within the Disciplines

In this third part of this book we focus on more discipline related applications of small group work. All of these articles were previously published in the *Cooperative Learning and College Teaching* newsletter. Although all articles in Part III were written in the 1990s, our reading of the literature suggests that most of the techniques are still in common use in higher education today. This should not be surprising since they embody the research articulated in Parts I and II, work on critical thinking/deep learning, brain based teaching, student centered pedagogy and other empirical and theoretical traditions.

The first article describes how Deborah Dentler teaches American History in her community college classroom. She takes the reader through activities, beginning with the first day of class, and then describes how she encourages students to read the textbook (ideas similar to Susan Prescott Johnston's article in Part II). She writes about how she makes the learning of terms more engaging and then moves to strategies that focus on more complex cognitive skills, including a history jigsaw procedure and an autobiography exercise, both designed to get at questions such as "What is history?" and "How is history best researched and written?"

Elaine M. Aschettino's article is next with a description of a compelling approach to teaching Print Journalism. Elaine identifies ways of using brainstorming and team posters to teach libel law and how journalists cover breaking news stories. In reading these two articles, as with much of the other work in this section, we kept thinking how engaging these classes would have been for us, had we taken them when we were undergraduates.

The third article in this part of the book is a summary of a variety of methods for using the ConcepTests procedure in college chemistry. ConcepTests were first popularized by Eric Mazur in physics at Harvard. The technique often involves stopping the class at frequent intervals and posing a question or issue to the students, usually in a multiple choice format. Students turn to a neighbor to discuss the item and then report their answers to the larger group. The teacher then discusses the responses with the whole class. Permutations of this technique have been adopted at the University of Wisconsin, as reported in this article, and around the country. Clickers are now a popular format of operationalizing ConcepTests, often in large lecture classes. The data of Mazur and others indicates using ConcepTests has a significant impact on higher order thinking, student attendance and engagement, particularly in large classes.

Kate Kinsella and Kathy Sherak next offer a thoughtful article about teaching English as a Second Language (ESL). They report on using surveys and questionnaires as vehicles for student engagement, along with cooperative learning, to address a variety of diversity issues that are common concerns in ESL classrooms.

The teaching of writing has been a long-standing challenge in education. The next two articles in Part III address this issue. Wendy Slobodnik discusses the basic writer in her article. She recommends forms of brainstorming as ways of selecting a topic and methods of developing the topic. She also presents peer critique as a procedure to help in the prewriting structure and rough draft stages of the writing process. Joe Cuseo's article deals with writing across the curriculum, a movement that has gained popularity in higher education in recent years. He notes that its popularity reflects the awareness that responsibility for increasing writing skills must include faculty outside of the traditional English/composition group. Joe asserts, and we agree, that it is the responsibility of the entire faculty teaching across the curriculum. He makes the case for a more analytical assessment of teaching writing, one that takes a process (rather than product approach). He argues for more systematic applications of structured group work if we are to address the serious weaknesses in the writing skills of our students.

Joe has also been a long time contributor to the cooperative learning newsletter and to our 2003 small group book, as has Richard Felder, whose article follows Joe's. Rich describes his journey in applying group work to engineering courses. He provides a history of applying cooperative learning to a five course sequence in chemical engineering and provides data, both empirical and narrative, regarding the effect of this pedagogy on students. Rich has a web site (http://www4.ncsu.edu/unity/lockers/users/f/felder/public/) which provides, excuse the pun, a rich array of materials he has developed over the years, including many works on active/small group learning and an interesting learning styles inventory.

Lisa Gray-Shelberg's article follows Rich's and describes how she used a Jeopardy game show format to teach a psychology class in history and systems. The procedure makes the learning of dates, historical names and other factual information an engaging and fun-filled experience.

Lisa's article is followed by one written by Edwina Stoll and her colleagues at De Anza Community College in California. The authors describe how they use active and small group learning in teaching their individual courses, including developmental writing, calculus, freshmen composition, British literature, and public speaking. This article brings home the idea that small group structures can be applied in most disciplines and with a wide range of student populations. It also reinforces the idea that a group of instructors working together is a rich source of ideas and can provide a kind of learning community of teachers who enhance the life of a professor. Too often college teaching is an isolating, competitive experience where instructors compete for limited resources, including tenure and promotion. This need not be the case, as the De Anza faculty proves. (In Part IV of the book, Cynthia Desrochers describes a more formal approach to developing faculty learning communities.)

The final entry in Part III is a second article by Rose Ann Swartz in which she describes how American and foreign-born students can work cooperatively in teaching and learning arrangements designed to develop student skills in international business. She has students work in teams of American and foreign students to develop modules of instruction, including library research, videos and class presentations dealing with cultural norms and traditions that impact doing business with persons from other countries. Rose Ann's work, along with Rachel Hertz-Lazarowitz's, emphasizes that cooperative learning can be one of the most powerful strategies for enhancing appreciation of diversity: this is one of the best documented student outcomes related to small group instruction.

Cooperative Learning and American History

Deborah Dentler

Fresh from colleague Mark Maier's seminar at Glendale College, I introduced a number of successful new Cooperative Learning (CL) teaching strategies in my American History class. There is a dearth of material on teaching college-level history using the CL method. I hope the following strategies will generate comments and inspire other history instructors to share what they are doing.

First Meeting Self-Introductions & Text Exercise

1. Self-Introductions

The first meeting of a history course is often considered a waste of time by all concerned. Students want the course syllabus, to quickly size up the professor, and get dismissed early. The teacher feels the students know nothing about history yet and so discussion is kept to a minimum. I have historically done most of the talking for the first and second class meetings, but since I began using CL this tradition has changed.

By doing all the talking in the first week, I realized, I must take some of the blame when it proves difficult to get students to contribute later. By employing exercises which require students to do most of the talking during the first and second class meetings teachers can convey in a very immediate way their expectations about class participation. The following strategies helped me use the first two class hours fully, built rapport among students, encouraged the formation of friendships, reduced student anxiety and competitiveness, and laid the groundwork for successful CL as the course progressed.

Seeing how few students I had (17 students during the semester in which I piloted these activities, rather than the usual 45) I quickly asked the class to rearrange chairs into a circle (this step alone generated cheers of approval; in larger classes students can be asked to stand and face their peers as they speak). We went around the circle stating what we'd had for dinner the night before and what music group or artist we were listening to this week.

At the second meeting, I did the textbook-reading exercise described below, preceded by another round of self-introductions. This time I asked each student to make a 30-second presentation about his/her name. (Students were free to say anything at all about their names—first, last, or both—and responses ranged from "how I feel about my name," to "who I was named after" and "what my name means in English.") I introduced this exercise by pointing out that a person's name and his/her feelings and experiences with that name is something unique to that person.

I hadn't predicted what lessons in multiculturalism these simple exercises would be. I had expected to encourage student friendships, develop the habit of class participation, and facilitate the learning of names. I did not anticipate the power of these self-introductions to demolish barriers like shyness, cultural myopia, and low self-esteem. I also underestimated the positive energy that flows from laughter. Stereotypes, including my own, crumbled when we learned the diminutive Vietnamese woman liked Hawaiian pizza and Mozart; the Pacific Islander of East Indian heritage eats curry but listens to Ice Cube just like his African-American classmate.

These exercises raised many questions in students' minds about their varying backgrounds, and gave me a springboard from which to lecture about the homogenization of American culture and the great pressure on immigrants and natives, starting from the early colonial period, to conform and assimilate.

The name exercise was even more useful for encouraging curiosity about different cultures and family traditions, and for breaking down barriers between students. A Korean-born student explained his parents had paid $200 to a naming advisor to select a propitious name for their newborn. Some names had been butchered by immigration authorities and others had been proudly adopted later in life by students themselves as an act of rebellion or self-invention. These exercises have continued to pay off throughout the semester. My students are more comfortable raising their hands to speak since they've discovered they all like the same music and food. For my part, all aspects of teaching are eased by the fact that, early on, I came to know something of the life dramas of individual students. I know who to call on for examples of immigrant experiences and perceptions, for instance. My stereotypes and expectations based on a set of bare names on a roster, were challenged and shaken, and I'm a better teacher for that.

2. Text Reading Exercise

At the community college where I teach, many of my students are still adding the course at the second class meeting, and the majority either haven't bought the text or haven't bothered to read any of it. There are many reasons for this, not the least of which may be procrastination. Even the best history text seems intimidating, dull, and irrelevant to those with no special interest in the field (which describes most of my students). Many students put off opening the text as long as they think they can get away with it.

For the second class meeting I devised an ungraded exercise that served three goals teachers have in the first week of a course: 1) to introduce students to the textbook, 2) to familiarize them with quizzes and tests, and 3) to provide the teacher with some initial data about students' skill levels.

I've used this exercise successfully on first, second, and third days of a course. For this exercise students read a portion of an assigned chapter, then answer a series of questions about the reading. I provide photocopies of the relevant text for those who haven't brought a book to class (always a majority). The students read silently alone, and then confer with a four-person team to work on the answers.

The questions to be answered are partly designed to develop textbook reading skills ("In five words or less, describe the main topic of the first page you read."). I even include questions whose main purpose is simply to teach reading/study skills like highlighting and research ("In the index, locate the term matrilineal, then underline or highlight that section of the text."). Other questions require higher-level critical thinking, asking students to interpret or apply what they've just read (e.g., "The author discusses ways in which Native American and British cultures differed. Can you think of three things these cultures have in common?"). To elicit higher-level critical thinking in a women's history course I might state "The text states that unmarried women had significantly more legal rights than married women in the seventeenth century." I would then ask, "Why do you suppose, then, virtually all women wanted to marry?"

The immediate benefits to the students are obvious: they start the course relating enthusiastically and openly with one another in a group exercise that is ungraded and therefore stress-free; they are forced to read the first few pages of the text—something many of them would otherwise put off for weeks; and they get fair warning in the first week of the semester of what reading level is expected and what my test questions are like. I have found this works much better than my former method, which consisted of exhorting them to read the book and to prepare on their own for the first quiz.

I've used the text-reading exercise successfully in classes of 40 and even 70 students by eliminating the team discussion process. It can be done as individual work sheets or in pairs rather than foursomes.

Teaching History Terminology: Term Teaming

As with any fact-based discipline, the study of history requires students to memorize terms and dates, such as Reconstruction, Calvinism, and the Enlightenment. It is this aspect of history courses that many students find intimidating and boring. How do most history teachers teach such terms and dates? Using the traditional approach, most of us hope students will read their textbooks and then we count on the presence of at least one bright, motivated student who knows at least one of the day's terms and will contribute the right answer. Then, when this approach fails, we resign ourselves to writing terms on the board and defining them while students passively copy them—often incorrectly—into notes. I now periodically employ a different approach to teaching my students lists of terms and dates. Essentially, I turn over a big chunk of the teaching to them. I call this Term Teaming.

As each new unit of the course begins, I place my students in their teams of four for at least one class session. Each team is given a list of four terms to research, define, and self-teach. The teams number off, meaning that there are several "number ones, twos, etc." in the classroom. All "number ones" are assigned the same term; all "number twos" are assigned another term, etc. When I've been able to prepare well in advance, I do something fancy like pass out individual strips of paper, assigning each student a term. More often, I list the day's terms on the board, numbered 1 through 4, or 1 through 8.

Term Teaming works this way: number ones must research in their text or notes the term they've been assigned (Social Darwinism, for example), and teach what they know about the term to the number two students. Meanwhile, the number three students teach their assigned term to the number four students. When the ones and threes have finished, the roles are switched. Then the partner pairs are rotated and the process repeated until all four concepts have been taught to all four team members.

At the end of this process (which takes 15 minutes), I ask each group to volunteer the definition the group feels it handled best. I like to encourage those who were passive listeners to report on what their partner taught them about a term. (I ask those who were number twos to report what they learned from number ones, for example.) Not all students can or will want to speak to the whole class, so this reporting process is fairly informal and fast. Correct definitions are repeated slowly by me and written on the board.

This technique empowers students to become responsible for their own learning, requires them to read their textbook and use the index, builds interpersonal rapport, and stimulates discussion. This approach takes more time than straight lecture, but is far more enjoyable, for both student and teacher, than the traditional method.

I use Term Teaming most profitably when reviewing fairly dry and date-ridden legal and political terms and events such as the series of acts by Parliament that preceded the Revolution (e.g., Stamp Act, Townshend Duties) or the various programs of FDR's New Deal and LBJ's Great Society. I also use this technique to help students with names of people I want them to remember such as Abigail Adams, John Brown and Henry Ford.

One of the great pleasures of this exercise is its spontaneity. Try it on those days you notice students' eyes are glazing over while you list terms on the board and you fear you're putting even yourself to sleep. Unlike most CL exercises, this one takes no advance planning.

Historiography Skill Building

Most course descriptions and textbooks adopted by colleges assume that college history courses will cover the topics "what is history?" and "how is history best researched and written?" Graduate students in history enjoy grappling with these issues, and teachers look forward to exploring them with students. When I raise these questions with my community college students, however, the abstraction of these topics makes for deadly classroom time.

This term I finally hit on two fresher approaches to the subject of historiography than the reading-and-discussion or term-paper methods by which I was taught. The first technique asks students to engage in a mini-research project during class time, using a variety of primary and secondary source materials. The other is a simple autobiography writing project done by each student outside class, but guided by ideas generated during in-class CL.

1. Research Jigsaw

For this exercise I divide students into groups of three or four. If there are excess students or late-coming stragglers, I find it preferable to permit a few pairs of two than to form larger groups.

Each group works on a different research assignment I hand out, and must collectively arrive at answers to my written questions by referring to primary and secondary sources I've provided. This project familiarizes students with the differences between primary and secondary historical sources, and graphically illustrates the difficulty of deducing facts from historical evidence. In the course of the project, students also master a variety of terms they'd otherwise learn more passively by listening to my definitions and copying from the chalkboard.

For example, one group studied the Mayflower Compact and answered a series of written questions such as "Describe the class, racial, and religious characteristics of the signers of the Compact." The sources I provided included the diary of Governor William Bradford containing his account of the Pilgrims' landing, and a facsimile of the Mayflower Compact I bought in New England last summer (one of those pseudo-parchment souvenirs available at tourist traps everywhere, and near Glendale College, incidentally, at Forest Lawn Cemetery).

While four students toiled over these and other materials, another group answered a series of questions concerning demographic characteristics of Puritans (life expectancy, age of marriage, fertility rates), using John Demos' classic account of Puritan family life, *The Little Commonwealth,* an original source town census roster dating from Puritan times, and modern compilations of data. Yet another group was asked to sketch a typical Puritan village on the blackboard, which required them to research such unfamiliar concepts (for Californians) as commons and meetinghouses.

I've used the textbook as a source of both primary

and secondary documents for shorter versions of the same exercise. Most history texts have maps, charts, diagrams and appendices containing a wealth of often-overlooked sources, such as the Constitution, excerpts of presidential speeches, and population tables.

Materials that can easily be culled from the college library to be used in the Research Jigsaw include: original Indian treaties, diaries kept by immigrant and frontier families, plays and poems from the period being studied, and art books showing furnishings, portraits, and costumes from which important insights can be drawn about how people of the past felt and lived.

For the Research Jigsaw, I allow forty minutes for group research and discussion, and then call for reports from each group. The first time I tried this I found presentations were more time-consuming than I'd anticipated, especially because I couldn't resist jumping in to correct misinformation. Reports resumed the following class period. At the end of this exercise, I led the class in a spirited discussion of how history is done by real historians, using materials identical to those the class had grappled with. It was much more fun for all of us than the historiography seminar I endured in graduate school.

2. Autobiography Exercise

One of my goals each semester is to instill in my students some appreciation for how challenging and fraught with dangers of misinterpretation is the process of writing about the past. No amount of lecturing on this topic ever sparked any discernable interest, until I stumbled on a new approach.

For this project, students are required to write a five-page essay. Two pages are devoted to describing the events of one month in the student's life three years ago. Two pages are then to be devoted to describing a recent week in the student's life. (The assignment reads "Describe your life last week.") Lastly, the student is to write a page relating the two sections, briefly discussing ways in which life three years ago impacted life last week.

I give my students a month to complete these autobiographical essays. When I hand out this assignment, I lead a class discussion about sources students might use to reconstruct their memories. To generate ideas, I use the cooperative technique known as Think, Pair, Share.

I ask each student to find a partner without moving chairs. "Look to the person on your right" usually suffices. Each pair must think of at least three documents or sources that might be helpful in researching the past. This takes less than five minutes of class time.

I then go quickly around the room asking each team to name one source. I list all suggestions on the board. This step takes five to ten minutes if done rapidly, and usually elicits several highly creative approaches to research. Calendars, diaries, and letters are obvious sources of information about events of the past. Less traditional are old computer files, high school yearbooks, checkbook registers, newspaper headlines from the period in question, clothes closets, and music collections.

This project focuses attention on a number of important questions simultaneously. How do historians sort out the important from the unimportant in a vast set of facts about the past? Which records are most reliable and useful in preserving evidence of the past? What can artifacts and objects like costumes and photographs reveal? How does the past influence the present? For their suggestion that students be encouraged to think about problems of sources, selection, embellishment and interpretation by writing their own autobiographies, I'm indebted to Julie Roy Jeffrey and Peter J. Frederick, authors of the teacher's manual that accompanies the text, *The American People* (2nd Brief Edition). The manual is entitled *Teaching The American People: A Guide for Instructors* (Harper Collins, 1992).

The Think, Pair, Share process encourages class participation, builds enthusiasm for the paper-writing work to come, and stimulates creativity. At the same time, it reduces barriers between students, encourages the formation of friendships and releases the teacher from the relative drudgery of pulling ideas out of unwilling or shy students in a more traditional, passive learning classroom.

I require students to submit a list of sources with their autobiographies, stating what documents or artifacts they used to jog their memories and to re-create their pasts. This is a very popular project with my students. A typical comment: "I'm so glad I had to write this paper because it has made me think about my life in ways I never did before." A final plus is the personal gratification I get from reading these papers. I learn all kinds of interesting and inspiring information about people I rarely get to know in a traditional course.

In my classrooms, this assignment is done for credit, but I grade these papers very liberally. It is the students' only opportunity to write without much concern for organizing and regurgitating history facts learned during the course. Even for those students utterly unmoved by matters historiographical, this essay serves to personalize the course and, at a minimum, gives them writing practice.

Conclusion

Why do CL techniques seem to work for community college students? Traditional methods of teaching and learning were good enough, after all, for most of us on the faculty. Why change what worked for us?

In thinking about why CL is important for community college students, I've come to believe the answer lies in the fact that who "us" is has changed dramatically since the current crop of college teachers began their careers. Largely white, heavily male, relatively affluent (compared to our students), and holding degrees from far more elite institutions than the ones that employ us, most faculty experienced their education as both a joy and a personal right. Most of us spoke up readily and often in class, and felt empowered, even entitled, to debate and contribute ideas. We were raised to question authority, to be self-learners, and we were taught skills early in life that equipped us to learn at advanced levels.

Our students, shaped by far different academic, economic, personal, and political experiences, typically do not feel empowered in the classroom. They are alienated from institutions, including colleges that too often serve to heighten their sense of exclusion from positions of power and privilege in society. Most importantly, our students do not have the self-esteem required to confidently participate in competition-based class discussions that follow the traditional passive-learning lecture methods. This is especially true of the large numbers of students who are in community colleges because they performed too poorly in high school to go elsewhere.

I've found it pays to break students into small discussion groups regularly throughout the term, even for something as relatively passive as viewing a documentary video. Early in my teaching career I wrongly assumed that it would be easy to generate enthusiasm and participation by simply showing a great film. I was at a loss to understand why most students didn't react the way I do to, say, Ken Burns' "Civil War" masterpiece. Now, after I show a film, I guide students' reactions and encourage dialogue by having student groups discuss thought-provoking questions I've written on the blackboard. I always preface this by pointing out that many people feel more comfortable talking in front of a small group rather than a large one. I encourage my students to practice talking in class by talking within their groups. I have found this eases the sense of isolation common to shy, anxious students; when we turn later to class-wide discussion of the film, I'm often pleased to see new hands raised.

This is a simple example of how CL experiences help transfer power from the teacher, as authority figure, to the students, serving to raise self-esteem and bolster confidence.

When we ask our urban community college students to find answers on their own and share them, non-competitively, with their classmates, we empower them in a way that wasn't even necessary for my generation of college students. When our students work with their peers on research projects—even very modest ones that take no more than 10 minutes of class time—we are literally inviting them to participate in the system. For many, this is the first time the system has welcomed them at the table.

Cooperative Learning Structures to Foster Student Involvement

Elaine M. Aschettino

Some of the good things about Cooperative Learning (CL) are that it works effectively for a variety of disciplines and there are many techniques that can be used in a CL classroom. I would like to share some of my successes with CL summarizers in my Print Journalism course. These examples can easily be replicated and adapted for many other courses.

Summarizers are exercises for "getting students cognitively active in summarizing for themselves what was important, what they have learned, how it is important, and/or how it fits with what they already know." I also took summarizers a step further and used them to help students think critically.

Print Journalism requires a study and understanding of libel—damage to a person's reputation caused by words, pictures or cartoons. Students need to know and understand the definition of libel as well as defenses against libel and the issue of fair comment and criticism. How could I get my students actively involved in understanding the complexities of these issues? I decided to use an exercise called "The Envelope Please." I used it as a summarizing format designed to help students understand and retain information about libel and a critical thinking exercise designed to help students sort out issues involved in libel suits.

At the beginning of the class, BEFORE I started lecturing, I gave each student a sealed envelope with a number on it. Envelopes were numbered one through six. The students were instructed NOT to open the envelopes until later in the class when I would give a signal. I told the students the envelopes contained questions related to the day's lecture which they would discuss during the CL part of our class, AFTER the lecture.

For homework, the students had to read about libel in their texts. During class, I gave a 25 minute presentation about media laws with an emphasis on libel. This included about five minutes of student generated questions and discussion. Then, I asked the students to look at the numbers on their envelopes and pair up by matching numbers. This meant that although most students were in pair, there were a few three-person teams.

I then told the students they could open their envelopes. The envelopes contained information about actual libel cases. Each team had a different case, but each team member had the same case. Altogether, six cases were being examined by student teams.

The students were instructed to read the short case studies and then as a team answer questions: Who sued for libel? Who got sued? What do you think was the outcome of this case? As the students discussed the cases, I circulated among the groups observing, answering questions the students asked me or asking students questions that would help them think through their reasoning or re-direct them if they seemed to be off course.

The students were given five minutes to work together as a team. Then, each team had to make a brief presentation to the class, which included an explanation of the libel case and their thoughts about who sued, who got sued and the outcome. Each team had to defend its answers based on its knowledge of libel. After each presentation, other students in the class were allowed to make comments about the case. We had some very lively discussions as students argued their points. Finally, I told the students the outcome of each case.

The students' favorite case involved a libel suit filed against a local newspaper by a well-known New England ski resort. The resort was investigating the idea of treating human sewage and converting it to snow which the resort would use on its ski slopes. There was a great deal of local controversy about this plan because it would require a change in town environmental regulations.

The local newspaper ran an editorial cartoon that showed two skiers in a chair lift wearing snow shoes on their feet and carrying toilet plungers in their hands. The caption read: "Uh-oh, looks like the snow machines are clogged again."

The ski resort filed a libel suit, saying the cartoon was totally false. However, the suit was thrown out of court because the judge ruled the cartoon was a recognizable joke and appeared on a clearly marked editorial page. The judge also criticized the ski resort for filing a "nuisance suit" and fined the resort for trying to stifle public opinion.

The students had a great time battling the issues involved in this and the other cases. In sorting out the questions of who sued, who got sued and what happened, the students were able to use their knowledge of libel and to apply that knowledge to understanding how libel laws are used and interpreted.

Since the students did not know the outcome of the cases until the end of class, this exercise gave them an opportunity to think critically about the parties involved in libel suits and how the courts handle libel cases—important issues for any journalist.

Another successful CL technique I used in my Print Journalism class was Carousel Brainstorming for getting students to summarize, retain and think critically about what they had been taught. One of the students' favorite Carousel Brainstorming exercises involved what they would do if they had to cover a disaster, accident or fire.

The students were assigned a chapter to read about these topics in their texts. The next day in class, I had a 20 minute lecture and discussion with the students about how reporters cover these situations. We went into the practicalities of getting to disasters, accidents and fires and writing the stories; the ethics of interviewing people who had suffered loss of family, friends or property and issues of personal safety for reporters covering these stories.

With about 30 minutes left, I divided the students into five news teams of three or four students. Each team represented a major newspaper whose reporters were assigned to cover a disaster, accident or fire. I had put up five poster boards throughout the room. Each poster contained information about an accident, fire or disaster.

I assigned each group a poster and told the students they would have four minutes to read about the accident, fire or disaster and to brainstorm a plan about how they would cover the story. Each group was given a different colored magic marker and had to write down its ideas on its poster.

Each reporter had to come up with at least one different idea and write it on the poster. Every four minutes, I rotated the groups clockwise, from one poster to the next. Each news team had to come up with different ideas; it could not duplicate what another team had already written.

There were all kinds of situations the students were forced to think about. For example, one poster described this scenario: "There has been an earthquake in San Diego that measured 8.5 on the Richter scale. You are a team of reporters from the Los Angeles Times that has been assigned to cover the disaster. Outline your group's plans for covering the earthquake. Include information about what sources you will contact, how you plan to get to San Diego quickly since the airport has been closed and it's a two-hour drive, who you will interview, what questions you will ask and any other information you can think of about the best way to cover this story."

After 20 minutes, we stopped and each group had to go back to its original poster. The team then selected one member to address the class and summarize the ideas that were on the poster. We did this for the last 10 minutes of class.

This brainstorming summarizer gave students the opportunity to practice using the information they had learned from the assigned reading, the lecture and discussion and to apply it to hypothetical, but realistic, situations. To do this, they had to recall what they learned and they had to think critically about how to apply their knowledge.

What I liked about these CL summarizers is that they actively engaged the students in the course content and helped them understand, retain and think about what they learned.

How Chemistry ConcepTests Are Used

Jim Cooper

The term ConcepTests is associated with the work of Harvard physicist Eric Mazur. In his book, *Peer Instruction* (1997), Mazur describes his dissatisfaction in the 1980s with traditional methods of teaching science and describes his movement toward a form of small-group instruction, which he terms Peer Instruction. Mazur reports beginning Peer Instruction in 1991. One assessment procedure identified with Peer Instruction in the large classes that Mazur taught was the use of ConcepTests throughout his class meetings. Mazur says that ConcepTests should: 1) focus on a single concept, 2) not be solvable by relying on equations, 3) be unambiguously worded, 4) have adequate multiple-choice answers, and 5) be neither too easy nor too difficult. Since Mazur's work in physics at Harvard, a number of teachers in science and mathematics have adapted his ConcepTest assessment procedures. The following applications of ConcepTests used in college chemistry classes were taken from the chemistry web site at the University of Wisconsin [www.chem.wisc.edu/concept/CTinfo.html].

Informal Groups in Large Lecture. (Art Ellis, ellis@chem.wisc.edu) There can be particular concern with the initial use of ConcepTests if it is the first time "the class is turned over to the class." Many of the ConcepTests on this web site have been used in large-lecture introductory general chemistry classes, of both majors and nonmajors, with typically 200 to 350 students, and in recitation sections of about two dozen. Introducing ConcepTests on the first day of class works well, although there is no reason why the introduction of the method could not occur at any time during the course. A typical introduction has been to pick an engaging topic, pose a question, and provide two to four choices to stimulate discussion. Of course, it is important to ensure beforehand that students are seated near enough to one another to be able to converse.

As an example, an equation is written on the board and the instructor asks, "Is this equation balanced?" After giving the class a few moments for reflection, a show of hands is requested: "How many of you think the equation is balanced? How many of you think it is not?" Usually some hands are observed for each answer. There are also students who don't commit to either answer. At this point the lecturer can say: "I'd like you to turn to your neighbor, introduce yourself, and then convince him or her that your answer is correct. There may be a moment of stunned silence, as though the class is thinking, "You mean, we can talk in class?" Then, typically, loud discussion ensues.

The intensity level of class discussion that follows often determines how much time to allot for each question. After a suitable period of time has passed, typically marked by a lull in the discussion level, the instructor interrupts and asks for another vote. If by show of hands most students have converged on the correct answer, the instructor can briefly affirm why it is correct and move on. If the class has converged on the wrong answer or not many hands are raised, this is a signal that the class is not following, and the teacher has some choices. One choice is to provide an additional clue, if the question lends itself to that, and repeat the process, with or without a discussion period; or, the instructor can try to explain why another answer is more appropriate. The value of the ConcepTest, as noted above, is that the pace of the course is adjusted as class mastery is assessed in real time.

Formal Groups in Large Lecture. (Grant Krow, krow@chem.wisc.edu) (Grantkrow@aol.com) At the beginning of the term, a short examination based upon general chemistry knowledge is given to each student. The results are used to assign students to permanent groups whose members are heterogeneous to some extent by ability, gender and race. A formal group size of five students has been found to be advantageous in dealing with the organizational component of ConcepTests and other group problem-solving techniques. In organic chemistry classes of 100-200 persons in large lecture halls, we have found that five-person groups of two students in one row and three in the neighboring row can conveniently interact. The formal group structure allows students to know immediately where to look for support and interaction when problems are posed for the class. Discussion of ConcepTests is facilitated as students become relaxed with their peer groups. Because students report out for their groups rather than as individuals, pressure created by the desire to avoid "wrong" answers is alleviated. We have found enthusiastic participation even when we ask for students' answers prior to giving a "desired" answer; students understand that ConcepTests can be a time to problem solve. For example, major concepts in a chapter on alkynes include the acidity of alkyne hydrogens, conversion of terminal alkynes to ketones, and keto-enol equilibria. A more advanced ConcepTest question, which required students to utilize all three concepts, asked whether 1-propyne could be converted to 1-D-acetone. Following group discussion, the groups who believed they could do the synthesis reported their method (deuterium exchange followed by mercury-catalyzed hydration of the alkyne) to the class on the board. This was followed by voting. "Will this work? Should we review the mechanism?" Further discussion of the mechanism by the students led to the insight that the keto-enol equilibrium during the hydration step would wash the deuterium out of the molecule so that the method would fail. Groups who had suggested the initial synthesis were able to easily change their answers as they integrated their knowledge of the keto-enol concept with their prior understanding of reagents and pathways for alkyne reactions.

Report Out. (Clark Landis, landis@chem.wisc.edu) Even in large lecture sections, ConcepTests provide a mechanism for easing students into interaction with the class at large. By extending the vote/discuss/vote sequence to vote/discuss/vote/report, students gain the opportunity to hear the reasoning of other students expressed in their own terms.

Imagine that a ConcepTest is tried which results in an initial vote split among two or more answers. After discussion with their neighbors, a second vote leads again to a mixed vote. At this point the instructor asks for quick reports of student reasoning for the correct answer only ("The correct answer is A, would someone who chose this response explain why?") or may ask for reports from two groups ("Both answers A and B received significant votes, would someone who chose A please explain why? Now someone who chose B?"). In practice it is paramount that the classroom supports students' reports in subtle ways. Students are far more likely to report out if they have discussed their answers with a group first; reporting out requires that the instructor support group discussion in lecture (and live with the cacophony and apparent loss of control). If the instructor chooses to have reports only on the correct answer, the class should be told what it is before the report out. Given the security of knowing that they are right, more students will volunteer to report. At the conclusion of the report the instructor should paraphrase the students' responses with an emphasis on the critical elements of their reasoning. Reporting of the reasoning behind both correct and incorrect choices is riskier: students who explain incorrect answers risk feeling publicly humiliated. DO NOT tell the students the answer before asking for reports: Who wants to explain publicly why they were wrong? Again paraphrase the reasoning by both groups, emphasizing the common elements of the two responses. Then reveal the correct answer and the reasoning. In some instances, the wrong choice will reflect an incorrect assumption, not poor logic. Praise the correct use of reasoning and point out the importance of checking assumptions. BE SUPPORTIVE IN ALL THAT YOU DO. LEARNING IS A JOURNEY IN WHIICH WRONG TURNS ARE INEVITABLE. Extending ConcepTests to public reports of reasoning can lead the entire class to deeper understanding of the thought processes that lead to correct answers and those based on common misconceptions. Use this method wisely; important and difficult concepts benefit most from this longer and more public application of ConcepTests.

Correct Answers to ConcepTests Are Rewarded with Bonus Points. (Michal Moeller, mmoeller@unanov.una.edu) Bonus points are given to all students if the class converges on the correct answer to a Chemistry ConcepTest question. If the class splits evenly on the answer then the entire class gets half of the original number of bonus points.

Give Student Groups Transparencies to Project Their Answers. (Art Ellis, ellis@chem.wisc.edu) A small group of students is given a transparency on which they write their answer to a ConcepTest question. For example, while the lecturer is demonstrating a set of precipitation reactions at the front of the lecture hall, several student groups are each assigned one of the reactions and are asked to write its net ionic equation on the transparency. The transparencies are then collected and the class votes on whether each equation is correct or not. In this method, the students providing the answers can remain relatively anonymous minimizing embarrassment if the group gives an incorrect answer.

Intensive Use in General Chemistry. (Judith Herzfeld, herzfeld@binah.cc.brandeis.edu) Concep Tests were designed to step sequentially through the material without any traditional lecturing. Students were expected to read an assigned part of the textbook before each class and follow up with traditional assigned problems from the textbook after each class. (The latter were discussed during recitations, not during "lecture" hours.) During the class, explanations were given only in the context of a specific ConcepTest, as the instructor's side of a dialog, first introducing a question and later summarizing the point. Students responded by using lettered and colored signs (the colors serving to aid long distance recognition), rather than a show of hands. The signs allowed a quicker pace, since all students could respond at once. The signs also minimized self-consciousness about wrong answers and allowed the instructor to coax those who hesitated to participate. The hour typically started with easy questions, to establish basics from the reading. Subsequent, more difficult questions then provided opportunities for "peer instruction" (or, if necessary, instructor's leading suggestions) for rethinking the problem. After the first thirteen hours in this format, students' opinions were surveyed. Out of a total enrollment of 200, there were 160 respondents. The students agreed that ConcepTests helped to keep them awake (83%), were an extra incentive to come to class (70%), helped them to understand how to work with the material (81%), clarified concepts (76%), were confidence building (62%), helped them to calibrate their understanding against the expectations of the professor (83%), and helped the professor to judge which concepts needed more explanation and which less explanation (85%). Students were ambivalent about whether the ConcepTests were "fun" and whether the teaching approach put too much reliance on the reading. From the instructor's point of view, the frequent feedback is extremely useful. Indeed, it is quite a revelation to realize how blindly we fly when we lecture. It is also personally satisfying to offer the students an experience that is less redundant with the textbook.

ConcepTests Used in Addition to Other Cooperative Learning Techniques. (Jeffrey Kovac, kovac@novell.chem.utk.edu) Student active-learning techniques, including ConcepTests, were used in a large general chemistry course at the University of Tennessee, Knoxville, during the fall semester of 1996. The course was the second semester of a mainline general chemistry course based on the fourth edition of General Chemistry by Darrell Ebbing. An absolute grading scale was announced at the beginning of the semester. ConcepTests were used regularly during the two weekly lectures. The number of ConcepTests varied depending on the material covered, but at least one appeared almost every lecture. Sometimes, as many as four were used during a 50-minute class. Some of the ConcepTests developed for this course have been posted on the ConcepTest web site at the University of Wisconsin-Madison. Other active learning methods were used and included cooperative-learning workshops during the teaching assistant-led discussions and cooperative take-home exams.

At the end of the semester student reactions were surveyed using a five-point scale: Strongly disagree through Strongly agree. The relevant survey questions and results were:
1. Having an absolute grading scale announced at the beginning of the semester was helpful.
   Strongly agree (16.1%) Agree (38.1%) Neutral (25.4%) Disagree (15.3%) Strongly disagree (5.1%)
2. The "ConcepTests" used in the lecture helped me learn the course material.
   Strongly agree (22.9%) Agree (44.1%) Neutral (23.7%) Disagree (6.8%) Strongly disagree (2.5%)
3. The overall format of the course helped me learn chemistry.
   Strongly agree (11.9%) Agree (44.1%) Neutral (31.4%) Disagree (9.3%) Strongly disagree (3.4%)

I found that the ConcepTests created a more interactive atmosphere in the classroom. Most students responded positively, but there were a few who defiantly sat alone and refused to participate in the discussions. On the other hand, groups of students began to sit together because they found the mutual interaction beneficial. The ConcepTests certainly were useful to me in providing feedback on the crucial question: Am I being understood?

I am still getting used to the technique, making decisions about what I can leave out of the lectures that I have given for twenty years to allow time for the ConcepTests. With a fairly standard departmental syllabus there are some difficult compromises to be made. Overall, however, I have found ConcepTests to be a powerful pedagogical technique and continue to use them in my teaching.

MultiStep ConcepTests. (Chuck Casey, casey@chem.wisc.edu) In a 200-250 student organic chemistry course that consists of lecture, without discussion sections separate from the lecture, the use of a somewhat more complex problem with several steps as a ConcepTest offers students the opportunity to talk amongst themselves about not just one concept, but about several in succession, thus allowing them to put the pieces of the problem together. A synthesis question such as "Can this ketone be made selectively from an alkyne?" requires making connections between the concepts of oxidation, correct choice of starting material, and selectivity. The instructor can walk the students through the different steps of the problem by casting the problem as a series of more specific questions and soliciting discussion from the class at each point. Sometimes students offer suggestions for answers at each stage; usually the instructor offers suggestions, but not until after the students have talked amongst themselves and thought about the problem. This postponement of presenting options removes the multiple-choice feel of the question and prevents the students from discussing only the possibilities that are already presented. These ConcepTests may take 10-15 minutes of lecture time.

ESL Students and the Cooperative College Classroom

Kate Kinsella and Kathy Sherak

Classroom experience and educational research have shown that structured small-group learning can be of immense value in multicultural classrooms where some or all of the students are still in the process of learning English (e.g., Bejarano, 1987; Long & Porter, 1985; McGroarty, 1991; Pica, 1987). Second language acquisition and concept development are promoted through the students' engaged participation in collaborative tasks that require active construction and negotiation of meaning. In a student-centered interactive classroom, many ESL students enjoy their only regular safe and supportive opportunities to share ideas and information in English with individuals outside their own communities. Well designed group activities, both in and out of class, can thus provide English learners with an authentic and enabling context for the development and application of a wide range of social and communicative skills in their second language, so vital to success in U.S. higher education and an increasingly interdependent workplace. In contrast, more traditional teacher-fronted classrooms marked by linguistic heterogeneity tend to reward and encourage participation from confident and competitive native speakers or students with native-like proficiency.

Despite the potential pedagogical, social, and personal benefits to be reaped by ESL students working in heterogeneous groups in any discipline, they are often the most reticent participants. Well-intended efforts to create a more democratic learning environment may be met with considerable reluctance and disorientation by some ESL students and yield fairly disappointing outcomes. The Cooperative Learning (CL) literature heralds the multiple attributes of an interactive classroom and cites the impressive gains made by minority students in particular (e.g., Kagan, 1986; Slavin, 1983), suggesting that the competitive, individualistic orientation of traditional teacher-fronted classrooms is at odds with the values of many minority groups and that the pervasive "transmission" mode impedes development of academic proficiency and oral fluency by not allowing students to become "active generators of their own knowledge" (Cummins, 1989). However, most currently available resources and professional development on small-group learning, while providing a plethora of potentially viable structures for purposeful, task-oriented communication, have been designed with the needs of native speakers of English in mind. The methods and materials do not adequately address the needs of extremely heterogeneous adult classes—diverse in age, personality, culture, home language, English proficiency, academic achievement, prior schooling, and educational attitudes and values. Students clearly enter the contemporary multicultural college classroom with differential preparation and predispositions to operate readily, willingly, and effectively in cooperative groups.

Our experiences as ESL Program faculty and teacher educators with the linguistically and culturally diverse student body at San Francisco State University have shown us that small-group activities can be extremely stressful and alienating for non-native English speakers, more so than traditional formats, particularly outside the relatively nurturing environment of the ESL classroom. This is in part due to the fact that many enter U.S. higher education having excelled or at least survived adequately in classes where instruction was solely delivered in the "transmission" mode. They also frequently lack the linguistic and pragmatic machinery that would enable them to approach cooperative ventures with native students with more confidence and competence. Unless small-group learning is introduced with an extremely compelling rationale following a solicitation of the students' prior educational experiences and attitudes, in manageable doses, truly structured for equitable participation, and regularly assessed, the ESL team member is likely to experience no more sense of voice or empowerment than in a conventional lecture/discussion. In this article we hope to provide some reflections and practical suggestions, largely gleaned from our own classroom observations and student feedback, for facilitating more receptive and inclusive group learning in classrooms where some students are still acquiring the language of instruction.

Adolescent and adult ESL students who have completed much or all of their prior education abroad generally need to be more carefully prepared for a transition to a constructivist model of teaching and learning. Although many study regularly with peers from their own cultural backgrounds, few tend to have engaged in CL on a formal basis as part of an organized course curriculum. International and immigrant students who have been educated in a comparatively traditional, hierarchical system customarily regard a college instructor as an unquestioned authority on subject matter. They may additionally have been raised to accept anything from a professor as truth and to never seriously entertain opinions different from those of the expert. They may consequently expect considerable direction from the instructor, in a context in which they may already feel at a cultural and linguistic disadvantage, and perceive little academic value in class discussions or group activities which require classmates to share and construct knowledge.

Individualistic learning styles are not innate, but they are certainly ingrained and affirmed. When given the opportunity to specify learning preferences, an adult learner who has experienced consistent academic success within a teacher-fronted classroom is not likely to indicate groupwork. After years of sitting in formal lecture classes, we have found that it is difficult for many students to distinguish between "what helps me learn" and "what I have grown accustomed to." In fact, Reid's (1987) seminal research on the learning style preferences of foreign-born students enrolled in pre-university intensive English programs across the U.S. yielded some rather startling, but revealing, data. Virtually none of the 1,200 respondents chose group learning as a major learning preference and many indicated that group learning was actually a highly negative style!

Some would argue that creating a learner-centered classroom warrants accommodating the learning preferences of students from diverse cultural and educational backgrounds, and in a class with strikingly negative biases, such as those of Reid's respondents, that would mean reexamining curricula and teaching methods and largely excluding groupwork. We feel strongly, however, that work and learning style surveys generally do not allow students to specify the conditions under which they do or do not find groupwork a gratifying or frustrating context for learning, thereby forcing many into a fairly simplistic individualistic learner profile. Yet when given the opportunity to describe their past schooling and to elaborate upon the factors which contribute to a positive or negative groupwork experience, we have found our foreign-born students to be both appreciative and insightful, providing us with important direction for our classroom practices. Moreover, openly acknowledging our students' backgrounds and biases helps to convey a sincere effort on the part of the instructor to tailor an informed collaborative experience that will indeed support their learning and morale.

Gaining knowledge of students' prior schooling and group learning experiences is perhaps the most critical stage in initiating unprepared or reticent ESL students to groupwork. At the beginning of the term, we invite this vital feedback in a variety of ways—by means of a survey, written experiential description, and/or an activity called Give One and Get One. The Classroom Work Style Survey in Figure 1 was designed to provide teachers of heterogeneous classes an instrument for eliciting and responding to their students' varied work style preferences. In one class, for example, you may find that the majority of your students have never had a positive prior experience working with peers in class; initial activities will understandably require considerable justification, structure, modeling, facilitation, and validation of both academic and social achievement. In another class, you may discover that the students are unanimously enthusiastic about working collaboratively, but want the instructor to form the small groups and structure the activities very explicitly, rather than leave the process up to each individual team's initiative.

The most consistent and initially surprising feedback we have gleaned from distributing this survey, in numerous classes with both undergraduate and graduate bilingual students, is that the majority prefer to work primarily in culturally heterogeneous groups established by the instructor rather than with their friends. The common and understandable reasons are that they want to meet students from different backgrounds and also practice English, but don't want to run the risk of alienating their friends or being rejected by others if forced to independently seek membership on a team. The majority predictably also appreciate the opportunity to work more regularly with a partner than with a team, particularly at the beginning of the term as they acclimate to cooperative structures. To accommodate these recurring preferences, we assign students to heterogeneous base groups of four for about a month's duration, yet allow them to get together with any partner or group of classmates for relatively quick, easy, and familiar cooperative structures, the most popular among our non-native speakers being Kagan's (1989) Think-Pair-Share and Numbered Heads Together.

Another way to gain insight into the qualitative

dimensions of your students' prior experiences working with peers is to distribute a questionnaire. We have found that students were most willing to respond to the following questions:

Where did you attend high school and/or undergraduate school?
Did you participate in many classroom group activities in your former school system?
Have you participated in classroom group activities in past high school or college classes in the U.S.?
In what kind of activities have you participated in other classes?
Did you enjoy these activities?
What did you like best about group activities?
What, if anything, did you dislike about group activities?
What conditions make you feel more comfortable working in a group?
What conditions make you feel frustrated or uncomfortable working in a group?
What are some of your favorite ways to learn in class?

With both the survey and questionnaire, it is important to discuss the results with the class. One easy way is to make a transparency with the tabulated data or representative comments, and to highlight some of the more salient findings. Students are always pleasantly surprised to learn that other classmates responded similarly, and that the instructor actually intends to take the feedback into consideration when structuring the class sessions. It is also an ideal opportunity to acknowledge students' reticence to participate in groupwork based on negative prior experiences, and to assure them that you will try to create a safe and supportive context for them to experiment and become comfortable learning with and from peers.

Reading our ESL students' responses to these questions over the past years has opened our eyes to the complex reasons an adolescent or adult English learner may exhibit anxiety or resentment at the announcement of a cooperative course curriculum. Beyond the more obvious fact that a large percentage of ESL students have simply never engaged in task-based group learning within a formal educational setting, many who already have come badly bruised from unsettling experiences in previous high school and college classes. We have seen a noticeable pattern to the variables which can sabotage the potential merits of learning with and from classmates for the student who is not fully proficient in English.

A widespread concern of ESL students about participating in a heterogeneous group is being intimidated and dominated by native students. They feel anxious about collaborative tasks, justifying that native English-speaking classmates are frequently intolerant of any linguistic awkwardness, impatient with more reserved participation, and seemingly less validating of their contributions. Many mention that some majority students seem only superficially engaged when an ESL classmate offers a perspective or rarely allow them the floor to make a point. Even ESL students with exceptional oral fluency can be extremely sensitive about their pronunciation and word choice and concerned about making errors in front of fellow team members. This is not surprising, considering that many ESL students go through the better part of any given day or week with little occasion for sustained interaction in English. Therefore, the most anxiety-provoking experience imaginable, other than being required to give an oral report, is to be thrust into a group task which has not been highly structured to ensure equitable, solicited, and validated participation from each member.

Frequently ESL students will be perceived by classmates and instructors as unprepared, uncollaborative, and passive because they lack the culturally-appropriate language strategies to participate dynamically in an English-speaking group. Every aspect of the necessary cultural knowledge for participation in a class discussion or cooperative working group has a linguistic correlate. ESL students must know how and when to enter the instructional conversation and what to say to have their specific needs met. It takes considerably longer than is commonly recognized to become both socially and academically proficient in a second language. According to Cummins (1989), although a student may indeed achieve competence in basic interpersonal language within two to three years, a minimum of five years is generally required to learn the academic and more sophisticated social aspects of second language proficiency. Thus, even ESL students who have completed high school in the U.S. generally need to become familiar with a wide array of communicative language functions if they are to contribute effectively to the group process and have their participation valued. Some of the language functions more critical to CL include the following: informing, interrupting, requesting clarification, expressing agreement or disagreement, apologizing, and persuading. Since these culturally-based language functions are not systematically integrated into the secondary or college English curriculum, ESL students are largely left to their own devices to either be very astute cultural observers and active listeners within mainstream classes, or to use inappropriate language and pragmatics and suffer the consequences. Olsen (1992) has compiled a useful array of language formulas or "gambits" used in English conversation to convey specific communicative purposes. We suggest making this information available to interested students, or at least a partial list of some of the most essential linguistic machinery for successfully gaining entry into a discussion such as illustrated in Figure 2.

Another common reservation ESL students voice about classroom collaboration is that they are often asked to do too much too soon. The prospect of spending nearly an entire class session interacting with a small group of classmates early in the term is overwhelming and alienating to most. In classes with high enrollments of non-native English speakers, we recommend beginning with what they are most comfortable, namely a more traditional presentation/discussion format, then easing them into cooperative structures, initially with a single partner. Many former students have admitted actually dropping out of classes outside the ESL Program after the first day if an instructor mentioned that there would be a heavy emphasis on groupwork. Therefore, to retain and sustain diversity in our classes, we make it known from the onset that the curriculum will include a balance of learning opportunities: with a partner or small group, independently, and with the unified class. We strive to validate their past educational experiences and begin with more familiar learning formats, then gradually implement change as they build the necessary sociolinguistic skills and confidence to embrace CL as a viable process within higher education.

Give One and Get One is a particularly nonthreatening, enjoyable, and motivating initial activity for students who have had few (or unpleasant) experiences with small group learning. This structured icebreaker provides the instructor with a quick and revealing overview of a class's reasons for liking and disliking cooperative work, and at the same time allows classmates to become better acquainted through a focused and manageable initial interaction. Developed by Harvey Silver and Associates for use in management training, we have adapted this structure for use as a schema-activator at the beginning of a lesson or for a quick review of material. It is both easy to implement and process. The activity begins with some "prepared participation," a feature we find essential for less fluent or confident English users. Students are asked to make two lists on the same page and to label them "Positive Factors" and "Negative Factors." They are then encouraged to jot down at least five factors which contribute to making groupwork a positive experience and five factors which contribute to making groupwork a negative experience. It is a good idea to elicit a few examples from volunteers or even offer a few yourself for each category in order to model for students the wide range of possible answers. After about eight minutes, ask the students to get out of their seats and take the next fifteen minutes to interact with as many classmates as possible, preferably people they don't already know. The object is to introduce themselves, compare lists and accurately copy interesting items their own lists (along with the contributing students' names).

During the follow-up processing of the activity, students need to be able to accurately convey a classmate's idea and correctly pronounce his/her name. An efficient way to process the activity is to focus first on the positive factors and solicit a volunteer to share one interesting factor selected from another student's list and at the same time acknowledge the source for the rest of the class. That student then takes the floor and shares a factor gleaned from another classmate's list while introducing that contributor. As each successive student shares an idea, the instructor can write these on the board or on the overhead projector, along with the contributor's name. Everyone tends to listen attentively, partly because the subject matter is interesting, but also because no one is certain who will be called upon next by a classmate. We usually continue this processing cycle until we have about a dozen items on each list, and then allow volunteers to add any factors which they feel ought to be included. For students who have had little or no opportunity to interact meaningfully with members of another community, Give One and Get One provides a comfortable and positive initial exposure. Furthermore, like the survey and questionnaire, this structured activity gives voice to students' concerns about engaging in CL and provides a safe communicative vehicle for focused, constructive discussion of educational values and norms. Moreover, it helps to build student buy-in and motivation to enter a community of learners with very different educational histories, values, and expectations.

Krashen (1981) refers to those emotional or personality traits that can greatly obstruct language and content acquisition for second language learners as the socio-affective filter. If a student is anxious, has little motivation, and lacks self-esteem and confidence, even understandable messages will be blocked or filtered and language and concept development will not happen.

In our years of classroom and personal interaction with ESL students from diverse cultures, we have seen that no instructional practice has greater potential for raising or lowering an adult English learner's socio-affective filter than groupwork. Creating a student-centered, interactive classroom in a multicultural setting requires a careful examination of the instructors' responses to diversity. Unless our cooperative classroom endeavors are designed with comprehensive preparation and inclusion of students who come less initially motivated and equipped, we cannot say that we offer a culturally-pluralistic setting for learning. However, by validating our students' educational histories and preferences, and orchestrating groupwork in manageable, safe, and structured doses, we can help bilingual/bicultural students make their unique contributions and benefit more fully from what U.S. higher education has to offer.

Classroom Work Style Survey

Directions: This survey has been designed to help you and your teacher better understand the way you usually prefer to work on assignments in class. Please read each statement, then based on your past educational experiences, decide whether you mostly agree or disagree with each statement.

1. When I work by myself on assignments (instead of with a partner or small group), I usually do a better job.
2. When I work on assignments by myself, I often feel frustrated or bored.
3. When I work by myself on assignments, I usually concentrate better and learn more.
4. I enjoy having opportunities to share opinions and experiences, compare answers, and solve problems with classmates.
5. I prefer working on assignments in class with a single partner rather than with a group of classmates.
6. Most of the time, I prefer to work by myself in class rather than with a partner or a small group.
7. When I work with a partner or a small group in class, instead of by myself, I often feel frustrated or like I am wasting time.
8. When I work with a partner or a small group in class I usually learn more and do a better job on the assignment.
9. Most of the time, I would prefer to work in class with a single partner rather than by myself.
10. Most of the time, I would prefer to work with a group rather than with a single partner or by myself.
11. I am more comfortable working in groups when I can select the group of classmates with whom I will be working.
12. Usually, I prefer that the instructor select the group of classmates who I will be working with.
13. I prefer working in groups when there is a mixture of students from different backgrounds.
14. I prefer working in groups when the instructor assigns a specific role to each group member.
15. I prefer working in groups when the instructor lets us figure out for ourselves which group member roles and responsibilities we each want.
16. Usually, I find working in a group to be a waste of time.
17. Usually, I find working in a group to be more interesting and productive than working alone in class.
18. I hope we will not do too much group work in this class.
19. I hope we will have regular opportunities in this class to work with a partner or with a small group.
20. I mainly want my teacher to give us classroom assignments that we can work on by ourselves.

Directions: Give yourself 1 point if you AGREED with the following questionnaire items and 0 points if you DISAGREED. Next, add the points under each heading. The greatest total indicates the way you usually prefer to work in class.

INDEPENDENT WORK STYLE
1. ___
3. ___
5. ___
7. ___
16. ___
18. ___
20. ___
TOTAL _____

COLLABORATIVE WORK STYLE
2. ___
4. ___
6. ___
9. ___
10. ___
17. ___
19. ___
TOTAL _____

Figure 1. Classroom Work Style Survey

Language Formulas/Gambits to Increase Communication

EXPRESSING AN OPINION
It seems to me that...
In my experience...
In my opinion...
From what I've read/heard...

GIVING REASONS
In addition...
What's more...
That's the reason...
And besides...

ASKING FOR CLARIFICATION
Could you repeat that?
In other words, you think that...
I'm not sure I'm following you.
What was that?

CORRECTING ONESELF
What I meant was...
What I'm saying is...
Let me put it another way...
Don't misunderstand me...

INTERRUPTING
Excuse me, but...
Sorry for interrupting, but...
Can I ask a question?
I'd like to add...

DISAGREEING
Yes, but...
I can see your point, but...
I see it another way.
My idea is slightly different from yours.

Figure 2. Language Formulas/Gambits to Increase Communication

Learning Techniques and the Basic Writer

Wendy Slobodnik

Profiling the "Basic Writer"

"I can't write... In high school I didn't have one English class where I wrote an essay... I freeze when I know I have to write anything... I hate writing!" Sound familiar? Such statements usually manifest the "the basic writer," a person who has had little to no training in writing and/or whose native tongue may not be standard English.

Enabling the basic writer to perceive the creation of an essay or a report as a positive experience and an achievable goal is, admittedly, no easy task. However, the philosophy underlying cooperative learning actually encourages such a transformation. A few of the strategies that encourage the basic writer to take a more active, optimistic view of writing are as follows:
- Effective monitoring of student comprehension concerning the writing assignment,
- Peer assistance in the prewrite stages of essay development, and
- Immediate peer and instructor feedback regarding the rough-draft essay.

The person who successfully links these strategies together is the instructor, who carefully monitors pairs/group work and who sets a time limit for each activity. The following illustrates how this technique works in the prewrite and postwrite stages of writing.

Pairs-Share Brainstorming

Often, the instructor will give what s/he thinks are excellent directions concerning the writing assignment, including possible topics upon which to write. However, if the student looks straight ahead with a blank stare and a nonplussed expression, the instructor may safely assume that the writing assignment is anything but understood (or appreciated).

To avoid the above scene, begin the writing assignment by pairing students. After explaining the assignment, have the pairs brainstorm applicable topics. These topics must be narrow enough to fit within the page limits of the assignment. A person from each pair is then selected to write two narrowed topics on the board. Time allotted for this activity is usually 5-15 minutes. Each student in the class may then select a topic from the board.

After selecting a narrowed topic, the student brainstorms possible related facts/ideas, either in class or as homework. In-class brainstorming is limited to 10-15 minutes.

Collaborating on possible writing topics encourages the student to immediately take an active interest in the writing assignment. Working with a partner often helps the student overcome the "I hate writing" syndrome that immediately stymies any further participation. In addition, a board full of possible topics may offer the basic writer possibilities that s/he had not considered.

Group Brainstorming Help

The student individually brain storms and selects a topic. S/he then reconvenes with a group and shares the results of that brainstorming. After listening, each group member may suggest additional concepts, examples, definitions, or illustrations for the author to consider. This activity continues until all group members have received feedback. If a particular subject is problematic and the group cannot come up with additional information for the author, the instructor may intervene and assist. Time allotted for this activity is usually five minutes for each student within the group.

Of all the peer-assisted writing activities done, this activity is often the one most appreciated by students. Peer comments and suggestions made in this collaborative effort often influence finished documents.

The homework for Group Brain storming includes selecting an organizational framework, or prewrite structure (e.g., mind mapping or outlining) and using it in constructing the essay.

Class Critiquing of the Prewrite Structure

After finalizing the prewrite structure (outline, concept map, etc.) each student puts a hard copy of his/her prewrite on a desk. Each student then gets up, walks around the room, quickly finds a prewrite which interests him/her, sits at the desk where that structure is displayed, and writes down any suggestions for improvement on the draft. The critiquers write their names on the drafts so the authors can ask for any needed clarification. After 3-5 minutes, each student then moves on to another prewrite and goes through the same procedure previously mentioned.

During this activity, the instructor needs to make sure that each student is participating and that each prewrite has comments. To ensure that each prewrite is scrutinized, the instructor places two stickers on each paper. After a student has critiqued a prewrite, s/he may remove and turn in the stickers for points.

Students' responses to this activity have been very favorable because the writers may choose either to incorporate or to discard the suggested input of the class. In addition, beginning writers usually enjoy the variety of this exercise. The timing for this exercise varies according to class size but usually runs from 15-25 minutes.

Peer Critiquing the Rough Draft

The next step involves each student's individually creating his/her first rough draft, which begins either in class or at home. After completing the rough draft, the student gives the essay over for peer critiquing.

Admittedly, peer critiquing by amateur writers represents one of the biggest challenges for students and instructors. However, as one writing expert stated, "Everyone can peer critique, even the most inexperienced." The secret to successful peer critiquing lies in discovering in which area(s) students feel most competent.

Let's assume that the instructor has created a peer critique sheet which covers the global issues, such as accurate spelling/homonym usage, effective word choice, clear, logical organization, and sufficient details. After introducing this assessment tool to the class, the instructor writes those global areas across the board and has each student put his/her name under the area with which s/he is most familiar. After critiquing his/her own essay, the student selects others who specialize in areas where the student feels s/he needs assistance. The instructor's job is to make sure that each student acts as a peer critiquer. The writer's job is to select three classmates who specialize in different areas. The combined efforts of these critiquers result in a total peer critiquing effort that covers most global issues/problems within the paper.

Most students feel comfortable with at least one area of essay development, so this exercise encourages participation within their linguistic comfort zones. However, of all the collaborative activities mentioned, this one represents the biggest risk in terms of coordinating time and including all students. One student may be more in demand than others because of his/her expertise in spelling or word choice. In addition, students critique at varying rates, so some students may temporarily be without a paper to revise.

To ensure a smooth operation of this activity, the instructor may select two or three assistants to act as monitors and make sure that all students are actively involved in critiquing. Students who have to wait for essays to critique may be given essays from other classes to critique.

Each student essay is peer critiqued by three different classmates. The instructor becomes the final critiquer, serving as the specialist in one area which has not been approached by the other critiquers. However, rather than specifically labeling or actually revising errors, the instructor highlights problematic areas; this method compels the student to discover what is wrong with the highlighted areas and to make the necessary changes. The peer critiquers described above may assist in clarifying the highlighted areas. Time allotted for this critiquing exercise is usually 30-45 minutes, depending on class size.

After the instructor critiques, the student-writer takes the essay, makes the necessary revisions, and submits the finished product.

Initially, these techniques may not produce a perfect finished essay or report. However, if practiced consistently, this collaborative process does create a positive classroom atmosphere where the basic writer develops confidence in the writing process.

College Writing and Cooperative Learning: Implications for Writing Across the Curriculum

Joseph B. Cuseo

The Crisis in Student Writing

Amidst general concerns about declining literacy and academic preparedness of college students during the mid-1970s (Carnegie Foundation, 1976, 1984) the crisis in student writing emerged as an issue in higher education (Smit, 1991), as evidenced by the proliferation of writing proficiency testing at colleges and universities (Connolly & Vilardi, 1986). In 1981, a major research report on student writing in high school revealed that less than 3% of students' class time and homework was spent on writing anything longer than a paragraph. When students did write, it typically consisted of summaries, descriptive reports, stories, or poems; virtually no persuasive writing was done in high school (Applebee, 1981). Comprehensive nationwide testing of high school seniors' writing skills by the National Assessment of Educational Progress (NAEP) revealed declining performance on a variety of writing tasks (Applebee, et al., 1990).

Decline in the frequency and proficiency of student writing has triggered alarming concern in higher education because the quality of student writing and the quality of student thinking have long been considered to be inextricably related. The importance of writing for focusing and developing thinking has rested on the following bedrock of arguments: (a) The act of writing is characteristically slow and explicit, making the thinking process more reflective and deliberately conscious of specific details. (b) Writing is an active process requiring a high level of cognitive engagement or involvement. (c) The visibility and indelibility of the written word encourages students to step back from their thinking so they can objectively reassess, refine, or rediscover thoughts (Applebee, 1984). As poet William Stafford (1982) articulates it, "A writer is not so much someone who has something to say as he is someone who has found a process that will bring about new things he would not have thought of if he had not started to say them" (quoted in Connolly, 1989, p. 3).

When viewed from this perspective, writing is not merely a vehicle for communication but is also a process for learning. This represents a paradigm shift from the old "product-oriented" approach to writing which emphasized that writing is the product of thinking (i.e., writing comes after the formulation of clear thoughts in a think-then-write sequence). The new writing paradigm takes a "process-oriented" approach in which the writer's thinking develops during the process of writing (Ambron, 1991). The phrase "writing to learn" has been coined to capture this process, reflecting a learning process that not only takes place in lower-division composition classes, but which can occur in all academic disciplines if students engage in writing with respect to the subject matter. To promote such cross-disciplinary writing, "Writing Across the Curriculum" (WAC) programs began to emerge at colleges and universities during the mid1970s (ERIC Information Bulletin, 1991). A 1987 survey revealed that 427 postsecondary institutions had adopted some type of formal WAC program which required at least one upper-division writing course (McLeod & Shirley, 1988); and a 1988 survey of community colleges indicated that "writing to learn" or "writing and thinking" ranked first as a faculty development topic, with over 70% of the responding institutions reporting that workshops on this topic had been conducted on campus (Stout & Magnotto, 1991).

The WAC movement has been fueled by the force of the following principles: (a) English faculty alone cannot remedy the serious shortcomings in student writing; faculty in all disciplines teaching both lower- and upper-division courses must be involved if these shortcomings are to be systemically redressed. (b) Relegating writing development to a few lower-level composition courses sends students the message that writing is merely a peripheral or preparatory experience that is not central to the college curriculum can, in turn, reduce students' motivation to improve their writing. It also sends faculty the message that teaching writing is tantamount to teaching elementary mechanics and form, as reflected in the following faculty member's comment, "I think students should be shipped over to English to learn form, then shipped back to me so I can pour the content in" (quoted in Graham, 1983-84, p. 17). (c) Writing is fundamental to the thinking-learning process, not merely a product of what has already been learned; thus, writing is an integral component of learning in all disciplines, and writing to learn and learning to write are complementary goals. (d) Different academic subjects place different demands on writers, so learning to write across different disciplines may serve to promote the ability to communicate for diverse aims and audiences (Griffin, 1982; Spear, 1988; Smith, 1983-84).

Implications of Cooperative Learning Groups for Writing Across the Curriculum

The upshot of these WAC principles and their implications for Cooperative Learning have been suggested by Spear (1988), "Once we accept these principles, it follows that we expect more writing of students and demand that it be of higher quality and conceptual maturity than before. Collaborative learning and peer response groups have not been explicitly tied to writing across the curriculum. However, if sharing writing is, by definition, central to the writing process, we cannot overlook the strongly implicit connections" (p. 10).

Historical precedent for these connections has been documented by Gere (1987) who conducted an extensive review of the history and use of writing groups. She reports that writing groups date back to "literary societies" in the colonial period and, during the late 1800s, student writing groups were formed in classrooms. She also notes that the number of publications on writing groups increased markedly during the 1980s, indicating that, "A variety of disciplines are moving toward a socially defined view of knowledge, and this transition suggests a need to expand the concept of writing beyond the sole performer" (pp. 3-4).

The scholarly literature on the teaching of writing points to the conclusion that peer groups are important to the development of effective student writing. One reason that peer groups are considered to be essential is that they provide the student writer with a real, live audience and an authentic community of people who speak the same language. Kenneth Bruffee (1983) argues that writing "is not an inherently private act but is a displaced social act," so collaboration with peers "is not merely a helpful pedagogical technique incidental to writing. It becomes essential to writing" (p. 165). If writing is a displaced form of conversation as Bruffee suggests, then the peer group becomes essential to the writing process because students can write effectively only if given some opportunity to write to people with whom they usually converse—their community of peers. Attempting to write exclusively for the instructor is akin to conversing with someone from a different community, someone who may be perceived as foreign, dated, and judgmental, thus increasing the likelihood that student writing will become excessively self-conscious or strained. As John Trimbur (1985) points out, "By emphasizing the social activity of writing, collaboration can play a significant role in helping students make the transition from one community (the peer group) to another (the academic community), from one discourse to another, from one identity to another. Collaborative learning can help students generate a transitional language to bridge the cultural gap and acquire fluency in academic conversation" (p. 101).

A second reason the peer group is important for student writing is its ability to provide the writer with distinctly different feedback than that provided by the instructor. Peer-group feedback may be uniquely effective because of its following positive features.

Peer-group feedback is multiple and diverse. As Gebhardt (1980) notes in his article on teamwork and feedback for collaborative writing, "Since any group of four or five participants will probably have quite a range of knowledge, attitudes, and assumptions on a given subject, such a discussion can provide a writer with a cross-section of possible audience diversity" (p. 74). Moreover, Moffett (1968) argues that, "multiple responses to a piece of writing make feedback more impersonal and easier to heed. Group reactions establish a consensus about some objective aspects of the writing" (p. 194).

Peer-group feedback is immediate, frequent, and continuous. As Trimbur (1985), points out, "A practical advantage of peer feedback is to reduce the teacher's paper load. Teachers can assign more writing, serial drafts, and revision while at the same time making sure the writing receives immediate feedback" (p. 98). Immediate and frequent feedback is critical to the contemporary process paradigm for writing because this approach views writing as a recursive process involving multiple drafts at different stages of the writing process. This is a theoretically sound principle but its practicality remains questionable unless the instructor shares the onerous burden of providing continuous feedback with other readers, such as the writer's peers. The value of frequent peer feedback during the writing process is underscored by research indicating that instructor feedback on final paper drafts has a negligible impact on improving students' subsequent writing, and if feedback is received prior to the final draft, it is equally effective whether it comes in the form of peer critique or instructor commentary (Dudenhyer, 1976; Thompson, 1981). Hillocks (1986) also found that high levels of peer interaction during the writing process resulted in higher levels of student involvement and commitment to writing. The value of having this peer interaction take place in small groups is strongly supported by Nystrand (1986), who conducted a semester-long study of 250 students' writing in 13 different college classes. He found that students working in groups of four or five evidenced greater gains in essay-writing performance and made higher-quality revisions in their writing by the end of the semester than did students who worked alone.

Peer-group feedback is more concrete and less anxiety-provoking than instructor feedback. As Peter Elbow (1973) points out in *The Teacherless Class*, "There are two conditions that help you produce words easily. These two conditions are usually absent when you write, but the teacherless class helps to produce them. The first condition is to know how people are reacting to your words. Usually you know this when you are having a conversation with someone, and so you don't find it hard to speak meaningfully and fluently. Before you go on to the second thing you have to say, you get a feel for how your listener reacted to the first thing. You can tell not only from what he says but from how he says it—little physical movements and postures—whether he is understanding you, whether he agrees with you at all, or whether he is beginning to think you are crazy. There's another condition that makes it easy to produce language: not worrying how the audience experiences your words ... . At first the class makes you depend on all this feedback you are getting: you wonder how you wrote anything before without it. But after a while you don't care about it so much. After a while you get enough reactions from enough people that finally you begin to develop a trustworthy sense of the effect of your words" (pp. 124-125, 126). Moreover, the less anxiety-provoking feedback provided by peers may embolden student writers, enabling them to react less defensively to constructive criticism. As James Moffett (1968) suggests, a student may "write off the comments of a teacher by saying to himself, 'Adults just can't understand,' or 'English teachers are nit-pickers anyway,' but when his fellow human beings misread him, he has to accommodate the feedback" (p. 195).

Peer-group feedback can have a positive reciprocal effect on improving the reading and writing skills of the peers who provide such feedback. As Hvitfeldt (1986) notes, "Peer critique offers the students an opportunity to develop their own critical reading skills with material that is at their own language level. It also functions as the first step in learning to look at their own writing more critically at the rewriting stage" (p. 5).

The Case for Cooperative Learning in Student Writing Groups

A wealth of compelling arguments have been marshaled in favor of the process approach to writing and the value of student writing groups; however, specific empirically-grounded practices for structuring writing groups have been given relatively short shrift in the scholarly literature. The need to attend to how writing groups are structured is highlighted by an extensive study of different instructional strategies for teaching writing (Hillocks, 1986). He found that pedagogical practices which, by far, were the most effective for improving student writing were those that had greater structure and focus with respect to both the group process and the writing task. These findings are consistent with calls for greater structure by scholars in the field of English and Composition who have been longtime proponents of collaborative writing groups. For instance, Harvey Wiener, who has been a key figure in promoting the collaborative writing movement, states firmly that, "Expecting students to engage in productive conversation simply by reshuffling chairs, by telling them to work together in groups, or by requiring, without further guidance, that they read each other's papers, can easily stymie collaboration and not stimulate it" (1986, p. 61). Similarly, Anne Gere, who has authored a book on the history and use of writing groups, argues that, "Writing groups... succeed, or fail in many ways. But in the most general terms we can assert that they are more likely to succeed when groups are sufficiently prepared and committed, when appropriate tasks are clear and/or agreed upon by all participants and when debriefing or evaluation is built into the life of the group" (1987, p. 112).

Cooperative Learning in a Sequence of Engineering Courses: A Success Story

Richard M. Felder

As part of an ongoing longitudinal study of engineering education, I taught five chemical engineering courses in successive semesters to roughly the same body of students, beginning with the introductory course on chemical process principles and ending with a senior course in chemical reactor design. The basis for the instructional approach in all five courses was the Cooperative Learning (CL) model articulated by Johnson, Johnson, and Smith (1991), with most deviations from their recommendations being due to either inexperience or timidity. The narrative that follows summarizes what I did and how it worked.

CL Format and Activities

In every course in the sequence, homework assignments were done by fixed teams of three or four students that, with few exceptions, remained together for an entire semester. The homework consisted of a mixture of standard quantitative problems, problems that called for verbal explanations of physical phenomena, brainstorming exercises, and occasional problem-formulation exercises. (e.g., Make up a nontrivial problem related to the material in Chapter 6 of your text. Make up a problem that involves what we covered this week and what was covered this month in your organic chemistry class.) The homework counted for about 15% of the final course grade, the rest being determined by grades on individual tests and the final examination.

I used in-class group exercises in every class period, varying them so that the students never knew what was coming next. Sometimes I would ask the same kind of question I would normally address to the whole class during a lecture. (e.g., What procedure could I use here? Is what I just said correct?) I might pose a problem and ask the class to outline a solution strategy, estimate the solution or guess what it should look like, get started on the solution procedure and see how far they could get in three minutes, fill in a missing step, or figure out a way to check an answer. I might ask for jargon-free explanations of course concepts. (e.g., Explain, in terms a bright high school senior could understand, the concept of relative humidity. Explain, in terms of concepts you learned in this course, why you feel comfortable in 65°F air and freezing in 65°F water.)

Sometimes I asked them to generate questions about material immediately after I had covered it, and at other times I had them write and hand in one-minute papers at the end of a class. (e.g., List the major points in the material we covered today. Then list the muddiest points.)

I also varied the structure of the in-class exercises, sometimes jumping directly into groups, sometimes doing Think-Pair-Shares, and occasionally having pairs work through critical derivations or examples from their text using a TAPPS (thinking-aloud-pair-problem-solving) format. The level of active student involvement in these exercises generally varied between 90 and 100 percent, which is not bad considering that the class size ranged from a high of 125 in the first semester to a low of 90 in the last. (The previous paragraph and this one comprise my response when anyone asks me in a workshop or seminar how they can teach large classes effectively.)

I tried to do a variety of things to help the students learn to function effectively in groups. I regularly required them to summarize in writing what they were doing well as a team, what their problems were, and what, if anything, they planned to do differently in the future. I advised and periodically reminded them to set up all assigned problems individually (no detailed mathematical or numerical calculations) and then meet as a group to work out the complete solution set. I warned the students about the drawbacks of one or two of them completing all the solutions and then quickly explaining those solutions to teammates who weren't really involved in solving the problems. (This message did not get through to some students until after they flunked the first test.) I admonished students not to put nonparticipating team members' names on solution sets, especially repeating no-shows. I invited teams having serious problems to meet with me to talk things over. Finally, I announced that a team by unanimous consent could fire a chronically noncooperative member and a team member who constantly had to do most of the work could quit, both options being available only if repeated attempts to correct the problem had failed. Fired students or students who quit had to find teams of three willing to accept them, or else they would get zeros on the remaining homework assignments. (I found that teams almost invariably found ways of working things out before either of those last-resort options was exercised.)

The narrative that follows might give professors of technical subjects like engineering, science, and mathematics an idea of what to expect if they try CL on students who have not experienced it before.

Chemistry 205

First day: Setting the stage. I announced that all homework must be done in fixed groups with one solution set handed in per group. I also gave the criteria for group formation (three or four members, no more than one of whom could have received an A in identified mathematics and physics courses), and specified individual roles within groups: coordinator, recorder, and one or two checkers, with the roles rotating on each assignment.

I spent some time explaining why I was doing all this, assuring the students that it wasn't just a game I was playing with them or something I designed to make my life easier (quite the contrary). I told them that both educational research and my experience indicated that students learn better and get higher grades by teaching one another some of the time rather than listening to professors lecture all of the time. I also guaranteed them that when they went to work as engineers they would be expected to work in teams, so they might as well start learning how to do it now. During the next two days, several students expressed strong reservations about group work and requested permission to work alone. Permission was denied.

Second day: Introduction to group work. I interspersed small group problem-solving exercises throughout my lecture. The student response was variable—the level of interaction generally decreased with distance from the front of the room. At the end of the period, I asked students who had not yet affiliated with homework teams to get together after class with teams of three willing to pick up a fourth member and work things out, which they did.

First homework assignment: Resistance to group work. Assignments were turned in by most students working in groups as instructed, but also by several individuals and one "group" consisting of a student and teammates Elvis Presley and Richard M. Nixon. I applauded that student for creativity but informed all those who had not yet joined groups that the fun was over and I would accept no further assignments from individuals. By the due date of the second assignment, all students were in homework teams.

Facilitation: Effective team functioning. I periodically included group self-assessment questions on homework assignments, and sometimes in class I offered suggestions for effective homework team functioning, trying not to be too preachy about it. I occasionally got complaints about team members not pulling their weight or missing group sessions or about personal conflicts between group members, and I met with several groups in my office during the semester to help them work out solutions. (By the semester's end, only one group actually dissolved out of roughly 35 groups in the class.) Dropouts during this period brought some groups down to two members. Some pairs combined, others disbanded and individuals joined teams of three. (In subsequent courses, I allowed some pairs to remain intact if dropouts occurred late in the semester.)

First test results: Some complaints. The class average on the first test was 66, brought down by some very low grades (as low as 10). Some students complained that their performance on the test suffered because the better members of their groups had been working out most of the problem solutions prior to the team meetings to discuss homework. I announced in class that students doing all the work in their teams were hurting their classmates rather than helping them, and I repeated the message about setting up problems individually and completing them in groups. Some students who had complained subsequently reported improved interactions within their groups.

Midsemester evaluations: Positive reactions. The students were overwhelmingly positive about group work. Almost on a whim, I announced that students who wished to do so could now do homework individually. Out of roughly 115 students remaining in the course, only three elected to do so, two of whom were off-campus students who were finding it difficult to attend group work sessions. (In subsequent courses I occasionally assigned individual homework but never again let the students opt out of assigned group work.)

Last half of the semester: Growth in class cohesiveness, problem-solving skills, and self-reliance. The student lounge began to resemble an ant colony the day before an assignment was due, with small groups clustered everywhere, occasionally sending out emissaries to other groups to compare notes and exchange hints (which I permitted as long as entire solutions were not exchanged). Homework grades were almost invariably in the 90s, and many students began to do outstanding work on problems that called for creativity and higher level thinking skills. The nature of my office hours changed considerably from the start of the semester, with fewer individual students coming in to ask "How do you do Problem 3?" and more groups coming in for help in resolving debates about open-ended problems. I inferred with considerable satisfaction that the students had begun to count on one another to resolve straightforward questions instead of looking to me as the source of all wisdom.

The final grade distribution in CHE 205 was dramatically different from any I had ever seen when I taught this course before. In the previous offerings, the distribution was reasonably bell-shaped, with more students earning Cs than any other grade. When the course was taught using CL, the number of failures was comparable to the number in previous offerings but the overall distribution was markedly skewed toward higher grades: 26 As, 40 Bs, 15 Cs, 11 Ds, and 26 Fs. Many of those who failed had quit before the end of the course. The course evaluations were exceptionally high and most students made strong statements about how much the group work improved their understanding of the course material. My conclusion was that CL led to improved learning in all but the least qualified and most poorly motivated students.

Subsequent courses: Using CL. At my encouragement, new teams formed at the beginning of each semester, even when all members of a team from the previous semester remained in the sequence. I continued to ask the teams to assess their performance periodically and to meet with me if they had persistent problems. The students' level of comfort with CL continually increased, although there were always problems that needed attention. No more than two times in any semester did a team fire a member or did a team member quit.

"Can I do all this stuff and still cover the syllabus?"

When I give teaching workshops and talk about CL, an inevitable question has to do with whether doing group work cuts down on the amount of material that can be covered in a course. I have several responses, but the principal one is to describe what I did in the experimental sequence. In all courses, except the first one, I put my notes in coursepaks which the students got on Day 1. The notes had gaps to be filled in and frequent questions like "Where did this figure come from?" and "How do you get from equation 4 to equation 5?" and requests like "Verify this result." and "Convince yourself." I promised the students that some of these missing pieces would show up on the tests and I kept my promise, so that most of the students actually read the notes—especially after the first test.

As a consequence of using these handouts, I saved untold hours of class time that would have been wasted on writing detailed derivations and prose on the board and instead used those hours for active learning exercises. By their own estimation and mine, the students learned far more from the exercises than they would have from the stenography involved in note taking from lectures, and I ended up covering more material in each course than I had gotten through when all I did was lecture. As indicated above, mastery of the course content was clearly higher than when I had used more traditional teaching techniques.

Evaluation. Several times during the experimental course sequence the students were asked to rate how helpful CL was to them. Their ratings of group homework were consistently and overwhelmingly positive. At the midpoints of the introductory sophomore course, the two junior courses, and the senior course, the percentages rating CL above average in helpfulness were respectively 83%, 85%, 87%, and 86%, and the percentages rating it below average were 9%, 7%, 7%, and 7%. The ratings of in-class group exercises were also positive, but it took many of the students longer to appreciate the benefits of these exercises. Above average ratings were given by 41%, 70%, and 86% of the respondents in the two junior courses and the senior course, and below average ratings were given by 24%, 12%, and 6%, respectively.

In the semester following the experimental course sequence, the students were asked to evaluate the sequence retrospectively. Of the 67 seniors who responded, 92% rated the experimental courses more instructive than their other chemical engineering courses, 8% rated them equally instructive, and none rated them less instructive. Ninety-eight percent rated group homework helpful and 2% rated it not helpful. Seventy-eight percent rated in-class group work helpful and 22% rated it not helpful. Women generally gave CL higher ratings than men, but they were also more likely to report that their ideas were devalued or discounted within their groups. They also indicated that they took take less active roles in group discussions.

Of the students who took the introductory course

as sophomores in the fall of 1990, roughly 80% had either graduated or were still enrolled in chemical engineering after their fourth year of college, a retention rate significantly higher than normal in this major. Sixty percent of the seniors considered the experimental courses very important factors in their decision to remain in chemical engineering, 28% considered them important, and 12% rated them not very important or unimportant.

My own observations corroborated the students' opinion that CL had improved their educational experience. For one thing, they came to class regularly: attendance on any given day was normally 90% or better, which is far from what we usually see in lecture classes of the size I was teaching. Students tended to do better on tests than any other class I ever taught, even though the tests called on them to exercise a greater variety of thinking and problem-solving skills than any I had previously given. I also observed a greater sense of community in this cohort of students than I had seen in any other chemical engineering class in my 25 years in the profession. Almost from the outset of the study, they worked together, partied together, and displayed a remarkable sense of unanimity in complaining about things in the chemical engineering program that they didn't like. One student commented, "This class is different from any I've been in before. Usually you just end up knowing a couple of people—here I know everyone in the class. Working in groups does this."

One episode in particular led me to believe that group work was having the desired effect on the students' intellectual development. In the third semester of the study, the class was taking fluid dynamics and heat transfer with me and thermodynamics with a colleague. My colleague is a traditional instructor, relying entirely on lecturing to impart the course material, and he is known for his long and difficult tests, with averages typically in the 50s or less. The average on his first test that semester was 72 and on the second test it was 78. He ended by concluding that it was perhaps the strongest class he had ever taught. Meanwhile, I casually asked the students how things were going in thermo, mentioning that I heard they were doing well. Several of them independently told me that they had become so used to working in groups, meeting before my tests, speculating on what I might be likely to ask, and figuring out how they would respond, that they continued to form groups for studying in their other classes. Cooperative Learning had done its job.

Moving to CL is not an easy step for professors of technical subjects (or any other subjects, for that matter). Instructors have to deal with the fact that while they are learning to implement CL they will make mistakes and may for a time be less effective than they were using more familiar teacher-centered methods. They may also have to confront and overcome substantial student opposition and resistance, which can be a most unpleasant experience, especially for teachers who are good lecturers and may have been popular with students for many years.

The message of this report, if there is a single message, is that the benefits of CL in technical courses more than compensate for the difficulties that must be overcome to implement it. Instructors who pay attention to CL principles when designing their courses, who are prepared for initially negative student reactions, and who have the patience and the confidence to wait out these reactions, will reap their rewards in more and deeper student learning and more positive student attitudes toward their disciplines and toward themselves. It may take an effort to get there, but it is an effort well worth making.

Epilogue: What Do I Do Differently Now?

When I began the study, I was fairly low on the CL learning curve. I still use it extensively in every class I teach, but I do some things differently than I did in the longitudinal study, in part because of what the study taught me. I now form groups myself rather than letting the students self select. On the first day of class I circulate a questionnaire asking for grades in selected prerequisite courses, gender, ethnicity, interests, and times available for group work outside class, and I form groups that are heterogeneous with respect to ability (as measured by reported grades). I put students in the same groups who have common interests and report similar possible meeting times. I also try to avoid forming groups in which women are outnumbered by men and ethnic minorities are outnumbered by white students; my study data and the literature suggest this gender and ethnicity policy. I discuss the rationale for CL up front more than I used to, using a variety of sales pitches that I have found effective for engineering students. Finally, I have increased the frequency of group self-monitoring exercises, where students assess and discuss how the groups are functioning, finding that the more frequently problems are placed on the table the less likely they will be to explode into crises.

Jeopardy 305: A Cooperative Learning Method for Teaching History and Systems of Psychology

Lisa Gray-Shelberg

The scheduling of a PSY 305: History and Systems of Psychology class during a three-week, intensive (four hours a day, four days a week) summer session necessitated an approach that would motivate students to read and learn a large amount of information in a short period of time. Therefore, a Jeopardy 305 game was developed combining aspects of the television game show, Jeopardy, and Aronson's Jigsaw technique using interdependent learning groups.

Each four-hour class session had three elements: 1) lecture, 2) discussion, and 3) Jeopardy 305. Students read 1-2 chapters a day and submitted ten Jeopardy-format questions per chapter on 3 x 5 cards, rated for five levels of difficulty. Each student, in addition to being responsible for reading and writing questions for the chapter(s), was assigned to an Expert Group and to a separate Jeopardy team. Expert Group members became in-depth authorities on a particular section of the assigned readings, such as, "Edward Chace Tolman" or "the subject matter of behaviorism." Expert Groups met to discuss the content and to assure that they had sufficient expertise to teach the topic to others.

After carefully studying assigned sections of the textbook Expert Groups broke up and Jeopardy Teams met; every Jeopardy Team had one member from each of the Expert Groups. The teams met to prepare for the Jeopardy 305 game in which members were required to take predetermined turns representing the team. Because Jeopardy Teams were composed of members with separate in-depth topic expertise, students had to teach and learn from each other in order to make their teams competitive.

During the class break, the instructor selected five questions from each of the different levels of difficulty for each of the five or so major topics within a given chapter and placed them on a "game board" in the front of the class.

After the break the class played Jeopardy 305 with the instructor as M.C. and a class member as her assistant. The M.C. read the question and a designated player from the first team that signaled readiness to respond gave the answer. A preselected noisemaker was used to signal that a team was ready to respond. Correct answers were assigned points according to question difficulty level.

Individual Student Activities

1. Read and learn the assigned chapter(s) in the textbook.
2. Prepare 10 Jeopardy questions and answers on 3" x 5" index cards using the following Jeopardy format:

Side 1
Category:
Text chapter & title:
Page number:
Name of student:
Difficulty level:
Question: (e.g., This young naturalist, while staying in the East Indies, developed the outline of a theory of evolution that was similar to Darwin's.)

Side 2
Answer: (i.e. Who is Alfred Russell Wallace?)

Thus each question consisted of the information to be identified and each answer consisted of the correct identification phrased as a question: "What is?" or "Who is?"

3. Review the sections of the textbook assigned to your Expert Group and know the material particularly well.
4. Watch the game show Jeopardy to gain knowledge of how the game is played.

In-Class Work Activities

1. Students work in Expert Groups for 1/2 hour to gain sufficient expertise in the assigned material to teach it to other students.
2. Students teach other Jeopardy Team members mastered material and learn material covered by other experts.

Expert Group Activities

1. Determine what facts, concepts, theories and examples are central to an indepth understanding of the material assigned to the Expert Group.
2. Review the essential information so that each group member has a solid understanding and can teach it to others.

Jeopardy Team Activities

1. Select and obtain a team noisemaker to use in the game to signal that your team wants to answer a question.
2. Choose a team name. Some examples have been "Introspectionists," "Behaviorists," "Functionalists," "Automata," "The Ids," and the "Freudian Slips."
3. Learn, review and teach each other the assigned reading material for each game.

Instructor Activities

1. Make a JEOPARDY 305 game banner for the front of the classroom above the space that will be used for the Jeopardy 305 board. The banner stays up for the length of the class.
2. Before each Jeopardy 305 game, make a banner describing the overall subject matter (usually the title of the textbook chapter to be covered) for the upcoming game and separate signs (large enough so the students in the back of the room can read them) for each category of questions (e.g., Behaviorists). Mount the banner and signs underneath the JEOPARDY 305 banner and above the Jeopardy board.
3. Make a facsimile of a Jeopardy board for the front of the classroom. The board should have room for a matrix with at least five subject categories across and five difficultly levels (Level 1 or $100 questions, Level 2 or $200 questions, Level 3 or $300 questions, Level 4 or $400 questions, and Level 5 or $500 questions). For one class this was accomplished by employing used file folders to make 11" x 8 1/2" question holders with pockets which were taped to the chalkboard with a special 3M tape which was easily removed. One class used a metal board approximately 4' by 4' to which the selected questions were under another card (both affixed with a magnet) which displayed the difficulty level ($100, $200, etc.).
4. Assign students to Jeopardy Teams, heterogeneous with regard to gender, race, class test performance and prior performance (using GPA or prior grades in particular classes). (Group assignments may need to be modified if one team proves to be much better than the others.)
5. Make and distribute Expert Group reading assignments, taking care that assignments are of similar length and that their position in the chapter is rotated by group.
6. Generate rules for Jeopardy 305 with the class and then prepare and distribute them, or prepare and distribute the rules yourself and entertain suggested modifications.
7. Make a timetable for class activities and distribute it to the class. A sample breakdown is:
   9:00-10:00 am Lecture/discussion
   10:00-10:30 am Expert Groups meet
   10:30-10:45 am Break
   10:45-11:15 am Jeopardy Teams meet
   11:15-11:30 am Jeopardy setup
   11:30 am-12:30 pm Play Jeopardy (once students get the hang of it, the game takes less time; the difficulty and complexity of the material also affects game length)
   12:30-12:50 pm Review, preview of the next day, and wrap-up
8. During the class break and/or while students are meeting in groups, prepare the Jeopardy 305 game by selecting five questions of different levels of difficulty for each of the major topics in a given chapter (sometimes overriding the difficulty ratings assigned by the question writer and editing poorly-worded questions).
9. Obtain class volunteers to serve as the game assistant and scorekeeper for the day (this can be done ahead of time as well). If you are lucky, a class member will volunteer to serve as a permanent scorekeeper and to tally the number of cards submitted by each class member.

Playing the Game

The class played Jeopardy 305 with the instructor as M.C. and a class member as assistant; we called the assistant "Vanna," (or "Danna"). The M.C. read the question and the designated player from the first team that sounded its noisemaker gave the answer. Correct answers were assigned points based on question difficulty level. The noise maker was held by the first member of each team who then passed it on to the next team member after each question round. This method gave each team member the opportunity to respond to questions and thwarted the teams that may have relied on their best players.

The instructor randomly chose the team that started the game. The member who held the noise maker on that team chose the category and the difficulty level for that first question.

The instructor read the question. The player holding the noisemaker in each team competed to answer the question. If none of the designated players could answer the question (which must be prefaced by "What is?" or "Who is?") the question was open to the floor (i.e., any player on any team could give the correct response). A correct response earned a score of one point (or $100) to five points (or $500). Points and monetary totals depended on how the class decided to score the game. "Vanna" distributed point/money cards to the team who correctly answered a given question. A previously determined scorekeeper collected and recorded the points for each team. The game continued in this manner until all questions in all categories had been asked. In terms of resolving disputes, "Vanna" ruled!

Course Grades

Students earned credit toward their course grade in four ways. Except for Participation all grades were based on individual performance rather than undifferentiated group grading. The final course grade was based on the following percentages:
Quality and quantity of Jeopardy questions 25%
Scores on the three class examinations 55%
Attendance 10%
Participation 10%

Evaluation of Jeopardy 305

On an informal level both groups of students spontaneously communicated to the instructor, the Psychology Department Chair and to other students positive reactions to the class. Positive comments were made about both learning the subject matter and class atmosphere.

The students in the first class were so eager to share their experience that they produced a video containing excerpts from two Jeopardy 305 games and interviews with class participants. Two of the students and the instructor made Jeopardy 305 presentations at meetings of the Western Psychological Association and the American Psychological Association.

Ten of the 15 members of one class completed an anonymous evaluation questionnaire. All respondents agreed that participation in Jeopardy 305 "increased my motivation to learn the assigned material;" "provided an effective framework for studying;" "compared with more traditionally taught lecture classes, the Jeopardy format required active involvement in higher than knowledge level thinking processes;" and that "teaching others increased my own learning."

Nine of the ten respondents indicated that because of Jeopardy 305 they "became better able to learn new concepts by expressing them in my own words," and "learned to handle questions requiring critical evaluation." Eight out of ten answered "true" to the statement that, as one effect of Jeopardy 305, "I was more apt than in the past to try to understand hard-to-learn material rather than just memorize it," and 3 out of 10 became "better able to summarize reading material in my own words," and thought that "my ability to see the difference between apparently similar ideas increased." Only 50% thought that "In trying to understand new ideas, I am not more likely to try to relate them to real life situations to which they might apply." This finding probably has less to do with the efficacy of Jeopardy 305 than it does to the fact that most people would find it inherently difficult to relate the history and systems of psychology to their everyday world.

My subjective evaluation is that the students were highly involved in all aspects of Jeopardy 305 and very motivated to master course content both in order to compete well in the game and to perform well on the class examinations (and on the GRE for the graduate school bound). Students entered eagerly into the game and showed neither embarrassment nor shyness. The public nature of the exercise did not appear to negatively affect either performance motivation or motivation to learn. The students were given three examinations very similar in content to those used in more traditionally-taught courses and they performed very well on them.

Integrating Jeopardy 305 into a traditional course takes a considerable amount of instructor organization. The preparation of a game board, daily signs and banners, question selection, and the like are fairly time consuming. However, the almost unanimous positive response from the students and the evidence of their learning made the extra time I spent worthwhile.

Classroom-Tested Collaborative Learning Tasks

Edwina Stoll, Barbara Illowsky, Jim Luotto, John Swensson, and Sally Wood

Instructors at De Anza Community College, Cupertino, California formed a Collaborative Learning Project group which has been instrumental in encouraging interested instructors to experiment with collaborative methodologies in their classrooms. Some instructors adopt Collaborative Learning (CBL) as the major teaching method which they use almost exclusively, while others use collaborative tasks to augment other teaching methods. Additional CBL structures at our college include instructors combining two classes which they team teach using CBL methods and instructors planning a progressive set of classes so that students can enroll in a series of CBL classes over several quarters.

In all cases, instructors have the option of having their classes listed in the college schedule as courses in which collaborative methods will be used. The listing in the catalog reads "Collaborative Learning Class. Open to all students." Also included in the schedule is an explanation of the Collaborative Learning Project which encourages students to enroll and gives specific descriptions of some of the Collaborative Learning Project classes. For example, "A Successful Combination of Reading and Writing" is a description of a combination of two developmental courses being team taught using CBL methods. The description lists the course numbers, times and instructors along with three advantages to enrolling in the combination course.

In this article we would like to share five CBL tasks that have been classroom tested at De Anza. We invite you to adapt our tasks to your content and classes and to call us with questions and feedback about the tasks.

Collaborating to Study Controversial Issues (Sally Wood)

CLASS: Developmental Reading and Writing (Pre-collegiate level)

This project requires students in collaborative groups of three-five to study a current controversial issue in depth. Since the goals of this project focus on strategies the students have been learning and practicing for several weeks, the assignment is given near the end of the term. The project involves reading, writing, and group collaboration skills and includes the following activities:

- research, read and thoroughly analyze three long articles on specified issues;
- collaborate with assigned classmates in planning and delivering an oral presentation that covers both the pro and con arguments of a common issue, and
- write an individual essay that not only explains both the pro and con arguments of an issue but also supports one side.

Procedure for Implementing the Project

The first stage of the project takes approximately two weeks. During this period, my colleague Jean Miller and I require that students find and read news articles on current controversial issues. Students typically find material on topics such as euthanasia, legalizing drugs, abortion, and gays in the military. At the end of this reading period, students participate in a brainstorming activity during which they state issues they would like to study further. I write the suggested issues on the chalkboard, and the class discusses each, considering whether there are definite pro and con arguments involved and if reading materials would be readily available to give enough information on the issue. Next, by a show of hands, students indicate which issues they like best, and the most popular are selected.

We do not allow students to self-select into groups. We collect notes on which students prioritize the three issues that most interest them, and then we form groups of three to five students based primarily on their choices but also on ability level, gender, ethnicity and age.

The second stage of the project is for students to find information on their assigned issues. We make arrangements with the library staff to give an orientation and to assist the groups in finding articles of appropriate difficulty and length. Though individuals are encouraged to find articles on their own, they are also allowed to share one or two with group members. Students are told that the group needs to find readings that cover both the pro and con arguments on the issue.

Next, individuals write an analysis of each of three substantial articles. Analyses are submitted to Jean and me. Each includes identifying the author's thesis, tone, purpose, approach (subjective or objective), and use of denotative and/or connotative language. In the final section of each analysis, students must write two to four paragraphs in which they state and explain why they are for or against the issue.

During the third stage of the project, groups meet both in- and out-of class to plan their fifteen- to twenty-minute oral presentations. Groups are encouraged to try to develop creative presentations which will interest their audience. Some popular presentation formats are listed in Figure 1. Ideas for Group Presentations.

Students are asked to present both the pro and the con arguments concerning the group's issue and to be sure all group members participate in some way. When groups have finished planning their presentation, they complete and submit a Group-Presentation Worksheet (see Figure 2).

After each group gives its presentation, the audience fills out an Evaluation Form based on explicit criteria (see Figure 3). For the final stage of the project, groups are given a week to draft, discuss, edit, and then write essays about their issues. In their essays they are required to explain both the pro and con arguments of their issues and state which side they favor. They must support their opinions with clear, concrete examples from their research or from personal experiences.

This project allows students to demonstrate and reinforce many reading, critical thinking, and writing strategies they have been working on for the term. Students enjoy the presentations and often become quite involved in asking questions and arguing their own views.

Though the project, in the above form, takes two to three weeks, it can be streamlined in the following ways:
- Instead of conducting an orientation and finding materials in the library, the instructor can assign articles from the anthology being used for the course or from news publications; and
- Requiring students to write an essay could be eliminated if the project is being used in a class that does not demand such writing.

COMMENTS: If this project is used as a whole, it is important to give students very specific instructions. We usually first present an overview of the assignment and explain the objectives, and then we provide individuals with specific directions for each stage of the project. It is especially helpful to explain the type and length of articles they should find, or they often will use short articles which lack substantial pro and/or con arguments.

Creature Volume (Barbara Ilowsky)

CLASS: Math 1B 2nd quarter of first year (theoretical) calculus

GOALS: To reinforce finding volume by revolving a curve around its axis or revolution. To practice curve-fitting techniques and determine equations of curves. To demonstrate that several extremely different types of equations and techniques may yield very similar solutions and that, even in math, there is not always "one right answer." To be able to recognize whether an answer is feasible or ludicrous.

MATERIALS NEEDED: Party decoration (the type that has crepe paper and unfolds to make a 3-D object such as a wedding bell, pumpkin or creature).

CLASS TIME: One full in-class period. Plus, students must meet outside of class. Also, approximately 20 minutes a few days later for each group to make a two-four minute presentation.

STEPS:

1. Divide the class into groups of three or four members.
2. Give each group a different creature. One person is in charge of the creature.
3. One person in each group sketches the shape onto graph paper.
4. The equation(s) of curve is/are decided by each group.
5. Each group determines integration techniques.
6. The group decides whether its answer is feasible or not.
7. Each group completes a worksheet to hand in to instructor (Figure 4).

HINTS: Assign and do the in-class part a couple of days before the presentations. Allow students to keep the creature until their presentations. Suggest to students that they set up their coordinate axes before trying to determine the curve. Also, remind them that the metric system is easier to work with.

COMMENTS: The instructor does not have the correct answer. Students have had minimal or no prior experience in curve fitting; this activity is often their first experience with curves that are not contrived for homework. The curve-fitting part takes time. Many curves have similarly-shaped graphs at first glance. It is important to stress fitting several points. Scaling is important. Often, what appears to be a reasonable curve could yield an absurd result.

Multiculturalism Using Both Homogeneous and Heterogenous Groups (John Swensson)

CLASS: Freshman English Composition

GOALS: To maximize students' experiencing other cultures in the classroom, increase communication skills and risk-taking and to increase cohesion between members of small groups and within the whole class.

STEPS FOR ACHIEVING THE GOALS:

1. The first day of class students play the Name Game which allows every student (and even the teacher) to learn the names of all the class members. Homework Assignment: Students list background information and if possible talk to family members about their family origins to add to that list.
2. The second day students are seated in a circle to share information about their family and ancestors. The goals of this exercise are to: a) extend the sharing, risk-taking and use of communication skills; and b) enable students to learn some background information about their peers.
3. The third day students form culturally homogeneous groups. A culture does not have to be determined by ethnic or national boundaries. For example, in past classes students have formed sports, music or single-parent cultures. Note: As the teacher, I exit the classroom so as not to insert myself into this process, except that I do warn students that I might make some changes in their groups. The students are told, "You are the teachers. You should decide what you wish to teach the class about your group. What defines your culture? What characterizes your society? Is your group one of country? Geography? Religions? Languages? Costumes? Foods? Traits? Are there stereotypes (generalizations) associated with your group that are correct? Incorrect? We would like to hear from each member of your group; each presenter will be graded separately, although a strong team effort will undoubtedly help everyone. Please coordinate all handouts, videos, and other audiovisual requirements in advance. Thank you."
4. After about two weeks the homogeneous group presentations are delivered to the class.
5. Now that the students have become well acquainted as a class, the instructor assigns them to heterogeneous Base Groups for the rest of the quarter. The following criteria are used: course skill level, culture or ethnicity, gender, and age. To help students build a community with their new teammates, Base Groups may be asked to select group names or participate in activities, such as free-throw shooting contests between groups or a scavenger hunt in the library for research material.

COMMENTS: The class time required for this activity is from three to nine hours depending on the amount of time the instructor allows at each step. These homogeneous group presentations are absolutely wonderful because students are more willing to take risks, share, and work hard to establish the standards for their groups' cultural presentations. The audience can see pride associated with sharing a culture whether it is based on ethnic or national boundaries or on sports, music or other common experiences.

The students use excellent teaching aids, such as short videos, costumes or ethnic foods. Another benefit of this activity is that third- and fourth-generation immigrants get exposure to those who have just arrived and subsequently learn much more about their former cultures than they previously knew. Students in groups based on regional cultures (Mediterranean, Asian, Middle Eastern) will discover, among other things, similarities in their national cultures.

Teaching Satire Using John Dryden's Mac Flecknoe (Jim Luotto)

CLASS: British Literature

GOAL: To better understand satire techniques by making a close analysis of a classic model.

MATERIALS NEEDED: Satire handout (see Figure 5) and a copy of John Dryden's Mac Flecknoe.

IMPLEMENTATION: Each group's task is to first paraphrase the assigned lines from Mac Flecknoe and then decide where it would place these lines on a continuum from invective to farce (see Figure 5). The intent of this procedure is to assess if groups understand Dryden's purpose for this passage. A recorder in each group writes the group's judgment(s), as well as the lines they would cite in support of their conclusion(s). After ten minutes, each group has about three or four minutes to report to the rest of the class. Groups are told to determine who will give the group's findings and who will read the significant lines in support of those findings. The readers are asked to read the lines quietly within their groups, so they can give the emphasis and intonation which they feel Dryden would have intended.

STEPS FOR ASSIGNING THE TASK:

1. Divide the class into groups and ask each group to appoint a recorder.
2. Assign each group a portion of the lines in the poem.

HINTS:

1. This activity takes about fifty minutes.
2. Encourage the students to make precise references to both the Satire handout and to Mac Flecknoe. Students' opinions need to be substantiated succinctly but concretely.
3. Make students aware that their passage may very well include different kinds of examples from the continuum shown in the handout.

Public Speaking Support Groups (Edwina Stoll)

CLASS: Any class where students deliver individual speeches to the whole class.

GOALS: To reduce student anxiety about speaking in front of a class. To receive and provide feedback at several stages of the development of a speech. To practice delivering a speech with a small group of classmates. To listen critically to speeches delivered by others. Support groups are formed at the same time an assignment is given and remain together through the presentation of the speeches. For example, in a public speaking class support groups are formed at the same time instruction is given about the specific type of speech (i.e., demonstration, persuasion) to be presented in the next round of speeches. Support groups meet during class several times throughout the various stages of the speech development in order to give and receive feedback. Some of the stages include: topic selection, potential sources of information, research ideas, construction of thesis and main points, support material for each main point, ideas for visual aids, writing the introduction and conclusion, and practicing the delivery of the speech.

STEPS: Each time the support groups are scheduled to meet, these steps are followed:

1. Each student comes to the group meeting prepared with the appropriate stage of the speech in written form.
2. A Timer is appointed within the group so that each group member receives the same amount of assistance from the group.
3. Group members take turns sharing their assignment preparations for the day.
4. All other group members listen carefully and provide feedback which may be in the form of questions, praise, critique, suggestions, etc.
5. A Recorder for each group hands a written report of its progress to the instructor (usually a sentence or two about each group member's progress).

HINTS:

1. Time management is critical so that each member receives feedback.
2. Insure accountability by awarding points or giving quizzes so that each student must come to class prepared to participate in the group activity.
3. Encourage groups to meet outside of class. This is especially helpful as the due date for speeches draws near.
4. Form groups heterogeneously using skill level, ethnicity, age, gender, and topic area if the topics are known in advance.

COMMENTS: This activity not only works well in speech classes, but also in any course where students are required to give a presentation to the full class as part of an assignment. Students report that working in the support group format reduces anxiety in two basic ways. First, since they are forced to prepare the speech well in advance because of the due dates, they feel secure with the content and organization. Second, practicing in front of group members builds confidence for the speaker and gives an opportunity to make changes if needed.

Your group may use one of the following formats or create one of its own.

Remember that having your audience participate makes the presentation more interesting to them and easier for you. You may want to use video or audio equipment, illustrations, handouts, or costumes. Also, consider allowing time after your presentation for the audience to ask questions and engage in some discussion.

1. Compare and/or contrast two people who have been involved in an incident concerning the issue.
2. Broadcast a radio or TV editorial and a response stating both sides of the issue (use sound effects or background music if you wish).
3. Debate both sides of the issue.
4. Dramatize an incident concerning the issue.
5. Hold a mock trial with defendant, plaintiff, and/or witnesses presenting various arguments on the issue.
6. Conduct an opinion poll of the class members and/or people outside of class and then relate their responses to arguments for both sides of the issue.
7. Make and explain an illustration about the issue.
8. Introduce your presentation by giving the class a quiz about the issue or ask them to state which side of the issue they favor.

Figure 1. Ideas for Group Presentations

1. Please provide a detailed explanation of the format of your group's presentation.

2. Please explain the role and contribution of each team member.

   a. Name:
      Contribution:

   b. Name:
      Contribution:

   c. Name:
      Contribution:

   d. Name:
      Contribution:

   e. Name:
      Contribution:

3. What handouts, if any, do you plan to use?

4. Will you need any of the following equipment? TV monitor ___VCR ___Tape player ___

Any other ___ (please explain):

Figure 2. Group Presentation Worksheet

Group Issue:
Criteria: 1 = inadequate; 2 = poor; 3 = average; 4 = good; 5 = excellent
1. Group presented both pro and con arguments (with statistics, examples and quotes): 1 2 3 4 5
2. A balance of pro and con arguments was presented: 1 2 3 4 5
3. Arguments presented were valid: 1 2 3 4 5
4. All members participated equally: 1 2 3 4 5
5. Creativity of presentation: 1 2 3 4 5
6. Thoroughness of presentation: 1 2 3 4 5
7. Audience participation: 1 2 3 4 5
8. Overall Group Score: 1 2 3 4 5
COMMENTS FOR THE GROUP:

Figure 3. Controversial Issue Presentation

Give the following information. Group members' names. Name of creature. Using complete sentences, describe the shape of the two-dimensional region you rotated. Sketch the region you revolved. Be sure to label the axis of revolution, the function(s) of the curve(s) and important points.

Figure 4. Volume Assignment

(Note: The editors have drastically reduced the length of this handout from its original length of approximately 1500 words to accommodate our format.)

Writing intended to criticize a person or society can be placed along a continuum: invective – lampoon – satire – comedy – farce. These are not absolute distinctions, of course; one category shades into the next

Invective: Direct personal attack. Although true satire is essentially ironic, invective is, basically, name calling.

Lampoon: Johnson defines lampoon as a "personal satire; abuse; censure written not to reform, but to vex." What distinguishes lampoon from purer forms of satire, according to Johnson's definition, is the author's intent. The satirist wants to point out some evil—personal or societal—with the purpose of alerting the reader and, possibly, even of correcting the evil. The writer of a lampoon, instead, wants only to annoy, not destroy, an enemy.

Satire: Nearly all good satire can be distinguished by certain characteristics in attitude or method:

1. The first is to describe a painful or absurd situation, or a foolish or wicked person or group, as vividly as possible.
2. The second is that when a satirist uses uncompromisingly clear language to describe unpleasant facts and people, he intends to do more than merely make a statement, he intends to shock his readers. By compelling them to look at a sight they had missed or shunned, he first makes them realize the truth, and then moves them to feelings of protest.
3. This leads us to the final test for satire; typical emotion which the author feels and wishes to evoke in his readers. It is a blend of amusement and contempt in some satirists, the amusement far outweighs the contempt. In others, it almost disappears; it changes into a sour sneer, or a grim smile, or a wry awareness that life cannot all be called reasonable or noble.

Comedy: The purpose of comedy is to cause painless, nondestructive laughter at human weakness.

Farce: Farce is an exaggerated form of humor, making use of broad improbabilities of plot and characterization for comic effect.

Figure 5. Satire Handout

Cooperative-learning Teams to Establish "International Connections"

Rose Ann Swartz

Major changes in business today include the use of work teams, the internationalizing of business, and the increased diversity of the workforce. Many students, however, have had little experience in productive teamwork and interacting with people from different backgrounds and cultures. The use of cooperative-learning teams and planned interaction with international students can help bridge this gap in student learning.

For the last ten years, I have been implementing cooperative-learning teams in all of my management courses in the College of Business. These learning teams have added to the energy in my classes and provided an opportunity for students to interact with others, to share ideas, and to accomplish tasks.

The following exercises describe my attempts to use teams as a basis for students to learn more about other cultures. The end result is that students are more job ready and hopefully will appreciate and embrace diversity more.

In each of these projects, I collaborate with professors in our Intensive English Program (IEP) at the university. The IEP attracts international students interested in improving their English skills, primarily in order to continue their academic education in the U.S. The IEP program has about 50 students representing approximately 15 different countries. This collaboration has benefitted students in both the College of Business and IEP. Through this interaction, business students have become more aware of different cultures and perspectives while working in a team setting. Professors in IEP have appreciated the opportunity for their students to meet and work with American students— and to practice their English skills.

The following International Connections projects were developed to provide opportunities for cultural interaction. The Cooperative Presentation project is task oriented and provides an experience for students from different cultures to interact while researching and preparing a business presentation. The Expert Panel project is an advanced activity that provides an in-depth experience for both the American and international students. The focus of the Expert Panel is to learn how to do business in other countries.

Cooperative Presentation

Purpose: To provide a structured experience for American students to interact with international students in preparing a business presentation. The presentations help all students develop their research and presentation skills and learn about current business practices.

Format: Existing management teams are assigned an "international representative" who will be a member of the team during this project. These teams do library research on a chosen topic in preparation for their presentations. Topics include: Diversity in the Workplace; Leadership Styles; Global Markets/Joint Ventures; Motivating Workers in a Diverse Workplace; Doing Business in Another Country; Legal Factors; and Affirmative Action. The management students are upper-class students who are familiar with our library and how to research a topic. The international students chosen for this experience are those enrolled in IEP speaking and writing courses. Their instructors use this experience to introduce them to the library and to explain how to do research. Teams are given instructions on how to make an effective business presentation, and taught how to use software graphics in the preparation of their visuals.

A written outline of the presentation and a bibliography are submitted by the teams prior to their presentations. Presentations are 20-30 minutes in length, depending on the number of student teams. Each student is required to speak and each is required to prepare an appropriate visual aid to support his/her topic. Some time is reserved for questions and answers.

Feedback: This project requires several class periods and coordination of meeting times for library research. The benefits, however, are great. American students gain experience working with students from different backgrounds and assisting the international students as they all complete a major task. The international students learn more about doing research on the college campus, using the existing technology, and working with American students on an assignment from start to finish.

Videotapes of the groups are used to provide feedback to all students on the effectiveness of their presentations and on their presentation styles. For the IEP students, the videotapes are used as an assessment of their developing English skills.

Grading: Instructors evaluate their own students according to their individual objectives for the presentations. For example, the IEP instructors evaluate not only the students' research abilities but also their individual improvement in speaking English. Each instructor carefully explains the evaluation process at the beginning of the project.

Expert Panels

Purposes: To structure a cooperative-learning experience between international and American students. To learn about business and social behavior in other countries. To develop skills in organizing a presentation and serving on an expert panel.

Format: Student teams composed of management and IEP students meet to do research on how to conduct business in another country. The country chosen is the one represented by the international student who serves as the cultural expert. In addition to traditional library research, students interview faculty and other students from the chosen country. Often parents and relatives of international students serve as resources.

Next, the team writes a script and develops several scenarios to illustrate such concepts as appropriate business greetings, the business luncheon, how to handle business negotiations, business after hours, etc. This script is used for the videotaped role-play students prepare outside of class. (At first I had our television production staff videotape the scenarios. Now, however, because many students have access to camcorders, students film their segments at their convenience.)

The final presentations include 5-8 minute videotapes illustrating important concepts followed by panel presentations. Entire teams can be on the panels which elaborate on specific areas and respond to questions from other members of the class. Students are required to participate in either the videotape OR the formal presentation; however, most students participate in both activities.

Project Timeline: One criticism of having team projects is that students have a difficult time meeting after class to work on these projects. My personal opinion is that if our objective is to have students develop team skills, then class time should be available for team meetings and projects. The entire 50-minute class period for eight meetings is dedicated to this project, including team meetings and library research. The timeline is as follows:
- Meeting 1: Get Acquainted Day (ice breaker exercise). Discuss project.
- Meeting 2: Team meetings. Begin research. Discuss role-plays.
- Meeting 3: Team research.
- Meeting 4: Complete outline of research. Finalize role-play. Determine props needed for videotape.
- Meeting 5: Videotape segment. (May be done in or out of class.)
- Meeting 6: Team review of videotape. Make final presentation plans.
- Meeting 7: Final presentations and discussion.
- Meeting 8: Presentations continued if needed.

Feedback: For the past five semesters, I have incorporated expert panels into my organizational behavior classes. Personal observations made throughout this activity showed a heightened interest in — and tolerance for — other cultures. Students were heard attempting to learn select words and phrases in other languages and asking questions about a particular gesture, habit, or perception. The videotaped segments showed American and international students joined in dancing to international music, singing songs from other countries, eating new kinds of foods, recreating cultural ceremonies, practicing appropriate greetings, and participating in sports such as volleyball and golf with their new friends. On several occasions, students have asked to see their videotapes again after the class was completed.

Grading: Team grades are given for this project along with a "Percent of Effort" evaluation. Students complete a form indicating the percent of effort they believe each team member contributed to the project. (Each can earn 100%.) The average "Percent of Effort" is then multiplied by the total team points and grades are awarded accordingly. Of course, students should be made aware of this "effort" evaluation before beginning the activity.

More Examples

For Expert Panel projects, teams are prepared by their respective professors. Example 1 is a handout that I use for my Management 302 (Organizational Behavior) class. This project provides questions for the initial get together and explains the project. Example 2 is used by an IEP professor. Collaboration and communication are key to the success of this project.

Example 1: International Guests/Expert Panel Projects Meeting 1 Form Sheet

Ice Breaker

You will have approximately 10 minutes with each guest. During that time try to find out as much as you can about his/her country. In return, the international students will want to know things about growing up in the U.S. Team Leaders: try and make the international students welcome! Although you should ask your own questions, here are some starters:

1. How do you like being a student in an American university? What impressions do you have of American students? American food? American customs? American dress? American music?
2. What have you noticed that is different in America than in your home country? What is the same?
3. How do American business and social customs differ from your home country?
4. What are your career plans after leaving Ferris State University?
5. What do you miss most from your country?
6. How can we help you to get the most from your American experience?

Project

With the help of your cultural representative AND library research, you are to become EXPERTS in your assigned area. Work to understand the sources of these particular cultural behaviors and why they are important. Follow these steps: 1) Research assigned area, 2) Share content, 3) Decide on important concepts to share in your presentation, and 4) COME TO CLASS PREPARED!

Decide on what to include in your videotape. Select behaviors that you can clearly demonstrate to your audience. You are to BECOME the individuals in the videotape by using appropriate language, customs, dress, mannerisms, etc. Decide on which topics/behaviors to elaborate in your 25-minute presentation. The videotape will be your visual aid. Organize your presentation. Present Dr. Swartz with two TYPED copies of your bibliography and presentation outline on ____. Sign up for videotaping. Be prepared for "one take."

TOPIC: _____

IEP STUDENT: _____ PHONE: _____

Example 2: Form for IEP Students

Level 5 Classroom Exchange Project with MGMT 302 Class

Purpose of the Project

To help foreign visitors to your country (particularly those in business) interact successfully in your culture. Your group will teach, through a short videotape role-play and a panel discussion, one aspect of your cultural behavior that you believe is important for foreign visitors to your country to know.

Project Description

You and your American group members are going to discuss and do light research upon a given area of your culture. You will function as the facilitator (cultural expert) for your group. Together you will work to really understand a cultural behavior and be able to explain why knowing that behavior is important for interacting successfully with people in your culture. Each group will have 25 minutes to present its information. Your presentation will be divided up into the following segments:

Segment 1: A 5-8 minute video role-play demonstrating the cultural behavior you will be discussing. You can take different approaches to this role-play, including showing how it is done correctly or demonstrating a cultural conflict that occurs as a result of not understanding the behavior. The role-play should be as authentic (true to life) as possible, using props if you have them.

Segment 2: A panel discussion in which you elaborate upon the concepts presented in the video. This discussion will explain the behavior demonstrated in greater detail and will also be used to discuss your research. Research should be done to help explain why the behavior is important, to help your audience fully understand the situations in which the behavior is appropriate, and also to understand any variations in the behavior that might occur in different situations. This section can take up to 15 minutes. Each member of your panel should have something to say about the cultural behavior.

Segment 3: A 3-5 minute question-and-answer period.

Your group may take the option of dividing into two teams: one to "star" in the video, and the other to function as the panel of experts.

Project Grading

You will be graded on your participation in the project and upon your presentation, either in the video or on the discussion panel. That means that you are expected to take an active role in group discussions by initiating conversations, sharing your insight and ideas, and guiding the group with information concerning your culture.

Conclusion

We all know the value of exposing our students to other cultures and learning how to work with people with different backgrounds, experiences, and values. Yet, these experiences may need to be structured and encouraged, especially in areas with limited diversity within the community or university. I learn something new every time I implement one of these projects in my classes. In addition, the opportunity to team with faculty in the IEP has been extremely rewarding. Establishing an "International Connection" is well worth all the time and organization necessary.

Part IV

Applications of Small Group Work and a Look to the Future

When we invited contributors to send new chapters for this book, we simply asked folks to write about what they had been thinking about in recent times. There were no requests regarding whether the chapters should be applied or research/theory focused, or any other constraints, other than that the work generally be related to research based active and small group work. As you might expect from this group of diverse thinkers, the chapters we received were similarly diverse in focus. Part IV reflects this diversity, as do the chapters in Part I.

Joe Cuseo, in his new chapter in Part I, described seven procedural principles of small group learning and David and Roger Johnson described five basic elements of their approach to cooperative learning in their Part I contribution. These two chapters serve, along with the first chapter in Part IV, written by Spencer and Miguel Kagan to illustrate the somewhat different views of small group learning that have emerged over the years. Jim and his colleagues wrote an article in *Change* many years ago, seeking to distinguish the forms of group learning, most prominently the distinction between collaborative and cooperative learning, differences that seemed important at that time. These distinctions now seem less important than simply using small group work in thoughtful ways, with a focus on the educational outcomes to be fostered among students serving as guiding principles to planning and implementing group work.

We don't think there is one best method of implementing group work, as the variety of strategies reflected throughout the book indicates. Ultimately, faculty members need to identify procedures with which they are comfortable, in light of their disciplines, student populations, course levels, enrollments, and other factors. Spencer and Miguel Kagan's chapter focuses on four fundamental principles of their approach to small group instruction: Kagan Structures. After introducing their four principles, they describe five Kagan Structures that increase student engagement and success. Some are designed to make relatively small amounts of material more meaningful to students and others focus on larger cognitive outcomes relating to successful longer term class projects.

David and Roger Johnson's chapter follows the Kagans' chapter and addresses a structure that they have developed over the years, Constructive Controversy, which is also known as Structured Controversy. They identify the benefits, both empirical and theoretical, of engaging in intellectual conflict and point out the benefits of managing such conflict in useful ways (versus less useful ways, such as debate and conflict). The Johnsons provide powerful data in support of Constructive Controversy, a procedure that we view as one that needs more attention as the world gets more complex and interdependent and as the skills for peacefully resolving conflict become more important, whether at home, in the workplace, or at national and international levels.

Following the Johnsons' chapter is one by Susan Prescott Johnston. Susan and Joe Cuseo are the two friends and colleagues who have been with us since the first issue of the newsletter in 1990. We cherish their friendship and will always be thankful for their high standards of professionalism. In her chapter, Susan provides a planning template for ensuring high levels of student engagement. This template can be used in any course, as teachers seek to actively engage their learners.

Cynthia Desrochers is Director of the Institute for Teaching and Learning in the California State University (CSU) Chancellor's Office, an office that coordinates faculty development among the 23 campuses of the CSU system. In her chapter, Cynthia calls for formation of Faculty Learning Communities to serve as support groups to foster innovation in teaching and learning. She outlines her experiences and offers advice on forming such a community using the theme of small group instruction as a focal point. Learning communities among students have been around for decades — including the landmark work of Jean MacGregor and Barbara Leigh Smith at Evergreen State College that is now carried on at Evergreen and across the nation by their intellectual descendents. The formation of Faculty Learning Communities provide similar support for faculty that is offered to students: systems for fostering cognitive and emotional growth.

Following Cynthia's chapter is one by Mark Maier, KimMarie McGoldrick and Scott Simkins who focus on how cooperative learning principles and practices can inform teaching and learning in higher education. They point to recent work in such areas as Just-in-Time Teaching, Context Rich Problems, forms of inquiry learning, Peer Instruction and Classroom Experiments. Many of these procedures were developed for use in specific disciples, primarily in science, mathematics, engineering and technology. Often they were developed without reference to the rich resources provided by the cooperative learning and other small group literature developed in higher education (and by K-12 researchers) over the decades. Mark and his colleagues note how the cooperative learning work can enrich applications of these pedagogies. It should also be noted that cooperative learning work can be enriched by greater attention to such issues as the nature of the problems offered by the areas identified by Mark and his colleagues, such as the Context Rich Problems field and the importance of technology as used in Just-in-Time Teaching; each pedagogy enriches the other.

Philip Abrami has been a distinguished contributor to higher education for decades. He and his colleagues at Concordia University in Quebec have addressed a variety of issues in K-12 and higher education. His chapter for this volume, completed with Rana Tamim, Robert Bernard and Eugene Borohovski, provides further evidence of the breadth and depth of the scholarly work that he has contributed. The chapter looks at factors that make a difference in distance and online learning. Drawing on the power of meta-analysis, the authors look at three forms of interaction: student-student, student-teacher and student-content. They determine that "guided, focused and purposeful activity may be the answer to the question of truly effective interaction" and ultimately to successful instruction. Many of us who have contributed to this book would roundly applaud their sentiment and suggest that careful instructional planning and implementation based on important educational outcomes serve as the basis for all good teaching. Regrettably, our graduate programs too rarely provide even the most fundamental preparation in the skills that prepare us to be teachers.

The final chapter in this book is written by Donald Bligh. Donald is well known around the globe, although perhaps best known in his home country of Great Britain, for his work addressing the questions of What's the use of lecturing? and What's the use of discussion? In his chapter, Intellectual Exploration Together (IET), Donald reflects on a life time of scholarly work. He offers a method of exploring the world, IET, and posits the proposition that one of the most powerful methods of doing research may be to focus on what a researcher does not know, or only partially understands. He calls for meetings, both live and virtual, in which groups of scholars, representing many disciplines, come together to brainstorm, speculate and synthesize. This chapter may be a fitting way to finish this volume, with its focus on the tentative nature of knowledge and how it changes over time, informed by changes within our own fields and from other disciplines.

We hope that the work presented in this book raises as many questions as it answers, and that it inspires beginners to start experimenting with their pedagogies and more experienced practitioners to share their work with colleagues in communities of learners on their campuses and beyond. We hope to foster a dialog among colleagues across the disciplines concerning what we should be teaching, how we should be teaching and what the next challenges to higher education are as we face a resource limited, interdependent world within academe and across the globe.

Five Must-Know Kagan Structures for Higher Education

Spencer Kagan and Miguel Kagan

Through structured interactions in pairs and in small teams, student learning becomes more effective; students more fully attend to, more deeply process, better store, and more completely recall academic content (Johnson & Johnson, 1989). The key to these improved outcomes, is carefully structuring the interaction among students. Many instructors feel they are doing effective cooperative learning when they simply have students talk in pairs or when they have small groups solve a problem or complete a project. Unstructured interaction of this type, however, does not lead to gains for all students. An unstructured pair discussion between a high achiever and a low achiever often is one student talking while the mind of the other student is wandering. Unstructured problem solving or project work in small teams is often some students doing the work while others take a free ride. By carefully structuring the interaction we produce increased engagement for students and significant improvement in their success.

In 1968, Spencer began developing simple instructional strategies that produce engagement among all students. These structures are carefully designed to put four principles in place, symbolized by the acronym PIES. First we will define PIES and then describe five structures that can be effectively used in many higher education instructional formats

PIES—Basic Principles of Cooperative Learning

PIES stands for Positive Interdependence, Individual Accountability, Equal Participation, and Simultaneous Interaction (Kagan & Kagan, 2009).

Positive Interdependence. Positive Interdependence exists when: 1) students have a common goal, and 2) when they cannot reach that goal without the contribution of each member of the pair or group. When Positive Interdependence is in place, students feel that they are on the same side.

Individual Accountability. Individual Accountability exists when each member of the pair or group is required to make a contribution that will be known by the instructor and/or the other members of the group. When Individual Accountability is in place, all students must make a contribution; they cannot hide.

Equal or Equitable Participation. Although perfectly equal participation is never possible, effective cooperative learning requires participants to participate and contribute approximately equally. In cases of discrepant abilities, we require Equitable Participation. When this principle is in place, students feel mutual respect and enjoy equal status.

Simultaneous Interaction. Rather than calling on one student or one group at a time to be actively engaged, effective cooperative learning maximizes engagement for all students.

Five Kagan Structures

All of the Kagan Structures are designed to ensure the PIES principles are in place, which in turn dramatically increases the probability of full engagement and student learning. Next, we present five Kagan Structures that promote cooperation and active engagement in higher education. We will describe them, provide some content examples at the university level, and reveal the benefits of these structures compared to traditional higher education teaching methods.

Overview of the Five Kagan Structures

1) **Listen Right!** transforms passive lectures into opportunities for students to actively process and assimilate new learning.

2) **Numbered Heads Together** converts review sessions into a highly engaging and memorable team review experience.

3) **RoundRobin** generates high levels of interaction in discussion groups and promotes equal opportunities for students to participate.

4) **RallyCoach** provides immediate feedback for peer tutoring during problem solving and practice.

5) **Team Project** encourages creativity and collaborative construction of deep processing of course content.

Structure #1: Listen Right!
Punctuate lectures with periodic breaks for interaction and information processing.

The instructor stops lecturing after approximately ten minutes. The instructor tells students to review their notes and process what they've learned so far. The processing can take many different forms depending on the lecture content. Students can write a summary of two or three of the key points. They can create or add to a mind map or concept map, or they can create or add to any number of graphic organizers.

After students have independently reviewed or summarized their learning, they pair up. Partner A shares his/her summary or reflections first, then Partner B shares. Students can take additional notes as their partners share. They also can add points of clarification or make corrections if necessary.

After this sharing, the instructor quickly summarizes key points. Then, the instructor resumes the lecture. The instructor continues to punctuate the lecture with periodic breaks for additional rounds of Listen Right!

Benefits of Listen Right!

A lecture is an efficient way for a teacher to pass along a body of knowledge to a large group of students. Some lectures are oratory. Some include visuals, such as outlines, slides, or multimedia data. Lectures vary slightly in format, but the basic concept is the same: The sage on the stage transmits knowledge to students who listen and take notes.

There are some inherent drawbacks to lectures. Some students get lost. Developmental lectures build on earlier information. If a student misses early information, the likelihood of comprehending and retaining additional information is diminished. Listen Right! corrects this problem. It allows students to stop, review, and process what they've heard so far. It gives them the opportunity to ask questions, make clarifications, and hear it again, often in more comprehensible terms from a peer.

Another drawback of lectures is that they can be boring. Although none of us would like to admit that our students could possibly be bored by *our* lectures, boredom is a reality. Some students pay exquisite attention, taking copious notes at the beginning of the lecture only to find their ability to maintain interest wanes as the instructor drones on. Boredom is often the result of a lack of variety and stimulation. Inactivity results in sleepy brains. Some students may find the lecture mentally stimulating and are able to keep focused for the entire lecture. Others need a state change. Listen Right! infuses variety and student interaction, converting a one-way lecture into an engaging learning experience.

Many instructors balk at the idea of stopping to process when there is so much content to cover. However, actively processing the lecture increases retention. Listen Right! gives students the opportunity to immediately apply course content and teach others. Admittedly, if we do not stop to have students process what we say, we can superficially cover more content. But the result is that students retain less (Bligh, 2000).

Another advantage of Listen Right! is that it clears working memory. Working memory is the content we retain in immediate consciousness. For example, it is the telephone number that the operator gives us to dial. If we do not stop and process the number, it is gone. To move information from working memory to long term memory, we must actively manipulate or process the information. Students' brains do not operate like recorders. They don't press the record button at the beginning of a lecture and the stop button at the end and remember everything in between. Working memory has limited storage capacity. To pour more content into working memory without allowing processing time is like pouring more water into a glass that is already full. These punctuated processing breaks allow students to clear their working memory to take in additional information.

Structure #2: Numbered Heads Together
Transform review sessions into highly engaging and memorable cooperative experiences.

Students sit in teams of four. Within their teams, they number off from 1 to 4. The instructor asks a question or poses a problem and provides think time. The question can be a problem to solve, such as: "What is the mode of the following set of numbers: 10, 10, 9, 9, 8, 7, 7, 7, 6, 5, 5?" The question can be a review question or prompt, such as: "Define mode." Or the question can be an open-ended question, such as: "In sociology, when might a researcher want to determine the mode?" Students independently write their answers on a response board or on a slip of paper. Next, team members put their heads together. They show and/or read each other their answers and reach consensus. Teammates make sure they all know the team answer and the steps of obtaining the answer because one of them will be selected to represent the team. They erase or hide their notes.

The instructor randomly calls a learner number from 1 to 4. The selected students on each team stand, ready to demonstrate they know how to solve the problem. The instructor selects one standing student to respond with the larger group. In this case, the other standing students indicate that they agree with a thumb up, or they indicate that they disagree with a thumb down, or they indicate partial agreement with a thumb sideways. The instructor may select others with a thumb down or a thumb sideways to share their answers. If the answers vary, the instructor may re-teach or reinforce the concept.

An alternative method for student sharing is to have the selected learner on each team answer simultaneously by holding up his or her response board. The instructor checks answers and re-teaches if there are any incorrect answers.

Benefits of Numbered Heads Together

Numbered Heads Together has a number of distinct advantages over traditional review sessions. First, it is extremely high on Individual Accountability, which requires individual public performance during teamwork. Students know that if they have to publicly perform independently, there is greater social pressure to excel. Students can't hide behind their teammates or take a free ride; everyone is motivated to learn and participate.

Numbered Heads Together creates Individual Accountability in two ways. First, when the instructor asks the question, every student is accountable to his/her teammates for coming up with an answer to share. This is not true in traditional review sessions. In many traditional review sessions, the instructor may ask questions and some hands may shoot up. By virtue of its structure, Numbered Heads Together keeps students actively engaged.

The second source of Individual Accountability is when the instructor selects a teammate to respond for the team. Students know that they must learn and retain how to derive the answer and be able to correctly represent the team. Again, there is social pressure to achieve. Research on cooperative learning suggests that Individual Accountability is a critical component to academic gains (Johnson, Johnson, & Smith, 2006). It distinguishes successful cooperative learning from unstructured group work. Cooperative learning consistently outperforms traditional learning whereas unstructured group work has mixed results. When we include Individual Accountability in small group instruction, we structure learning for all students.

Numbered Heads Together makes the review content more "brain-friendly." Some information is easy for students to remember and some is more difficult. Students can easily remember what they had for dinner, but have more difficulty memorizing academic content. The key difference is how the memory is encoded. Events or episodes are encoded in episodic memory. Academic facts and information are encoded using semantic memory pathways. Numbered Heads Together transforms the review session into a social experience. Compared to memorizing discrete facts, students are better able to recall information that is constructed in a social context.

Structure #3: RoundRobin
Create greater engagement and equalize student participation in discussion groups.

RoundRobin is a very simple structure easily integrated into discussion group sessions. The instructor asks a question or poses a problem or task for students. For example, in a psychology lecture on obedience and power the instructor may say, "Do a RoundRobin. Everyone describe one example of coercive power."

Students break into their small groups. The instructor indicates who in the small group will respond first. If, for example, students in groups of four have numbers, the instructor may randomly select a number from 1 to 4. Or, the instructor may select one student to start and directs the turn taking. For example, "The tallest student on your team will share first, then going clockwise, each teammate will take a turn." The first student may share that parents have coercive control over their children. The next teammate clockwise may share that a manager has coercive power over an employee. Each student in the group takes a turn to share an example.

For discussion items that may require a long explanation, the instructor may do a Timed RoundRobin: Every student has one minute (or any predetermined time) to share. Some discussion topics work well with multiple short rounds of sharing, so the instructor may use a Continuous RoundRobin. For example, "On the board there is a list of political events in European history. Starting with the student with the most colorful clothing and going around clockwise, share a brief description of one event." Each student takes multiple turns sharing. In a Continuous RoundRobin, students continue to share until they cover all the topics, or until the instructor calls time.

Benefits of RoundRobin

There are two major benefits of RoundRobin. First, compared to traditional whole group discussions, RoundRobin creates greater Simultaneous Interaction. Let's say the instructor asks a discussion question in a typical discussion group and one student responds for one minute. To give each of the 30 students in the group one minute to verbalize course content, it would take us 30 minutes. During an hour discussion group, every student would get a maximum of two minutes of participation time. But of course, this is an overestimate. The instructor spends much more time talking and students much less. Plus, in traditional group discussions some students take more than their two minutes of talk time, while others do not say a word the entire hour.

Using RoundRobin, we give every student the same one minute using much less class time. In a team of four, if every student shared for one minute, then it would only take four minutes of our discussion time. Contrast four minutes with 30 minutes. In four minutes of class time we accomplish the same goal as it would normally take us in 30 minutes. And even more telling is how students spend their time. During the RoundRobin, each student is active for a quarter of the time. During traditional group discussion, each student is active for only a small fraction of the class time. Inactivity is the antithesis of what we're trying to accomplish in discussion sections. Many higher education courses are structured with a lecture and a discussion component. The goal of the discussion group is to overcome the inactivity of the lecture and allow students to express their own ideas and interact, making the content come alive. Yet, traditional discussion groups do a poor job of truly engaging students. Small group discussion structures, such as RoundRobin help remedy that problem.

A second major benefit of a RoundRobin is Equal Participation. Participation during a large group discussion is far from equal. The more vocal and extroverted students speak frequently while the more timid or introverted students remain silent. In RoundRobin, every student receives an equal opportunity to share. A Timed RoundRobin not only gives each student an equal opportunity to share but also provides an approximately equal amount of sharing. Since there is a correlation between engagement and learning (Pascarella & Terenzini, 2005) we should structure our courses to promote many opportunities for interaction, and equal opportunities so everyone has a chance to vocalize and internalize the course content.

Structure #4: RallyCoach

Provide immediate feedback and support through peer tutoring.

RallyCoach is a peer tutoring structure for problem solving and practice. The instructor assigns the class or group a set of problems. The problems can be on a worksheet, textbook problems, problems posted on the board, or problems displayed digitally. For example, in an integral calculus course the problems can be summation notation problems.

Students break into pairs. Pairs can be assigned by the instructor based on ability level or students can simply select a partner. In pairs, there is a Partner A and a Partner B. Students can pick who is Partner A and who is Partner B; it doesn't matter since they will have equivalent roles.

Partner A solves the first problem, talking out each step aloud. "The first thing is to re-write the problem using the summation rules. Next, we solve for the exponents. Four squared becomes 16. Next, we re-write the problem again solving for the square root. Then it just becomes simple addition." Partner B watches and listens. If Partner A doesn't understand how to solve the problem or makes an error while solving the problem, Partner B can step in to coach.

Partner B solves the next problem while Partner A watches, listens, coaches, and praises. For each new problem Partner A and Partner B alternate solving the problem.

Benefits of RallyCoach

Many courses that involve problem solving are merely demonstrations by the professor. Modeling how to solve problems is helpful for students to see a positive model. However, later when students attempt to solve the problems themselves, they sometimes discover they need help.

RallyCoach promotes cooperative problem solving. Students who discover that they need help have a coach who provides immediate tutoring and support. But as has been demonstrated by Slavin (1995) and others, tutors benefit at least as much as the tutees. As they teach their tutees, the tutors reinforce and refine their own skills.

Structure #5: Team Project

Encourage research, creativity, and content exploration with a cooperative project.

Team Project is a powerful structure for teams to create products or presentations. The product can be anything. In chemistry, it can be an experiment; in engineering it can be a structural design; in architecture it can be a set of blueprints for a commercial building; in programming, it can be an internet application.

The instructor assigns the project and assigns teams or allows students to form their own teams based on their interests. We recommend teams of four. Teams that are too large minimize active engagement and cooperation. Some students get lost in the shuffle. Pair projects work very well too. With pair projects, however, there is less synergy than with a team of four. If the projects will be presented to the class, pair projects generally take longer since there are twice as many projects to present.

An important feature of a Team Project is to equalize participation. Simply stating, "work on this project in your team" may spell disaster. Too often one student takes over the project, while another takes a free ride. The goal is to have every student contribute to the project. Using roles and responsibilities is the most powerful way to ensure everyone has a part to play. If the project is pre-defined, the instructor may assign different roles to each teammate.

Many higher education projects, however, are not pre-determined. They are initiated by students. A very important part of the project planning process is for teammates to plan out the project, then to formally assign each teammate a specific role. We encourage students to create and use a project planning sheet.

The sheet describes the team's goal and the role and responsibility for each teammate. It is almost a contract among teammates. Although some instructors may resist the idea of overly structuring team projects, unstructured group work is wishful thinking. In some groups there will be unequal participation, with some students taking a free ride.

Team Projects are a collaborative effort and many instructors are tempted to give a group grade to the project. However, we advocate against group grades (Kagan, 1995). Individual grades should be a reflection of individual work and individual learning. Students can be individually graded on their contributions to the team project or on their individual write-up of the project, or their individual test scores.

Benefits of Team Projects

Project-based learning has many distinct benefits whether done independently or collaboratively. Students construct a deep and real understanding of the course content by researching it thoroughly and applying their knowledge to real-world projects. Students develop their creativity and ingenuity, two key skills in an information-based workplace. Students can develop presentation skills as they present their projects to others.

Cooperative projects have the added benefits of increased teamwork skills. To successfully reach their team goals, students must interact, negotiate, make decisions, divide the labor, and coordinate efforts. The modern day workplace places a high premium on teamwork and interpersonal skills (Kagan, 2010). Interpersonal skills are especially salient for workplace leaders, including supervisors, managers, and executives.

Well-structured Team Projects implement both components of Positive Interdependence. First, students work together to reach a team goal. Second, well-structured team projects have team goals that cannot be reached without the contribution of every teammate. This is not necessarily true of unstructured team projects. To ensure the participation and learning of everyone involved, the task is structured either by the instructor or by the team to require the contribution of each team member.

In Conclusion

The five Kagan Structures presented in this chapter can be integrated into many course presentation formats across a wide array of academic disciplines. Each has a different purpose, but all of them are designed to implement well-established principles of effective cooperative learning. By including structured interactions in our higher education courses we can transform the learning experience.

Lectures become more interactive and often allow students to process their learning. Review sessions become more engaging and memorable. Group discussions become more equitable and create a greater rate of participation. Problem-solving becomes cooperative and provides students peer support and immediate feedback. And projects allow students to coordinate efforts as they apply their knowledge.

With these structures, learning is converted from an independent act to a social act. Learners are converted from passive recipients of knowledge to active constructors of their own knowledge. These changes in instruction can revolutionize student learning.

Constructive Controversy: Energizing Learning

David W. Johnson and Roger T. Johnson

Throughout the southwest region of the United States there are communities built about a thousand years ago high on cliffs. The builders and inhabitants, known as the Anasazi, lived in their cliff dwellings for almost a hundred years and then abruptly abandoned them. In a three to four year period, the Anasazi walked away from their communities and never came back. Why? No one knows. Many classes are to students what their cliff dwellings were to the Anasazi. Students enroll in a course, pay the tuition, and spend considerable time attending class sessions, completing assignments, and passing tests, but when the course is over, they walk away and intellectually, never come back. Why? No one knows.

It is possible for students to become so involved in the subject they are studying that they sparkle with energy, get deeply involved in the topics being discussed, rush to the library or internet to get more information and resources, continue discussing the topics over lunch and at night, seek out experts in the field to consult, and impatiently wait for the next class session to begin. How do you get students that interested in what you are teaching? An essential and often overlooked part of the answer is, "Stir up intellectual conflict."

Conflict gains and holds attention and interest. All drama, for example, hinges on conflict. When playwrights and scriptwriters want to gain and hold viewers' attention, create viewers' interest and emotional involvement, and excite and surprise viewers, they create a conflict. A general rule for television shows is that if there is not a conflict portrayed in the first 30 seconds, viewers will change the channel. Creating a conflict is an accepted writers' tool for capturing an audience. A general rule of modern novels is that if a conflict is not created within the first three pages of the book, the book will not be successful. There should be a general rule of teaching that states that if an instructor does not create an intellectual conflict in the first few minutes of a class period, students will not intellectually engage in the lesson and their attention will drift away to other things. By avoiding conflicts, instructors miss out on valuable opportunities to capture and emotionally involve students and enhance their learning

Intellectual conflict provides the spark that energizes students to seek out new information and study harder and longer. By structuring intellectual conflict in a lesson, instructors can grab and hold students' attention and energize students to learn at a level beyond what they may have intended.

Cooperation and Controversy

Conflict is an inherent part of cooperation. Intellectual conflict among group members, if not essential for cooperation's success, has the potential for enhancing the effectiveness of cooperation. The more cooperative learning is used, the more group members need to understand how to disagree with each other's ideas, conclusions and opinions, and challenge each other's reasoning and information in constructive ways.

It is difficult to discuss cooperative learning without discussing intellectual conflicts. There is a dual relationship between cooperation and conflict (Johnson & Johnson, 2005, 2007). On the one hand, to be constructive, conflict must occur in a cooperative context. On the other hand, to be most effective, cooperation must involve conflict among students' initial: (a) answers and conclusions; (b) strategies for completing tasks or solving problems, ways in which their groups' work could be organized, and approaches to completing assignments; and (c) perspectives, points of view, and frames of reference. In order for these conflicts to be managed constructively, students need a procedure for engaging in intellectual conflicts and to master the social and cognitive skills inherent in the procedure. In this chapter, the nature of constructive controversy will be explained, the instructional procedure will be discussed, the underlying theory will be outlined, and the validating research will be discussed.

Nature of Constructive Controversy

Constructive controversy exists when one person's ideas, information, conclusions, theories, and opinions are incompatible with those of another, and the two seek to reach an agreement (Johnson & Johnson, 1979, 1989, 2007). Constructive controversies involve what Aristotle called deliberate discourse aimed at synthesizing novel solutions. Related to controversy is cognitive conflict (which occurs when incompatible ideas exist simultaneously in a person's mind or when information being received does not seem to fit with what someone already knows). Constructive controversy is most commonly contrasted with concurrence seeking, debate, and individualistic learning. Concurrence seeking occurs when members of a group emphasize agreement, inhibit discussion to avoid any disagreement or arguments, and avoid realistic appraisal of alternative ideas and courses of action. Concurrence seeking is close to Janis' (1982) concept of groupthink (i.e., members of a decision-making group set aside their doubts and misgivings about whatever policy is favored by the emerging consensus so as to be able to concur with the other members). Debate exists when two or more individuals argue positions that are incompatible with one another and a judge declares a winner on the basis of who presented the best position. Individualistic efforts exist when individuals work alone without interacting with each other, in a situation in which their goals are unrelated and independent from each other (Johnson, Johnson, & Holubec, 2008).

Constructive Controversy Instructional Procedure

Have you learned lessons only of those who admired you, and were tender with you, and stood aside for you?

Have you not learned great lessons from those who braced themselves against you, and disputed the passage with you?

Walt Whitman, 1860

A United States history instructor is presenting a unit on civil disobedience. The instructor notes that in numerous instances, such as in the civil rights and antiwar movements, individuals wrestle with the issue of breaking the law to redress a social injustice. In the civil rights movement in the United States, individuals broke the law to gain equal rights for minorities. In the past few years, however, prominent public figures felt justified in breaking laws for personal or political gain. The central question is, "Is civil disobedience in a democracy constructive or destructive?" Students are placed in groups of four members and given the assignments of writing a report and passing a test on the role of civil disobedience in a democracy. Each group is divided into two pairs. One pair is given the assignment of developing and advocating the best case possible for the constructiveness of civil disobedience in a democracy and the other pair is given the assignment of developing and advocating the best case possible for the destructiveness of civil disobedience in a democracy. The overall group goal is for students to reach consensus as to the role of civil disobedience in a democracy. To develop their positions, students draw from such sources as the *Declaration of Independence* by Thomas Jefferson, *Civil Disobedience* by Henry David Thoreau, *Speech at Cooper Union, New York* by Abraham Lincoln, and *Letter from Birmingham Jail* by Martin Luther King, Jr. The students are to learn the information relevant to the issue being studied and ensure that all other group members learn the information, so that: (a) their group can write a high-quality report on the issue, and (b) all group members can achieve high scores on tests.

Constructive controversy may be used with almost any topic being studied. In doing so, the teacher organizes students into cooperative learning groups of four, divides each group into two pairs, assigns the pro position on an issue to one pair and the con position to the other pair, and then guides students through the following steps (Johnson & Johnson, 1979, 1989, 2007):

1. **Research and Prepare a Position**: Each pair develops the position assigned, learns the relevant information, and plans how to present the best case possible to the other pair. This involves both cognitive generation and cognitive validation. Pairs are encouraged to compare notes with pairs from other groups who represent the same position.
2. **Present and Advocate Their Position**: Each pair makes its presentation to the opposing pair. Each member of the pair has to participate in the presentation. Students are to be as persuasive and convincing as possible. Members of the opposing pair are encouraged to take notes, listen carefully to learn the information being presented, and clarify anything they do not understand.
3. **Engage in an Open Discussion in Which They Refute the Opposing Position and Rebut Attacks on Their Own Position**: Students argue forcefully and persuasively for their position, presenting as many facts as they can to support their point of view. The group members analyze and critically evaluate the

information, rationale, and inductive and deductive reasoning of the opposing pair, asking them for the facts that support their point of view. While refuting the arguments of the opposing pair, students rebut attacks on their position. Students keep in mind that the issue is complex and they need to know both sides to write a good report.
4. **Reverse Perspectives**: The pairs reverse perspectives and present each other's positions. In arguing for the opposing position, students are forceful and persuasive. They add any new information that the opposing pair did not think to present. They strive to see the issue from both perspectives simultaneously.
5. **Synthesize and Integrate the Best Evidence and Reasoning into a Joint Position**: The four members of the group drop all advocacy, and synthesize and integrate what they know into factual and judgmental conclusions that are summarized in a joint position to which all sides can agree. They may: (a) finalize a report on the issue, (b) present their conclusions to the class, (c) individually take a test covering both sides of the issue, and (d) process how well they worked together.

Theory of Constructive Controversy

Conflict is the gadfly of thought. It stirs us to observation and memory. It instigates invention. It shocks us out of sheep-like passivity, and sets us at noting and contriving...conflict is a 'sine qua non' of reflection and ingenuity.

John Dewey

A number of developmental, cognitive, social, and organizational psychologists have theorized about the processes through which conflict leads to positive outcomes. On the basis of their work, we have proposed the following process (Johnson & Johnson, 1979, 1989, 2007):

1. When individuals are presented with a problem or decision, they have an initial conclusion based on categorizing and organizing incomplete information, their limited experiences, and their specific perspective. They have a high degree of confidence in their conclusions (they freeze the epistemic process).
2. When individuals present their conclusions and rationales to others, they engage in cognitive rehearsal, deepen their understanding of their positions, and discover higher-level reasoning strategies.
3. When individuals are confronted with different conclusions based on other peoples' information, experiences, and perspectives, they become uncertain as to the correctness of their views and a state of conceptual conflict or disequilibrium is aroused. They unfreeze their epistemic process.
4. Uncertainty, conceptual conflict, or disequilibrium motivates epistemic curiosity, an active search for: (a) more information and new experiences (increased specific content), and (b) a more adequate cognitive perspective and reasoning process (increased validity) in hopes of resolving the uncertainty.
5. By adapting their cognitive perspectives and reasoning through understanding and accommodating the perspectives and reasoning of others, new reconceptualized and reorganized conclusions are derived. Novel solutions and decisions that are qualitatively better are detected.

The process may begin again at this point or it may be terminated by freezing the current conclusion and resolving any dissonance by increasing the confidence in the validity of the conclusion.

Conditions Determining the Constructiveness of Controversy

He that wrestles with us strengthens our nerves, and sharpens our skill. Our antagonist is our helper.
Edmund Burke

Whether controversy results in positive or negative consequences largely depends on the conditions under which it occurs. These conditions include the context within which the constructive controversy takes place, the heterogeneity of participants, the distribution of information among group members, the level of group members' social skills, group members' ability to engage in rational argument, and the active involvement of all participants (Johnson & Johnson, 1979, 1989, 2007).

Cooperative Goal Structure

The context in which conflicts occur has important effects on whether the conflict turns out to be constructive or destructive (Deutsch, 1973). There are two possible contexts for conflict: cooperative and competitive. In a cooperative context, constructive controversy tends to result in open-minded inquiry which leads to refined conclusions (Johnson & Johnson, 2007). It also tends to induce feelings of comfort, pleasure, and helpfulness in discussing opposing positions, an open-minded listening to opposing positions, motivation to hear more about opponents' arguments, more accurate understanding of opponents' positions and perspectives, and the reaching of more integrated solutions (Johnson & Johnson, 2007; Tjosvold, 1998). These patterns of interaction in turn promote social support and safety, creativity, performance, and quality solutions to which participants are highly committed (Tjosvold, 1998). Controversy within a competitive context tends to induce competence threat and result in closed-minded rejection of opponents' ideas and information while rigidly adhering to the same conclusion (Johnson & Johnson, 2007; Tjosvold, 1998).

Skilled Disagreement

For successful implementation of constructive controversy the following norms need to be developed (Johnson, 2009; Johnson & F. Johnson, 2009).

1. I am critical of ideas, not people. I challenge and refute the ideas of the other participants, while confirming their competence and value as individuals. I do not indicate that I personally reject them.
2. I separate my personal worth from criticism of my ideas.
3. I remember that we are all in this together, sink or swim. I focus on coming to the best decision possible, not on winning.
3. I encourage everyone to participate and to master all the relevant information.
4. I listen to everyone's ideas, even if I do not agree.
5. I restate what someone has said if it is not clear.
6. I differentiate before I try to integrate. I first bring out **all** ideas and facts supporting both sides and clarify how the positions differ. Then I try to identify points of agreement and put them together in a way that makes sense.
7. I try to understand both sides of the issue. I try to see the issue from the opposing perspective in order to understand the opposing position.
8. I change my mind when the evidence clearly indicates that I should do so.
9. I emphasize rationality in seeking the best possible answer, given the available data.
10. I follow the *golden rule of conflict* (i.e., I act towards opponents as I would have them act toward me). I want my opponents to listen to me, so I listen to them. I want them to include my ideas in their thinking, so I include their ideas in my thinking

Rational Argument

During a constructive controversy, group members are encouraged to follow the canons of rational argumentation (Johnson & Johnson, 2007). Rational argumentation begins with each side constructing its pro and con arguments. An argument consists of an assertion or claim, a rationale, and a conclusion (which is the same as the claim). Constructing an argument includes generating ideas, collecting relevant information, organizing it using inductive and deductive logic, and making tentative conclusions based on current understanding. One person's position is then presented to another person holding the opposite point of view. A dialogue subsequently takes place. Rational argumentation requires that participants keep an open mind, changing their conclusions and positions when others are persuasive and convincing in their presentation of rationale, evidence, and logical reasoning.

Active Involvement of All Participants

The likelihood of controversy resulting in positive outcomes tends to increase as the active involvement of both partners increases. Participants must not be able to avoid the conflict, yield to the other, be passive, or have the power to impose his or her view on others without explanation. In a constructive controversy, all participants tend to engage actively in open-minded inquiry which includes advocating their positions and critically challenging the opposing positions, while remaining focused on creating a synthesis that incorporates the best reasoned judgment of everyone involved.

Outcomes of Controversy

General Characteristics of Controversy Research

The research on constructive controversy has primarily been conducted in the last 40 years by researchers in a variety of settings using many different participant populations tasks in both lab-experimental and field-experimental formats. (Johnson & Johnson, 2009). In eighty-two percent of the studies participants were randomly assigned to conditions. All but two of the studies were published in journals. Participants ranged from first grade students, to college students, to adults. The duration of the study ranged from one to over twenty sessions. Taken together, their results have considerable validity and generalizability.

Achievement, Retention, and Quality of Decision Making and Problem Solving

Controversy tends to result in greater mastery and retention of the material and skills being learned than does concurrence-seeking (ES = 0.70), debate (ES =0.62), or individualistic learning (ES = 0.76). More specifically, participation in a constructive controversy tends to result in: (a) significantly greater ability to recall the information and reasoning contained in own and others' positions; (b) more skillfully transferring of this learning to new situations; and (c) greater generalization of principles learned to a wider variety of situations than do concurrence-seeking, debate, or individualistic efforts (Johnson & Johnson, 2009). In addition, constructive controversy tends to result in higher-quality decisions (including decisions that involve ethical dilemmas) and higher-quality solutions to complex problems for which different viewpoints can be developed.

Cognitive and Moral Reasoning

Students who participate in academic controversies end up using more higher-level reasoning and metacognitive thought than students participating in concurrence seeking (ES = 0.84), debate (ES = 1.38), or individualistic efforts (ES = 1.10). In these studies, students progressed in their stage of reasoning when confronted with reasons that opposed their own views and were one stage above their way of reasoning. Students also developed cognitively when confronted with counter arguments at the same stage of reasoning.

The same result happens with students' levels of moral reasoning. There are a number of studies that demonstrate that when participants are placed in a group with peers who use a higher stage of moral reasoning, and the group is required to make a decision as to how a moral dilemma should be resolved, advances in the students' level of moral reasoning result (Johnson & Johnson, 1989). In a recent study, Tichy, Johnson, Johnson, and Roseth (in press) found that controversy tended to result in significantly higher levels of moral motivation, moral judgment, and moral character.

Perspective Taking

In order to discuss difficult issues, make joint reasoned judgments, and increase commitment to implement the decision, it is helpful to understand and consider all perspectives. Constructive controversy tends to promote more accurate and complete understanding of opposing perspectives than do concurrence seeking (ES = 0.97), debate (ES = 0.20), and individualistic efforts (ES = 0.59). Engaging in controversy tends to result in greater understanding of another person's cognitive perspective than the absence of controversy and individuals engaged in a controversy tend to be better able to predict what line of reasoning their opponents would use in solving future problems than were individuals who interacted without any controversy. The increased understanding of opposing perspectives tends to result from engaging in controversy regardless of whether one is a high-, medium-, and low-achieving student. Increased perspective taking tends to increase individuals' ability to discover beneficial agreements in conflicts (Galinsky, Maddux, Gilin, & White, 2008).

Open-Mindedness

Individuals participating in controversies in a cooperative context tend to be more open-minded in listening to the opposing position than individuals participating in controversies in a competitive context (Tjosvold & Johnson, 1978). The researchers note that when the context was competitive there was a closed-minded orientation in which participants comparatively felt unwilling to make concessions to opponents' viewpoints. Within a competitive context the increased understanding resulting from controversy tended to be ignored for a defensive adherence to their own positions (Tjosvold & Johnson, 1978).

Creativity

Proponents of creativity often view conflict as necessary for creativity to occur. From the research it may be concluded that controversy tends to promote creative insight by influencing individuals to: (a) view problems from different perspectives, and (b) reformulate problems in ways that allow the emergence of new orientations to a solution. There is evidence that controversy increases the number of ideas, quality of ideas, feelings of stimulation and enjoyment, and originality of expression in creative problem-solving (Johnson & Johnson, 2009). Controversy encouraged group members to dig into problems, raise issues, and settle them in ways that showed the benefits of a wide range of ideas being used, as well as resulting in a high degree of emotional involvement in and commitment to solving problems. Being confronted with credible alternative views has resulted in the generation of more novel solutions, varied strategies, and original ideas. Individuals with a cooperative orientation tend to produce more creative syntheses than do individuals with individualistic or competitive orientations.

Task Involvement

Creating knowledge through disagreement tends to arouse emotions and increase involvement. Task involvement refers to the quality and quantity of the physical and psychological energy that individuals invest in their efforts to achieve. Task involvement is reflected in participants' attitudes. Individuals engaged in controversies tend to like the task better than do individuals engaged in concurrence-seeking discussions (ES = 0.63) or individualistic efforts. Individuals involved in controversy (and to a lesser extent, debate) liked the procedure better than did individuals working individualistically, and participating in a controversy consistently promoted more positive attitudes toward the experience.

Motivation to Improve Understanding

Participating in a controversy tends to have more continuing motivation to learn about the issue and come to the better reasoned judgment than does participating in concurrence seeking (ES = 68), debate (0.20), or individualistic efforts (ES = 0.59). Participants in a controversy tend to search for: (a) more information and new experiences (increased specific content), and (b) a more adequate cognitive perspective and reasoning process in hopes of resolving the uncertainty. There is also an active interest in learning others' positions and developing an understanding and appreciation of them.

Attitudes Toward Controversy

Individuals involved in controversy liked the procedure better than did individuals working individualistically (and to a lesser extent, debate), and participating in a controversy consistently promoted more positive attitudes toward the experience than did participating in a debate, concurrence-seeking discussions, or individualistic efforts (Johnson & Johnson, 2009). Controversy experiences promoted stronger beliefs that controversy is valid and valuable. Overall, individuals who engaged in controversies tended to like the controversy task better than did individuals who engaged in concurrence-seeking discussions (ES = 0.63).

Attitudes Toward Task

If participants are to be committed to implementing decisions and participate in future decision making, they must consider the decisions worth making. Individuals who engaged in controversies tended to like the decision making task better than did individuals who engaged in concurrence-seeking discussions (ES = 0.35), debate (ES = 0.84), or individualistic efforts (ES = 0.72).

Interpersonal Attraction Among Participants

Within controversy and debate there are elements of disagreement, argumentation, and rebuttal that could result in individuals disliking each other and could create difficulties in establishing good relationships. They seem, however, to have the opposite effect. Constructive controversy has been found to promote greater liking among participants than did concurrence-seeking (ES = 0.32), debate (ES = 0.67), or individualistic efforts (ES = 0.80). Debate tended to promote greater interpersonal attraction among participants than did individualistic efforts (ES = 0.46).

Social Support

Constructive controversy tends to promote greater social support among participants than does concurrence-seeking (ES = 0.50), debate (ES = 0.83), or individualistic efforts (ES = 2.18). Debate tended to promote greater social support among participants than did individualistic efforts (ES = 0.85). Constructive controversy has been found to be significantly correlated with both task support and personal support.

Self-Esteem

Participation in future controversies may be enhanced when participants feel good about themselves as a result of being involved in the current controversy, whether or not they agree with it. Constructive controversy tends to promote higher self-esteem than does concurrence-seeking (ES = 0.56), debate (ES = 0.58), or individualistic efforts (ES = 0.85). Debate tends to promote higher self-esteem than does individualistic efforts (ES = 0.45).

Psychological Health

Predisposition to engage in constructive controversy has been found to be significantly positively correlated with life satisfaction and optimistic life orientation (Tjosvold, XueHuang, Johnson, & Johnson, in press). In addition, controversy was significantly related to a sense of empowerment and egalitarianism/open-mindedness values.

Values

Participating in the controversy process implicitly teaches values such as: (a) you have both the right and the responsibility advocate your conclusions, theories, and beliefs; (b) "truth" is derived from the clash of opposing ideas and positions; (c) insight and understanding come from a "disputed passage" where ideas and conclusions are advocated and subjected to intellectual challenge; (d) issues must be viewed from all perspectives; and (e) you seek a synthesis that subsumes the seemingly opposed positions (Johnson & Johnson, 2000, 2007). In addition, it teaches hope and optimism about the future, a sense of empowerment, egalitarianism, the importance of keeping an open-mind, mutual respect and support, and respect for organizational superiors (Tjosvold, XueHuang, Johnson, & Johnson, in press).

Ability to Engage in Political Discourse

For students to be "good" citizens, they need to learn how to engage in collective decision-making about community and societal issues (Dalton, 2007). Such collective decision making is known as political discourse (Johnson & Johnson, 2000). Thomas Jefferson, James Madison, and the other founders of the American Republic considered political discourse to be the heart of democracy. The clash of opposing positions was expected to increase citizens' understanding of the issue and the quality of decision making, given that citizens would keep an open mind and change their opinions when logically persuaded to do so. When students participate in a controversy, they are also learning the procedures necessary to be citizens in a democracy. The combination of cooperative learning and constructive controversy has been used to teach students in such countries as Azerbaijan, the Czech Republic, Armenia, and Lithuania how to be citizens in a democracy (Johnson & Johnson, 2010).

Concluding Comments

It is difficult to discuss cooperative learning without discussing intellectual conflicts. The effectiveness of cooperation depends largely on the occurrence of intellectual conflict among group members and the constructiveness with which it is managed. The more cooperative learning is used, the more group members need to understand how to disagree with each other's ideas, conclusions, and opinions and challenge each other's reasoning and information in constructive ways. Students need a procedure for managing intellectual conflicts constructively. Constructive controversy is a procedure that teaches students how to improve the quality of the cooperative efforts to achieve mutual goals. The underlying theory posits that intellectual opposition will result in uncertainty, which will lead to epistemic curiosity and then to a more refined conclusion. The conditions under which controversy is effective include a cooperative context, skilled disagreement, rational argument, and active participation.

The outcomes that result include higher achievement, higher level reasoning, greater motivation to learn, greater creativity, more positive relationships, and greater self-esteem. In addition, each time students participate in a constructive controversy, they are also learning how to engage in political discourse and how to be citizens in a democracy.

References

Bligh, D. A. (2000). *What's the use of lectures*. San Francisco: Jossey-Bass.

Deutsch, M. (1973). *The resolution of conflict*. New Haven, CT: Yale University Press.

Galinsky, A. D., Maddux, W. W., Gilin, D., & White, J. B. (2008). Why it pays to get inside the head of your opponent: The differential effects of perspective taking and empathy in negotiations. Psychological Science, 19(1), 378-384.

Johnson, D. W. (2009). *Reaching out: Interpersonal effectiveness and self-actualization* (10th Ed.). Boston: Allyn & Bacon.

Johnson, D. W., & Johnson, F. (2009). *Joining together: Group theory and research* (10th Ed.). Boston: Allyn & Bacon.

Johnson, D. W., & Johnson, R. (1979). Conflict in the classroom: Controversy and learning. Review of Educational Research, 49 (1), 51-70.

Johnson, D. W., & Johnson, R. (1989) *Cooperation and Competition: Theory and Research*. Edina, MN: Interaction Book Co.

Johnson, D. W., & Johnson, R. (2000). Civil political discourse in a democracy: The contribution of psychology. *Peace and Conflict: Journal of Peace Psychology, 6*(4), 291-317.

Johnson, D. W., & Johnson, R. (2005). New developments in social interdependence theory. *Psychology Monographs, 131*(4), 285-358.

Johnson, D. W., & Johnson, R. (2007). *Creative Controversy: Intellectual conflict in the classroom* (4th ed.). Edina, MN: Interaction Book Co.

Johnson, D. W., & Johnson, R. T. (2010). Teaching diverse students who to live in a democracy. In F. Salili & R. Hoosain (Eds.), Democracy and multicultural education (pp. 201-234). Charlotte, NC: Information Age Publishing.

Johnson, D. W., Johnson, R., & Holubec, E. (2008). *Cooperation in the classroom* (8th ed.). Edina, MN: Interaction Book Company.

Johnson, D. W., & Johnson, R. (1989). *Cooperation and competition: Theory and research*. Edina, MN. Interaction Book Company.

Johnson, D. W., Johnson, R., & Smith, K. A. (2006) *Active learning: Cooperation in the college classroom*. Edina, MN. Interaction Book Company.

Kagan, S. (2010) An instructional revolution for higher education: Rationale and proposed methods. In P. Robinson & J. Cooper (Eds.), *Small group learning in higher education: Research and practice* (pp.   ). Stillwater, OK: New Forums Press.

Kagan, S. (1995). Group grades miss the mark. *Educational Leadership*, 52(8):68-71.

Kagan, S. & Kagan, M. (2009). *Kagan Cooperative Learning.* San Clemente, CA: Kagan Publishing.

Lowry, N., & Johnson, D. W. (1981). Effects of controversy on epistemic curiosity, achievement, and attitudes. Journal of Social Psychology, 115, 31–43.

National Training Laboratories Institute for Applied Behavioral Science. The Learning Pyramid. Alexandria, VA: 2006.

Pacarella, E. T., & Terenzini, P. T. (2005) *How college affects students: A third decade of research.* San Francisco: Jossey-Bass.

Slavin, R. E. (1995) *Cooperative learning: Theory, research and practice* (2nd Ed.). Needham Heights, MA: Allyn & Bacon.

Tichy, M., Johnson, D. W., Johnson, R. T., & Roseth, C. (in press). The impact of constructive controversy on moral development. Journal of Applied Social Psychology

Tjosvold, D. (1998). Cooperative and competitive goal approach to conflict: Accomplishments and challenges. Applied Psychology: An International Review, 47, 285–342.

Tjosvold, D., & Johnson, D. W. (1978). Controversy within a cooperative or competitive context and cognitive perspective taking. *Contemporary Educational Psychology, 3,* 376–386.

Tjosvold, D., XueHuang, Y., Johnson, D. W., & Johnson, R. T. (in press). Is the way you resolve conflicts related to your psychological health? An empirical investigation. Peace and Conflict: Journal of Peace Psychology.

The Missing Link: Planning for Student Engagement

Susan Johnston

In over thirty years of working in professional development with college faculty, I have consistently noticed how the lack of a specific and intentional plan to engage students during instruction often prevents instructors from meeting their goal to ensure that all students are actively processing new ideas as they are presented throughout a lesson. I have developed and field-tested a generic lesson planning template designed to ensure that students from all disciplines will be active participants in their own learning process.

This chapter will include: the planning template with guidelines, a blank form, and completed lesson example templates from two subject areas (which may be helpful for reference as readers progress through this chapter). The connection between intentional planning and student engagement is a crucial one and is often overlooked. Instructional plans that specify the knowledge to be learned— as well as when and how students will be expected to interact with that knowledge— can effectively overcome common obstacles to establishing effective student engagement, such as instructors who are overwhelmed by content coverage and students who are reluctant to participate.

The structure of the Interactive Lecture Plan is based on the rationale that students need to be presented with: a) knowledge intentionally pre-selected by instructors who teach for transfer by resisting excessive focus on content coverage, b) explicit and sufficient instruction in order to narrow the considerable gap between expert and novice, c) opportunities to be actively engaged in constructing understanding of new content throughout the entire lesson (Cooper & Johnston, 1997), and d) guided practice tasks in order to apply newly gained knowledge prior to evaluation on an exam or graded assignment. By implication, instructors then need to: a) take responsibility for selecting the most essential content (that which has maximum transfer value and is most challenging for students to understand independently), b) engage in backward planning and think like an assessor by first considering desired evidence of student learning, and c) write learning outcomes that require application of key content.

The Interactive Lecture Plan provides a coherent framework to use when planning instruction and enables instructors to resist the temptation to focus on content coverage at the expense of frequent and sufficient opportunities for student engagement during instruction. The direct instruction lecture format was initially selected as the basis for this lesson template because it is often the most familiar teaching model.

Below are specific guidelines for completing the Interactive Lecture Plan followed by a blank planning template and two subject matter examples.

Guidelines

The Interactive Lecture Plan is divided into two main sections: the Preliminary Preparation Phase and the Lesson Phases with Students. The purpose of the Preliminary Preparation Phase is to enable instructors to clarify their thinking with regard to: a) the content to be addressed in the specific lesson, and b) how students will demonstrate their understanding of that content. Without those fundamental decisions in place, focusing on the teaching strategies to be used when interacting with students is premature because effective planning requires that we first design with the end in mind (Wiggins & McTighe, 2005). The purpose of the second section of the plan, Lesson Phases with Students, is to enable instructors to clarify their thinking with regard to how the most essential content points will be sequenced and presented in order to best ensure that students will be successful when asked to demonstrate their understanding at the end of the lesson.

Preliminary Preparation Phase

Unit Title: In the Preliminary Preparation Phase, the second item is the Unit Title. The unit serves as the source for the individual lessons and is broad enough to encompass all lessons contained within that unit. Units often range from 2 to 4 lessons; topics that cluster together because of a common subject matter theme belong to the same unit. A course unit represents a large category (or chunk) of knowledge and semester courses may contain from 3 to 6 units depending on how the catalogue description, syllabus, or text organizes the material. The numbers of units and lessons in a course are also influenced by the number of class meetings each week; as the frequency of class meetings per week increases, so might the number of lessons within a unit increase. Students benefit from seeing how the major and minor topics are structured within a course, so lessons do not appear to be isolated, fragmented, and disconnected topics.

End of Unit Assessment: The third item within this phase is the *End of Unit Assessment* which describes the major ideas or procedures to be assessed as well as the type of assessment (test item, project, paper, essay, etc.) to be used to assign grades or points to students. Even if this assessment does not occur until a midterm or final exam, the content to be assessed is stated on the lesson plan well in advance of the exam to ensure that the eventual assessment is supported by the previous instruction provided to the students.

Lesson Information: The fourth item within this phase is titled Lesson Information and contains: a) the lesson title which is a very brief descriptor of the lesson's essential content, b) the lesson number within the unit sequence, and c) the number of total lessons in the unit.

Lesson Content Focus: The fifth item within this phase is the Lesson Content Focus which clearly states the essential content to be learned by students (the priority take-away big idea or skill that forms the basis of the specific lesson). The focus statement is determined by whether the lesson's final outcome will measure conceptual understanding or procedural knowledge.

Concepts are mental categories, sets, or classes with common characteristics. A concept's characteristics are its defining features. When learners construct understanding of a concept, they generalize from the characteristics. By generalizing from specific examples to describe broad categories, concepts help us simplify our world; we remember the categories instead of each individual instance. Concepts (with their definitions and critical features) are learned through the process of generalization and discrimination (using contrastive analysis of example vs. non-example or strong vs. weak example) and involves pattern recognition.

Procedures are required when we perform a series of mental or physical steps in a specific situation. Procedural knowledge reflects the expert's efficient approach to a problem or task and needs to be made explicit in order to serve as a guide to allow students to independently apply a skill. Concepts generally precede procedures in an instructional sequence. For example, the concept of editorial and its critical features would be presented prior to the demonstration of the procedure of how to write an editorial. When procedural knowledge is taught without prior related conceptual understanding, instruction lacks meaning and context. The content focus in a lesson plan will state the learning that is intended by the end of the lesson. If the endpoint of a lesson is procedural knowledge, the related concepts that first need to be addressed will be placed in the instructional points sections of the lesson plan template.

Declarative knowledge consists of factual content items. Factual information should lead to and support more important content, and because declarative knowledge cannot be applied, that type of content is rarely the endpoint of a lesson. Factual knowledge is included in a lesson to support the learning of larger conceptual or procedural understandings which can then be transferred to new scenarios or problems.

The Lesson Content Focus provides crucial clarity for the instructor who needs to plan instruction for the novice learner who cannot succeed when overwhelmed by a lesson that is packed with information delivered from an expert perspective. The content focus statement targets the most essential content within the unit topic to serve as the basis for individual lessons.

Essential Question: The sixth item within this phase is the Essential Question which requires students to reflect on their understanding of the essential content but does not ask students to practice or apply understanding in the same way that the Learning Outcome does. It provides a crucial focal point for students at the lesson's start and an opportunity for closure at the lesson's end as they are asked to consolidate their understanding. The question is not highly abstract and time-consuming; it can be answered in one or two sentences. It is carefully framed to require students to think about an essential element of what was learned in a way that demonstrates understanding and not merely recall of information. Students can record the answer in their notes at the end of class and those answers can be reviewed at the beginning of the next class session. A well structured set of lesson-based essential questions can serve as an effective study guide for students throughout the course as they prepare for midterm and final exams.

Learning Outcome: The seventh item within this phase is the Learning Outcome, a statement that describes a brief task requiring students to demonstrate their understanding by end of the lesson. The Learning Outcome is a statement of student performance that reflects what the instructor expects students to be able to do at the end of the lesson in order to provide evidence that the lesson's Content Focus has been learned.

This statement is based on the need for instructors to think like assessors and take responsibility for planning instruction "with the end in mind" prior to planning specific lecture points. The analogy of planning a vacation illustrates this point well. Without a pre-determined end destination, the traveler can only guess as to what items should be packed in the suitcase and will certainly arrive without some crucial or desired gear. Instructors who function as "curricular travel guides" for their students are engaged in a high stakes endeavor and are obligated to "pack their lessons" with only the most essential items that will best assist learners to successfully reach their learning destination. The Learning Outcome statement begins with the term Given which is followed by a description of the materials or prompts provided to students at the time of the task performance in order to provide structure and context for the practice task and is referred to as the "conditions under which the task will be performed" (Mager, 1997). Examples include: Given a new case, problem, sentence stem, graph, photograph, error in reasoning, artifact, text segment, brief article, example, conclusion, or data set, etc. (Given does not refer to or describe prior instruction just covered by the instructor, as in *Given a lecture by the teacher on the topic of soil erosion,....*)

The need for measurable student task behaviors precludes the use of verbs such as: *understand, learn, know, discuss, analyze, evaluate, appreciate, and identify.* These vague verbs lead to vague tasks causing confusion and frustration for both students and instructors. Useful task verbs (all of which have the potential to be used for lower or higher level thinking tasks) include: complete, record, solve, sort, list, support, illustrate. Selecting this type of specific task descriptor in advance enables instructors to clearly design a task that can effectively function as a practice opportunity as well as an indicator of student understanding. When the tasks in Learning Outcomes require thinking that is similar to future graded assessments, students perceive these tasks (that do not require grading by the instructor) as valuable practice opportunities that serve to prepare them for future graded exams, quizzes, or projects.

Lesson Phases with Students

Phase 1: Introduction

Many students benefit when instructors contextualize the new content and activate prior knowledge before the explanation of new content formally begins. Students are presented with a very brief real world description, scenario, case, past experience, or problem related in some way to the conceptual or procedural knowledge about to be learned. In place of technical explanations, a stimulating question is posed based on the real world context just presented in an effort to engage students by initially connecting them to the new content in a non-intimidating manner. This simple step serves to engage all students and to increase interest in the new content about to be presented. In the Introduction activity, instructors must avoid asking students questions that they could not possibly know until completion of the lesson.

Phase 2: Presentation

This phase addresses the presentation points that are required to ensure that students have sufficient information in order to successfully complete the Learning Outcome and the Essential Question found in the Preliminary Phase of the Interactive Lecture Plan. Instructors need to "deconstruct" the hoped for evidence of student learning at the end of the lesson in order to identify a logical sequence of points to present to the students. The number of points selected can typically range from four to eight, depending on the length of the class session. Each instructional point consists of three components for which instructors plan how they will: a) Explain and/or demonstrate each new content element to be introduced, b) Provide sufficient examples to establish concrete meaning for abstract content, and c) Insert brief partner Quick-Thinks that function both as checks for understanding for the instructor and as active thinking engagement tasks for the students. Guidelines for these three components include the following:

a. Explain/demonstrate each new content element to be learned. Each instructional point represents a subtopic the instructor must explain so students gain the requisite knowledge to successfully complete the task in the Learning Outcome. Therefore, instructors need to provide sufficient instruction that relates directly to the content in the Lesson Content Focus statement. Another challenge for instructors is to effectively plan and sequence the explanations in a manner appropriate for novice learners who are unfamiliar with the content and to avoid the assumption that students have somehow managed to gain deep understanding of the lesson's content from assigned textbook readings or from previous coursework.

b. Provide sufficient examples. Unless abstract explanations are accompanied by concrete and specific examples, students will fail to derive meaning from a presentation. Examples can be visual, auditory, or kinesthetic in nature. Instructors who succumb to the perils of content coverage will often omit the very examples so desperately needed by novices who struggle to make sense of the potentially meaningless theories, definitions, and rules often rapidly presented by expert instructors.

c. Insert Quick-thinks. These are tasks or questions that are tightly structured, very brief, and directly connected to the corresponding explanation. Quick-Thinks function as both instructor checks for understanding and as brief student engagement tasks. Because all students need to be actively engaged and thinking throughout the lesson, partner collaboration on Quick-Thinks following each explanatory point can effectively support this goal. This strategy is a low-risk instructional intervention that has the power to transform the classroom from a passive to an engaged learning environment. Students are held accountable for participation while being given a safe opportunity for cognitive processing as each new element in the lecture is presented.

In addition to instructor generated questions, Quick-Think options include eight generic forms that can be applied across disciplines: Select The Best Response, Correct the Error, Complete a Sentence Starter, Compare or Contrast, Support a Statement, Reorder the Steps, Reach a Conclusion, and Paraphrase the Idea (Cooper & Johnston, 1997). The key to effective implementation of Quick-Thinks is to shift from the traditional questioning strategy of posing the question to the entire class, then calling on volunteers, to the strategy of posing the question to the entire class, then requiring all students to collaborate with their work partners to answer the question. Instructors who have effectively made this shift, report a remarkable transformation in student participation, engagement, and content understanding (Mazur, 1997).

Phase 3: Guided Practice

The Guided Practice task in Phase 3 is an exact match with the task described in the lesson's Learning Outcome previously entered above in the Preliminary Preparation Phase. Phase 3 is where students actually perform the task. This element was included in the lesson plan format to ensure that students would actually be asked to complete the Learning Outcome task within the context of the lesson instead of for homework, hence the label guided practice vs. independent practice. A well-designed Guided Practice task serves as a final check for understanding for both instructors and students. Because grades/points are inappropriate when students are initially applying new understandings, this Guided Practice task is designed to serve as a formative assessment (diagnostic in nature) as opposed to a summative assessment (evaluative in nature). Phase 3 allows instructors to monitor and support students and to provide helpful feedback even if the task is a brief one. Some lessons take more than one day to complete if instruction or the practice task requires more time.

Phase 4: Consolidation

In this phase, students are given the opportunity to reflect on their learning by answering the Essential Question that served as a focus for students throughout the class session. In Phase 4 of the plan, instructors need not record the Essential Question, but record their selection of one of the following strategies: a) Whole class discussion followed by students recording individual answers, b) Individuals record answers and then share with partner, and c) Partners discuss potential answers and then individually record answers. Which option to implement may depend on the confidence level of the learners. Many students appreciate the option to engage in dialogue with their partners prior to recording their answers. Novice learners benefit from conversation using academic terminology in order to process and integrate their understanding of unfamiliar concepts and procedures. If time permits, some partners might volunteer to read their answers to the class so the instructor can provide affirmation or modification as necessary. Some instructors ask students to write their answers under the Essential Question recorded at the top of their notes, while others have students keep ongoing learning logs in their course notebooks that provide effective course summaries of essential content that can be used as study guides for quizzes and exams.

Shown on the following are the Interactive Lecture Plan blank template and two examples applied to lesson topics in Sociology and English courses.

References

Cooper, J. & Johnston, S. (1997). Quick-thinks: The interactive lecture. *Cooperative Learning and College Teaching, 8*(1), 2-6: Stillwater, OK: New Forums Press.

Mager, R. F. (1997). Preparing instructional objectives: A critical tool in the development of effective instruction, 3rd ed. Atlanta: Center for Effective Performance.

Mazur, E., (1997). *Peer instruction: A user's manual,* Upper Saddle River, NJ: Prentice Hall.

Wiggins, G., & McTighe, J., (2005). *Understanding by design* (2nd ed.). Alexandria, Virginia: Association for Supervision and Curriculum Development (ASCD).

Interactive Lecture Plan Blank Template

Preliminary Preparation Phase		
Course		
Unit Title (Lesson Source)		
End of Unit Assessment		
Lesson Information	**Lesson Title:**	**Lesson # within unit:**
		Number of total lessons in unit:
Lesson Content Focus: Conceptual or Procedural knowledge statement.	**Discipline Content: (Conceptual ___ Procedural ___)**	
Essential Question: Question for reflecting on essential content presented at start of lesson, but answered in Phase 4.		
Learning Outcome: Describes task requiring students to demonstrate their understanding by end of the lesson.	Given , students will be able to	
Lesson Phases with Students		
Phase 1: Introduction: Contextualize new content & activate prior knowledge.	Strategy to contextualize new content and activate prior knowledge:	
Phase 2: Presentation a. Explain/demonstrate each new content element to be learned. b. Provide sufficient examples. c. Insert Quick-Thinks that function both as checks for understanding and as brief student engagement tasks.	Point #1	a.
		b.
		c.
	Point #2	a.
		b.
		c.
	Point #3	a.
		b.
		c.
	Point #4	a.
		b.
		c.
Phase 3: Guided Practice: Statement describing task requiring students to demonstrate their understanding by end of the lesson. Matches Learning Outcome above.		
Phase 4: Consolidation Students answer the **Essential Question** posed at start of lesson.)	Strategy for answering the essential question:	

Interactive Lecture Plan -- Sociology Example

Preliminary Preparation Phase		
Course	Introduction to Sociology	
Unit Title (Lesson Source)	Basic Concepts of Sociology	
End of Unit Assessment	Unit exam: Write captions with correct terminology to explain 10 different real world scenarios.	
Lesson Information	**Lesson Title:** Society's Glue: Relationships, Rules, and Responsibilities	**Lesson # within unit:** 1 **Number of total lessons in unit:** 3
Lesson Content Focus: Conceptual or procedural knowledge statement.	Discipline Content: (Conceptual X Procedural ___) Societies can function in spite of competing individual differences when relationships, rules, and responsibilities are clearly established.	
Essential Question: Question for reflecting on essential content presented at start of lesson, but answered in Phase 4.	How can our college function as a community when the members (instructors, students, and staff) vary so widely in their belief systems, economic status, family structure, gender, age, ethnicity, nationality, etc.?	
Learning Outcome: Statement describing task requiring students to demonstrate their understanding by end of the lesson.	Given two newspaper articles (one describing a successful interaction with people of varying interests/backgrounds and one describing a violent interaction), students will be able to write one explanation for each event using the following terms: relationships, rules, and responsibilities.	

(continued on page 128)

Interactive Lecture Plan -- Sociology Example (continued)

Lesson Phases with Students		
Phase 1: Introduction Contextualize new content and activate prior knowledge.		**Strategy to contextualize new content and activate prior knowledge:** Ask partners to list differences they have noticed among members of the campus community. Several pairs volunteer to share ideas with class.
Phase 2: Presentation a. Explain/demonstrate each new content element to be learned. b. Provide sufficient examples. c. Insert Quick-Thinks that function both as checks for understanding and as brief student engagement tasks.	Point #1	a. Explain that the discipline of sociology is the study of society and social groups: how societies establish social order. The following features provide "social glue" when members of a group have different cultures/status/values/etc.: Relationships, Rules, and Responsibilities.
		b. Show on a matrix with columns for each of the "3 R's" above, examples of student behaviors (attendance, cooperation, homework, effort expended) influenced by those features. Volunteers participate also.
		c. All students (with partners) record one additional student behavior that could be added to each category in the matrix. Several share with class.
	Point #2	a. Explain that relationships often bind individuals together because common group values and status differences establish certain norms of behavior for the individuals within a relationship.
		b. Use the following campus relationships as examples: student/teacher, office manager/staff, deans/instructors. Lead discussion of how behavior within each different relationship is influenced by status, values, and norms.
		c. All students (with partners) record an example of campus behavior (seen or experienced) that has been influenced by a relationship. Several share with class.
	Point #3	a. Explain that rules are externally imposed sanctions that govern individuals' behaviors within a community. Violation of the rules carry a punishment or penalty.
		b. Lead discussion of examples of rules within the college community and impact on the community when rules are both obeyed and violated.
		c. All students (with partners) record examples of one rule that they think has maximum and one that has minimal impact on the functioning of the community. Several share with class.
	Point #4	a. Explain that responsibilities are assumed by individuals in a civil society who choose to act in a manner that reflects respect for the interests and collective life of the community.
		b. Provide examples of responsible and irresponsible behavior and impact of each on the collective life of a community.
		c. All students tell partners one example of students within the college community engaging in both responsible and irresponsible behavior. Several student volunteers share with class.
Phase 3: Guided Practice Statement describing task requiring students to demonstrate their understanding by end of the lesson. Matches Learning Outcome above.		Given two newspaper articles (one describing a successful interaction with people of varying interests/backgrounds and one describing a violent interaction), students will be able to write one explanation for each event using the concepts: Relationships, Rules, and Responsibilities.
Phase 4: Consolidation Students answer the Essential Question posed at start of lesson.)		**Strategy for answering the essential question:** Student partners discuss and agree on the three key terms to include in their written homework answer. (Instructor will call on students randomly to share their answers at next class session).

Interactive Lecture Plan – English Example

Preliminary Preparation Phase		
Course	English 57 – Basic Reading and Writing	
Unit Title (Lesson Source)	The Art of Persuasion (3 class sessions)	
End of Unit Assessment	Persuasive essay to convince someone to take action.	
Lesson Information	**Lesson Title:** Opinions & Evidence	**Lesson # within unit:** 2
		Number of total lessons in unit: 3
Lesson Content Focus Conceptual or procedural knowledge statement.	**Discipline Content:** (Conceptual ___ Procedural X) How to use evidence to support an opinion.	
Essential Question Question for reflecting on essential content presented at start of lesson, but answered in Phase 4.	How does the use of logical evidence to support your opinion affect your ability to persuade others?	
Learning Outcome Statement describing task requiring students to demonstrate their understanding by end of the lesson.	Given a hot topic from campus life with data related to the issue, students will be able to write a statement of opinion and provide three supporting evidence statements.	

Lesson Phases with Students		
Phase 1: Introduction Contextualize new content and activate prior knowledge.	**Strategy to contextualize new content and activate prior knowledge:** Read a recent editorial from the LA Times out loud. Ask all students to signal agreement or disagreement with the writer's message and then tell their partners one thing they heard that influenced their decision.	
Phase 2: Presentation a. Explain/demonstrate each new content element to be learned. b. Provide sufficient examples. c. Insert Quick-Thinks that function both as checks for understanding and as brief student engagement tasks.	**Point #1**	a. Explain distinction between fact and opinion: facts can be verified and opinions cannot.
		b. Show facts and opinions from a new editorial.
		c. Display a mixed list of 5 facts/opinions and have partners number to 5 in notes and label each item as fact or opinion.
	Point #2	a. Explain that opinion statements must be clearly stated for the reader.
		b. Show a strong and a weak example (an opinion statement that is clear and one that is vague).
		c. Ask partners to tell each other how the weak example could be improved and have some volunteers share with class.
	Point #3	a. Explain that persuasive opinions require supporting evidence. Discuss criteria for convincing evidence.
		b. Show a strong and a weak example (an opinion supported by facts and an opinion supported only by more opinions and unverifiable claims).
		c. Ask partners to tell each other how the weak example could be improved and have some volunteers share with class.
	Point #4	a. Explain that opinion statements and evidence need to flow logically.
		b. Show a strong and a weak example of opinion with evidence in logical order.
		c. Ask partners to tell each other how the weak example could be improved and have some volunteers share with class.
Phase 3: Guided Practice Statement describing task requiring students to demonstrate their understanding.	Given a hot topic from campus life with data related to the issue, students will be able to write a statement of opinion and provide three supporting evidence statements.	
Phase 4: Consolidation Students answer the Essential Question posed at start of lesson.	**Strategy for answering the essential question:** Partners discuss possible responses and then record individual answers in their notes under the pre-recorded essential question.	

Faculty Learning Communities as Catalysts for Implementing Successful Small Group Learning

Cynthia G. Desrochers

Last year, as I attended a national conference of predominantly faculty developers, I was reminded how it feels to be in a poorly run small group learning activity. Ours was a group of five all seated in one row along one side of a table. The task was to categorize 30 items listed on one sheet of paper. The paper was given to the person farthest from me at the opposite end of our group. Initially, I attempted to bend forward in order to participate, but I still couldn't read the paper; in addition, one individual quickly dominated our group by barking out her category selections in a competitive manner to beat the rest of us. After a few minutes, I sat back in my chair—smoldering just a bit—until the group task was completed. I thought it puzzling that the session facilitator was the director of a university center for teaching and learning, yet she gave no guidelines for accomplishing the small-group task, such as encouraging all groups to sit in a circle and placing the paper in the center, including everyone in the discussion, and equalizing talking and listening.

How could this scenario occur? I am a founding director of a teaching and learning center and have come to realize that one-shot workshops on topics as complex as teaching and learning rarely produce faculty change. The workshop continues to be the standard program offering of many teaching and learning centers. This is even more surprising when considering that almost 30 years ago Joyce and Showers alerted the education community to this problem. In their study of the transfer of training from staff development sessions, they found that only a small percentage of an innovation was transferred from a workshop setting to classroom practice without the presence of these components: (a) study of the theoretical basis of a teaching method; (b) demonstrations by persons who are relatively expert in the teaching method; (c) practice and feedback in protected conditions; and (d) coaching one another as individuals work the new teaching method into their repertoire, providing companionship, helping one another to learn appropriate responses, and figuring out optimal uses of the teaching method (1983).

Over the past four years, many of our 23 teaching and learning centers in the California State University (CSU) system have created faculty learning communities (FLCs) to promote changes in faculty teaching practices that are not typically attainable from even the best one-shot workshop. I posit here that the components called for by Joyce and Showers occur within a well-run FLC.

In status reports on the use of small group learning, experts in the field continue to raise concerns that although this powerful intervention is generally well accepted, there are still obstacles to its wider use among faculty (Cooper, Ball, & Robinson, 2009). And although both Karl Smith and Barbara Millis call for faculty to engage in conversations and collaborations with like-minded colleagues about their use of group work, they fall short of recommending FLCs. I submit that small group learning for college students parallels small group FLC learning for faculty and is perhaps the missing faculty development link for overcoming obstacles to faculty change.

Moreover, based on our CSU experiences with FLCs, this chapter encourages college leaders who are interested in developing small group learning expertise among faculty to use FLCs as the vehicle to develop and internalize the requisite skills to accomplish this. This chapter further presents a concise *Faculty Developers' Guide* for FLC implementation in order to provide initial direction for establishing small group learning FLCs, addressing the following key issues: (1) the research base for using small group learning with college students and for using small group FLC learning with college faculty; (2) suggestions for FLC structure, incentives, curriculum, activities, assessments, deliverables, and facilitation; (3) small group learning structures and teaching tips; and (4) resources on both FLCs and small group learning.

FLCs and the Miami University Projects

The concept FLCs as an approach to faculty development was developed by Milt Cox at Miami University in 1979. Initially created to develop the teaching abilities of junior faculty through a Lilly Endowment grant, national interest in FLCs was generated in 2001-2004 through support from the Fund for the Improvement of Postsecondary Education (FIPSE). In the 2003-2004 academic year, Richlin and Essington identified 132 institutions hosting 308 FLCs across the United States and Canada (Beach & Cox, 2009).

Typically, FLCs consist of a cross-disciplinary faculty group of 8-14 members, engaged in a yearlong curriculum focused on exploring a specific issue. There are two types of FLCs, cohort-based and topic-based. Cohort-based groups share the same cohort attributes, such as all being junior faculty, senior faculty, or department chairs. These FLCs collaboratively study the unique developmental needs of their cohort (Cox, 2001). However, for the purpose of this chapter, our focus is the topic-based FLCs, and the topic theme is *implementing successful small group learning in our college classrooms*.

A recent review of the impact of FLCs, published in the first volume and issue of the *Learning Communities Journal*, reported the outcomes of a large-scale survey of FLC participants, including their perceived changes in their teaching and their students' learning as a result of their FLC participation. There were responses from 395 faculty at six universities, with 79% reporting that student learning was improved and 73% reporting changes in their beliefs and attitudes about teaching (Beach & Cox, 2009).

What might account for the success of FLCs over traditional workshops includes the components of theory, modeling, practice and feedback stressed by Joyce and Showers, as well as the community/social structure of FLCs. Beach and Cox (2009) describe the benefits of FLCs when compared with other forms for faculty development (e.g., workshops, brown bags, and teaching circles) as FLCs being more: (a) structured, (b) intensive, (c) focused on completing the deliverables, (d) focused on the social aspects of building community, (e) focused on the scholarship of teaching and learning, and (f) focused on the team aspect while developing individual projects. In addition, the process of working on individual projects deeply engages each community member in efforts that may include: (a) trying out a new pedagogy and assessing the student learning that results from its use; (b) revising a course and assessing the results; (c) creating a new course, teaching it, and assessing the results; or (d) action research in a course, followed by presentations of results at conferences. It should come as no surprise to the reader that, much as small group learning with students builds community and positive social learning gains, so do FLCs with faculty.

To further support FLCs as an effective faculty-development practice for implementing small group learning, the spring 2005 FLC FIPSE grant follow-up survey conducted by the external evaluator found that the FLC themes that faculty perceived as resulting in the greatest changes in student learning involved active, student-centered, and group learning (Beach & Cox, 2009). Where 4.0 indicated *substantial amount* and 3.0 indicated *moderate amount* in changed student learning, the data revealed the following:

Teaching and Learning Approach	Mean	SD	Total
Active learning	4.07	1.06	244
Student-centered learning	3.99	1.05	236
Cooperative or collaborative learning	3.84	1.13	236

The California State University Projects

In fall 2006, Sonoma State, one of 23 CSU campuses, was working on a U. S. Department of Education grant to implement Universal Design for Learning at Sonoma and six other CSU campuses, in order to increase access for college students with disabilities. At approximately the same time, the CSU was also awarded a FIPSE grant to develop digital-case stories on various pedagogical themes to be used in faculty development. An unexpected nexus occurred between the two grants when faculty involved in the FIPSE grant decided to used Universal Design for Learning as their digital-case pedagogical theme. Moreover, after a two-day FIPSE-group meeting regarding the creation of Universal Design for Learning digital cases, participants recognized that this theme was so complex that its implementation would require in-depth engagement over time; hence, the CSU Institute for Teaching and Learning suggested that each campus form FLCs and offered to fund stipends of $500 per person, January to June, 2007.

Because I was personally involved in the early stages of the FIPSE digital-case project as the faculty development lead, I previewed the project at the Southern California Faculty Developers' June 2007 meeting at CSU Long Beach, asking the eight faculty developers present what information they would deem essential for a *Faculty Developers' Guide*. The following four components were unanimously suggested by these center directors, representing two University of California campuses, three CSUs, and three private colleges:

1. The literature base for the pedagogical theme, emphasizing its impact on student learning.
2. A condensed summary of the basic vocabulary, concepts, and information associated with the pedagogical theme.
3. Suggested learning outcomes, learning activities, and assessments.
4. An online commons for faculty to discuss their use of the pedagogical theme.

The first three components were subsequently incorporated into the *Faculty Developers' Workshop Guide* for the digital case in production, and the fourth item, an online commons, was developed for the entire FIPSE project. Because of the positive feedback from the FIPSE grant's *Workshop Guide*, the first three components are either directly included in the following *Faculty Developers' FLC Guide* or are listed in the *References and Resources* end-section for further study. However, because the digital cases were conceived as a faculty development *workshop* tool, as opposed to an *FLC* tool, where bi-weekly face-to-face gatherings are a key component, it is less essential to develop an online commons during the period of time in which an FLC is actively meeting.

Faculty Developers' FLC Guide on Using Small Group Learning

Pedagogical Theme

Successful Use of Small Group Learning in College Classrooms

Literature Base

The use of small group learning, a term synonymous with cooperative learning for the purposes of this *FLC Guide*, has a strong research base associating its use with student achievement and success. Among the numerous studies, three offer significant insights.

- Walberg (1984) studied the effect of selected alterable variables on student achievement. The effect size for cooperative learning was .80 with a percentile equivalent of 79. This indicates that under cooperative learning instruction, the average student is above 79% of the students in the control teaching conditions.

- Many of the *Seven Principles for Good Practice in Undergraduate Education* (Chickering & Gamson, 1987) are fulfilled when using small group learning, specifically: student-faculty contact, cooperation among students, active learning, prompt feedback, and respect for diverse talents and ways of learning.

- Astin (1993) conducted a comprehensive longitudinal study of the impact of attending college on undergraduate students, looking at factors that determine influences on students' academic achievement, personal development, and satisfaction with the college. He found that student-to-faculty and student-to-student interaction had the greatest impact on general education outcomes. For the commuter students on our urban campuses, it is likely that for many the only student-to-student interactions they experience are in small group learning classroom settings, as they hurriedly race from work, to school, to class, to home.

Vocabulary, Concepts, and Information[2]

- Small Group learning, also called cooperative learning, is a form of interactive learning among two or more students to complete a common task. Many teachers prefer to design four-person groups, seated in a circle facing one another, where all group members can focus on both the task and each another. Odd-numbered groups should be monitored for inclusion, as they increase the likelihood of producing an "odd man out" when individuals lean towards forming pairs.

- There are many small group structures, each defined by a set of student actions and interactions that are designed to promote small group learning. These structures fall on a continuum from simple structures (e.g., Think-Pair-Share) to complex structures (e.g., Jigsaw) in their degree of complexity of steps, social interaction, classroom organization, student responsibility, and time to complete.

- The formation of student groups also falls on a continuum from student selected, to random, to teacher-designed. Teacher-designed groups are typically formed with the intent of establishing within-group heterogeneity and between-groups talent-balance.

---

[2] This summary of small-group learning represents my interpretation of the dozens of articles and books I have read over the last 25 years, as well as my participation in dozens of workshops, on occasion as a participant, but more frequently as the workshop leader. However, if I were to cite one person whose resources most shaped my understanding, it would be Spencer Kagan's workshops and books, especially the book *Cooperative Learning*.

However, with cause, grouping by any desired attribute may be prescribed (e.g., grouping less-chatty students together so they have greater opportunity to be heard). Random groups can be accomplished by having students count off. To do this easily, divide the size of class by the size of the group desired, and ask students to count off by the quotient (e.g., in a class of 40, where groups of 4 are desired, divide 40 by 4, to yield 10, and then ask students to count off by 10, forming 10 groups of 4), or distribute playing cards and ask students to find their like number (e.g., the 4 suits for each number equal a group of 4), or use another creative grouping method drawn from course content (e.g., excerpts from Shakespearian plays, where students locate group mates who have excerpts from the same play).

- Key elements of successful small group learning include positive interdependence, individual accountability, and attention to social skills.
  > Positive interdependence is essential because small group learning stresses cooperation among group mates as compared with other situations that are designed to foster student competition with one another (e.g., running a 5K race to beat the other runners) or with yourself (e.g., running a 5K race to beat your personal best time). Positive interdependence can be established by designing a task so that each group member's success enhances the success of the entire group—captured in the image of "We all swim, or sink, together." Positive interdependence is often built into a small group structure. For example, in the Numbered-Heads Together structure, small groups are typically asked a higher-order-thought question that has a convergent answer and given sufficient time to discuss it. This is followed by one person from the group being randomly called upon to provide the group's answer. This practice encourages students both to share information they possess and to listen to the information provided by others, given the 25% chance that they will be randomly selected to report for their group. This motivation to share and listen for the good of the group is called positive interdependence.
  > Individual accountability refers to each learner attaining the course learning outcomes. The opposite of individual accountability occurs when one student does the majority of the work, while the others hitch-hike, contributing little and showing no evidence of learning, but all receive the same group grade. This scenario likely explains why some students wince when a small-group project is announced. However, unfair group-grading practices can easily be prevented through projects designed with individual accountability. It may be useful to think of the wording: small group learning and cooperative learning are both modifiers for how students are learning. But when the time comes for final testing, each individual student must demonstrate his or her learning. This can be accomplished in a variety of ways in classrooms where small group learning occurs. Three examples include:

  1. Limit small group learning to the use of simple structures that are not graded.
  2. Use complex small-group structures, followed by an individual assessment activity where each student is asked to integrate the contributions of all group members into an essay, outline, graphic, or on an exam.
  3. Assign group projects that require a substantial amount of research, integration, planning, and a culminating class presentation. Consider implementing some of the following tactics: help orchestrate virtual meetings for working-commuter students to connect outside of class (e.g., wiki, blog, Google.docs, and teleconference); ask students to keep track of the group roles each fulfills and a time-spent-on-project record; periodically during class, ask groups to give each other feedback on individual contributions to both the task and social well-being of the group (this can be done anonymously); use low-stakes grading on the project (pass/fail), but give letter grades for individual reports submitted by each group member on his or her individual sub-topics for the project.

  > Small group social skills encompass the myriad human behaviors that can make or break a group's effort to work together in order to solve a learning problem. Social skills include talking, listening, asking and giving help, encouraging others, gently querying reticent group mates, acknowledging the good ideas of others, recapping messages in order to affirm clarity, staying on task, summarizing where the group has been and where it still needs to go, and so on. It may be assumed that most college-aged students should already have these skills, but experience shows otherwise. Three methods of addressing social skills include:

1. Embed social-skill suggestions in each structure as you teach it. When explaining the steps for a small-group structure, embed some social steps as well. These may include asking each group of four to form a square (either by moving their chairs, or by two students moving to the other side of a table, or by two students turning around in their theatre-style seats), equalize talking and other forms of participation, include everyone's ideas, and ask for and give help as needed. And then it is wise for the teacher to circulate among the students in order to capture a few good examples of groups behaving nicely in order to report back to the total class without attribution to any one group; this way, many groups will surmise that you caught them in these good social acts and appreciate your nod.
2. Role-play appropriate and inappropriate social skills. Briefly role-play examples of good listening behavior and perhaps a humorous inappropriate example, asking a willing student to tell you the plot of the last movie he saw while you playfully yawn and look inattentively at your watch.
3. Debrief social dynamics at the middle or end of group-project sessions, in small-groups or with the whole class, and publicly or anonymously.

Briefly check the functioning of groups in order to air valid grievances and provide suggestions before problems fester. A few simple questions often suffice: What are we doing well as a group? What are we doing as a group that may be hindering our progress on the tasks at hand? What group rules should we implement in order to improve our group's functioning?

Now, to offer a word of comfort to the teacher who laments those small-group discussions that are too social and roam off-topic: students who are not working in small groups, but appear to be quietly listening to your lecture, may in fact be off-topic as they think about the latest pop-culture topic and daydream right through your eloquent prose. The difference in a lecture situation is that you have scant physical evidence of students' lack of engagement until the exam. Bottom line: humans go off-task when interesting thoughts enter their brains or too much time is devoted to a non-engaging task. Hence, it is probably wise to hit the repeat and recap buttons periodically when using any pedagogy.

And lastly, social skills are a topic of concern to many, at work, at play, and on the highway. If you have ever muttered under your breath that so-and-so clearly has never learned how to act civilly, acknowledge that this same so-and-so may be in your college classroom, and your efforts to promote student civility will allow other students to learn in a prosocial environment.

FLC Organization and the Call for Faculty Participation

Although FLCs typically last a year, a small group learning FLC can produce results in six months because this theme involves modifications of instructional delivery, learning activities, and formative assessments (i.e., processes), and many faculty, when they begin using small group learning, do so without altering their curriculum, final student products, or syllabus.

The Call for Participation inviting faculty to join an FLC on small group learning should be specific in terms of meeting dates and times, responsibilities, and deliverables in order to avoid scheduling conflicts and misunderstandings later, but loose enough to allow for members' input and subsequent buy-in to this community process. The Call might include the following:

1. **Timeline**
   This should include the *exact* dates and times of all FLC gatherings so faculty can determine if their schedule fits with the FLC's and mark on their calendars the FLC gatherings far in advance.

2. **Skeletal FLC Agenda Sample**
   Up to eight faculty will meet face-to-face with the FLC facilitator for two hours on six separate occasions from January to June, culminating in a four-hour session where each FLC member will share his/her results with the community in a 30-minute presentation, followed by a provost-hosted luncheon at the Faculty Development Center.
   #1: Introductions and sharing of small group learning resources for at-home study
   #2: Guest speaker(s); discuss resources
   #3: Plan for projects; classroom implementation
   #4: Share/discuss individual progress
   #5: Share/discuss individual progress
   #6: Share/discuss individual progress
   #7: Project presentations (30-minute final reports by all eight community members)

3. **Application and Selection Suggestions**

Faculty might be asked to write a one-page essay describing their instructional methods, problems or concerns they have about student learning, and why they would like to join this FLC. A simple check-off and sign sheet on the Application to Participate should determine that participants are teaching during the January to June timeframe of the FLC, plan to contribute to the community, are open to new ideas, can participate during the dates of the project, and have discussed with their department chair the FLC deliverable of sharing results with their academic department.

4. **Small Group Learning Project — Sample Deliverables**

In addition to the learning assignments/activities and classroom practice agreed upon by the FLC members, each FLC member:

a. Gives a 30-minute final presentation to the FLC, sharing classroom findings.
b. Shares findings at a departmental meeting.
c. Submits a 500- to 750-word article summarizing findings to the FLC facilitator; select articles will appear in the Teaching and Learning newsletter to be distributed campus-wide.

5. **Incentives**

Although many faculty would likely join an FLC for the intrinsic rewards, and others would join only if they were given 3-units released time, we have taken the middle road and offered a $500 professional development stipend to each faculty member upon his or her completion of the deliverables and a final project.

FLC Faculty Learning Outcomes

Throughout the duration of this FLC (six months is suggested), faculty will be supported as they:

1. Design small groups (2-4 students) to complete classroom learning tasks together using simple and complex structures.
2. Incorporate key elements of successful small-group work, including
   a. Positive interdependence
   b. Individual accountability
   c. Social skills (e.g., inclusion, equal participation, and mutual support).
3. Assess the efficacy of small group learning in their classrooms, using simple classroom assessment techniques, such as Minute Papers, to determine how students are learning in small groups (Angelo & Cross, 1993).
4. Revise to improve the use of small group learning in their classrooms.
5. Share interim results with the FLC at bi-weekly gatherings.
6. Deliver individual project final results in a 30-minute presentation to the FLC.
7. Prepare a final written report (500-750 words) to submit to the FLC facilitator.
8. Make presentations to local, regional, and national audiences.

FLC Curriculum, Learning Activities, and Assessments

The small group learning FLC curriculum includes a variety of small group learning structures. Below is a starter toolbox of eight structures. The first seven are considered to be simple structures, with the last structure, Jigsaw, classified as complex. [For additional structures, see References and Resources at the end of this chapter.] Note that because structures are content-free, faculty are challenged to find authentic disciplinary issues/problems and format the structures to them in purposeful ways that will illustrate to students that two or more heads are better than one.

1. **Think-Pair-Share**

This simple structure is likely the most familiar and a starting point for teachers who have never used small group learning. It can be used to solve problems in mathematics, economics, or chemistry, as well as to generate possible solutions for political, environmental, or educational issues. For a thorough analysis of this structure, see Millis & Cottell, 1998.
   1. Problem posed by teacher.
   2. Think time occurs.
   3. Pairs work together to solve the problem.
   4. A few pair solutions are shared with total class.

2. **Think-Ink-Pair-Square**

This is a variation of Think-Pair-Share. Teachers are encouraged to see how structures are built from a set of student actions and interactions, and they should feel free to modify structures to fit their students' learning needs.
   1. Problem posed by teacher.
   2. Individuals write responses.
   3. Pairs share and discuss responses.
   4. Pairs meet with another pair (a square) and share and discuss responses.

3. **RoundRobin**

   This structure involves students sharing information to solve a learning task. They might each be asked to give a separate incident from the class novel that demonstrates the main character's unwarranted distrust of others.
   1. Students grouped in 3s or 4s, count off.
   2. Teacher gives the learning task.
   3. Students take turns orally contributing in order.

4. **Three-step Interview**

   This structure is a not only useful get-acquainted activity, but also an outstanding method for having students share (and learn from) completed individual assignments prior to submitting them (e.g., original narratives and reports, research articles, current event summaries, service-learning experiences, and artistic products).

   Although labeled as three steps, it is beneficial for the instructor to insert two additional steps at the beginning: (1) Discuss how a good interview is conducted, encouraging the interviewer to pose a question and then listen to the interviewee. Role-play an inappropriate interview where a TV personality keeps interrupting the guest. (2) Allow time for students to draft 3-5 appropriate interview questions.
   1. Students pair up and one in each pair interviews the other.
   2. At the teacher's signal, students reverse roles.
   3. At the teacher's signal, the pairs square with another pair, making a foursome, and RoundRobin share what they learned in their interview of the other person. This promotes listening and learning from others.

5. **Numbered-heads Together**

   This structure works well when: (a) it is used to check understanding of higher-order thinking, (b) the answer has multiple parts, and (c) answers are divergent.
   1. Students seated in groups of four, number off 1, 2, 3, 4.
   2. Teacher presents a problem and asks students to put their heads together to solve it.
   3. Group-discussion time occurs.
   4. One number is randomly called (e.g., number 4), and that person answers for his or her group. For problems with multiple parts, different groups can give one part. If there is only one answer, one number 4 responds and then the other number 4s may be asked to agree/disagree or to add to the response.

6. **Send-a-Problem**

   This structure gives each small group the opportunity to write review questions to trade and solve with another group, perhaps in preparation for an exam. To increase the complexity of this structure, see Millis, 2008, pp. 159-161. [This Millis article is an excellent FLC group reading selection, particularly for teachers with prior experience using small group learning.]
   1. Students grouped in 3s or 4s write a high-consensus verifiable course-review question on a separate 3 x 5 card (e.g., Who is considered the father of psychoanalysis?).
   2. Group members test the clarity of their questions with group mates, revise as needed, and write a final question on one side of the card and the answer on the other.
   3. Group questions are stacked and clipped together and sent to another group to solve as a group by reading each question aloud, solving together, and checking the answer when all agree to do so.
   3. If needed, groups send diplomats to a question's author in order to solicit additional information.
   5. After answers are checked, the receiving group writes a comment on the answer side of each card, indicating their agreement or disagreement with the original answer. The cards are then returned to the groups of origin or to another group to solve.

7. **Categorizing with Post-Its**

   This structure promotes a visual group analysis of a course issue, and requires small Post-It pads, large sheets of chart paper, masking tape, and markers.
   1. Students, grouped in 4s, brainstorm ideas on an announced topic, write one idea per Post-It. [Example topic: list ways to improve the K-12 public schools.]
   2. Striving for a dozen or more ideas on Post-Its, students then categorize their ideas in groupings they can justify on a large piece of chart paper, labeling each category.
   3. Completed charts are posted around the room and one group member from each group remains with the chart as the chart explainer while the rest of the group gallery walks around the entire room to study the other charts. Charts are accessible during break for the chart explainers to view other charts.

8. **Jigsaw**
   Designed by Elliot Aronson, Jigsaw is a division of labor strategy that is particularly useful in getting students to read the assigned chapters of a text. In this scenario, each student in the foursome specializes in one of four chapters and studies it in order to teach its contents to his or her group mates, after which all group members are responsible for understanding all four chapters. To assess individual accountability, each student completes an integration-of-chapters assignment alone. This may sound a lot like the age-old graduate school study group — or a pot-luck dinner — where you are responsible for only a piece of the puzzle, but ultimately view the entire picture!
   1. If using small groups of four, the teacher divides the material to be "jigsawed" into four equal parts in terms of length and complexity, assuring that each part is independently comprehensible to the reader.
   2. Each student in a heterogeneous home group is assigned a different part to independently study in order to master key concepts and then teach them to group mates. At the initial introduction of Jigsaw to a class, consider teaching the Jigsaw process by using four one-page information sheets and guiding students through all the Jigsaw steps during a class session. Allow sufficient time for students to master their sheets, design a teaching strategy, and then teach the concepts from all four sheets to group mates.
   3. Each student independently completes an instructor-designed integration assignment that requires using the concepts from all four sheets.

An alternate form, Expert-group Jigsaw, increases student interaction and complexity. In this version students with the same parts are asked to meet as experts to discuss their mastery of key concepts and teaching strategies before they meet with their original group to teach their parts. Students learn to appreciate the insights of others in expert groups and are often reluctant to select the first version of Jigsaw over this modification in the future.

Two teaching tips: (1) When using either form of Jigsaw with large classes, reproduce the four sheets on four different colors of paper and ask students to form rainbow or like-color groups when meeting as home or expert groups. (2) Always give students access to all of the material, not just their own parts, so that all can check the accuracy of what's being presented by group mates.

Additional Learning Activities

In addition to the activities that are offered as FLC Faculty Learning Outcomes, additional learning activities include guest speakers, both local and national, who are experts on using small group learning; conference attendance; reciprocal classroom visitations and coaching among FLC members; lesson videotaping and review; and student-panel discussions. Moreover, all these activities can be used as assessments in order to determine the effectiveness of the FLC in promoting small group learning.

Two Concluding Caveats

- Not all students think and learn well in small groups; some need solitude to study and master concepts. Only at that point do they work effectively in groups by sharing what they have discovered by themselves. Teachers might allow the more reflective learner to be successful by announcing at-home readings that can be done prior to class small-group work in order to prepare for it.
- Not all faculty learn well in groups either; hence, some may shy away from using small groups in their teaching as a result of their experiences. These faculty will likely need to take smaller steps to be convinced of the worth of small group learning.

References and Resources

Angelo, T. A., & Cross, K. P. (1993). *Classroom assessment techniques.* San Francisco: Jossey-Bass.

Aronson, E. (1978). *The jigsaw classroom.* Beverly Hills, CA: Sage.

Astin, A. W. (1993). *What matters in college: Four critical years revisited.* San Francisco: Jossey-Bass.

Beach, A. L., & Cox, M. D. (2009). The impact of faculty learning communities on teaching and learning. *Learning Communities Journal,* 1 (1), 7-27.

Bransford, J. D., Brown, A. L. & Cocking, R. R. (Eds.) (2000). *How people learn: Brain, mind, experience, and school* (Expanded ed.). Washington, DC: National Academies Press.

Chickering, A. W., & Gamson, Z. F. (1987, June). Seven principles for good practice in undergraduate education. *AAHE Bulletin,* 39, 3-7.

Cooper, J. L., Robinson, P., & Ball, D. (Eds.). (2003). *Small group instruction in higher education: Lessons from the past, visions of the future.* Stillwater, OK: New Forums.

Cooper, J. L., & Robinson, P. (2009). The status of small-group instruction, 2008: What the experts say. In J. Cooper, P. Robinson, & D. Ball (Eds.), *Small group instruction in higher education: Lessons from the past, visions of the future* (2nd ed) (pp. 357-368). Stillwater, OK: New Forums.

Cox, M. D. (2001). Faculty learning communities: Change agents for transforming institutions into learning organizations.

In D. Lieberman & C. Wehlburg (Eds.), *To improve the academy: Vol. 19. Resources for faculty, instructional, and organizational development* (pp. 69-93). Bolton, MA: Anker.

Cox, M. D. (2003). *Faculty learning community program director's handbook and facilitator'shandbook.* Oxford, OH: Miami University.

Cox, M. D. (2009). A journey to scholarship development: The role of learning communities—A message from the Editor-in-Chief. *Learning Communities Journal,* 1 (1), 1-5.

Desrochers, C. G. (1999). Multi-purpose lecture breaks. *The Teaching Professor,* 13 (10), 1-2.

Desrochers, C. G. (2009, February). Classroom civility: Is it just me? *Thriving in Academe, NEA Advocate* (pp. 5-8). Washington, DC: NEA.

Jaques, D. & Salmon, G. (2007). *Learning in groups: A handbook for face-to-face and online environments* (4th ed.). New York: Routledge.

Johnson, D. W., & Johnson, F. P. (2006). *Joining together: Group theory and group skills.* New York: Pearson.

Joyce, B. R., & Showers, B. (1983). *Power in staff development through research on training.* Alexandria, Virginia: Association for Supervision and Curriculum Development.

Hubball, H., Clarke, A., & Beach, A. (2004). Assessing faculty learning communities. In M.D. Cox & L. Richlin (Eds.) *Building faculty learning communities* (pp. 87-100). New directions for teaching and learning, No. 97. San Francisco: Jossey-Bass.

Kagan, S. (1994). *Cooperative learning.* San Clemente, CA: Resources for Teachers.

MacGregor, J., Cooper, J. L., Smith, K. A., & Robinson, P. (Eds.) (2000). *Strategies for energizing large classes: From small groups to learning communities.* New directions for teaching and learning, No. 81. San Francisco: Jossey-Bass.

Michaelsen, L. K., Sweet, M., & Parmelee, D. X. (2008). *Team-based learning: Small-group learning's next big step.* New directions for teaching and learning, No. 116. San Francisco: Jossey-Bass.

Millis, B. J., & Cottell, P. G. Jr. (1998). *Cooperative learning for higher education faculty.* Phoenix, AZ: American Council on Education/Oryx.

Millis, B. J. (2007). Structuring complex cooperative learning activities in 50-minute classes. *To Improve the Academy.* In D. Robertson & L. Nilson (Eds.), *To improve the academy: Vol. 25. Resources for faculty, instructional, and organizational development* (pp. 153-169). San Francisco: Jossey-Bass.

Ortquist-Ahrens, L., & Torosyan, R. (2009). The role of the facilitator in faculty learning communities: Paving the way for growth, productivity, and collegiality. *Learning Communities Journal,* 1 (1), 29-62.

Petrone, M. C., & Ortquist-Ahrens, L. (2004). Facilitating faculty learning communities: A compact guide to creating change and inspiring community. In M.D. Cox & L. Richlin (Eds.) *Building faculty learning communities* (pp. 63-70). New directions for teaching and learning, No. 97. San Francisco: Jossey-Bass.

Sandell, K. L., Wigley, K., & Kovalchick, A. (2004). Developing facilitators for faculty learning communities. In M.D. Cox & L. Richlin (Eds.) *Building faculty learning communities* (pp. 51-62). New directions for teaching and learning, No. 97. San Francisco: Jossey-Bass.

Walberg, H. J. (1984). Improving the productivity of America's schools. *Educational Leadership,* 41 (8), 19-27.

Cooperative Learning and Disciple-Based Pedagogical Innovations: Taking Advantage of Complementarities

Mark Maier, KimMarie McGoldrick and Scott Simkins

A large body of literature has developed emphasizing and illustrating the benefits of cooperative learning for improving student learning in higher education [see, for example, Millis (2010) and the references included in that volume]. But cooperative learning is just one of many pedagogical practices available to instructors today that have been shown to improve student-learning outcomes. Many of the innovative classroom-tested teaching practices developed over the past twenty years, primarily in the STEM (Science, Technology, Engineering, and Mathematics) disciplines and often with support from the National Science Foundation, were intentionally designed to identify and/or address specific student "learning gaps" (McDermott, 1991) that hindered student learning in the targeted disciplines.

Among pedagogies developed in this context, Just-in-Time Teaching, Context-Rich Problems, Process Oriented Guided Inquiry Learning (POGIL), Peer Instruction, Interactive Lecture Demonstrations (ILDs), SCALE-UP, and Classroom Experiments are arguably the most familiar to instructors. Although some of these teaching techniques explicitly integrate group work in the learning process, they often overlook important recommendations from the cooperative learning literature that could further enhance student learning. For teaching techniques developed without an explicit group-work component, we believe that incorporating cooperative learning activities in a systematic and intentional manner is likely to further increase student-learning gains.

More generally, we believe that using cooperative learning practices *in conjunction with* discipline-based pedagogical innovations is more likely to increase student-learning outcomes than using either pedagogical practice *alone*.[1] Complementarities between cooperative learning and other pedagogies are, of course, not a new insight. Context-rich problems, for example, were first introduced in the physics education literature as small group activities (Heller, Keith, & Anderson, 1992) and therefore offer a model for purposeful integration of cooperative learning with other instructional practices. Pedagogical innovations, such as SCALE-UP (physics), Peer Instruction (physics) and POGIL (chemistry), developed with a disciplinary focus, have also incorporated cooperative learning structures in specific ways. Just-in-Time Teaching (physics), Interactive Lecture Demonstrations (physics), and Classroom Experiments (economics), however, were developed with little explicit reference to research on group work and could, in our view, benefit significantly from greater integration of formal cooperative learning structures.

In this chapter we describe how cooperative learning principles and practices can improve the potential for student learning in the discipline-developed teaching practices listed above, while also noting how cooperative learning practices can be enriched when integrated with discipline-based pedagogies developed to intentionally address student preconceptions, development of expert-like knowledge, transfer of learning to new situations, and metacognition.

Just-in-Time Teaching

One of the original motivations for developing Just-in-Time Teaching (JiTT) pedagogy was to "help students structure their out-of-class efforts and to get more out of precious in-class student-instructor face time" (Novak & Patterson, 2010, p. 5). This goal is accomplished in the Just-in-Time Teaching approach by posing carefully constructed questions on material that will be covered in the next class period (using an online learning management system, such as Blackboard or Moodle) and requiring students to respond to these questions by a preassigned deadline a few hours be-

---

[1] Watkins & Mazur (2010) provide evidence that supports this claim, highlighting the improved student-learning performance when combining Peer Instruction (a type of cooperative learning technique) with Just-in-Time Teaching (a pedagogical innovation first developed in physics).

fore class. Instructors then review students' JiTT responses before class and use them to organize and modify the upcoming classroom session in the hours leading up to the class – hence the "just-in-time" label.[2]

Just-in-Time Teaching provides a number of benefits, especially for instructors who use cooperative learning techniques regularly in their classes. First, JiTT encourages students to come to class prepared. If students are unprepared for class, then cooperative learning may be ineffective, perhaps even more so than a traditional lecture approach in which the instructor simply reviews what was missed. Many cooperative learning structures require content input from students and thus fail if students have not completed assigned reading before class. In addition, those students who are prepared will resent group members who are not and perhaps reject group work as an effective way for them to learn. JiTT promotes structured time on task between classes, leading to more productive in-class learning. Before the class begins, students have already begun an important step in learning by asking themselves questions, such as: "What do I already know about the concept?" And, "why do I hold these views?" Because all students have just thought about the same issues, they are better able to engage in small group discussions or other cooperative learning activities.

Second, Just-in-Time Teaching exercises provide a window into students' learning in real time. Seeing students' thinking processes – in the form of student responses to the JiTT exercises – also helps instructors to be better prepared for class, knowing what students understand and what they don't before class begins. Student responses to JiTT questions typically reveal significant learning gaps that instructors can then target through focused in-class exercises that direct learning where it is most beneficial. JiTT helps instructors teach more efficiently and effectively. In addition, student responses often provide the raw material for cooperative learning exercises. Working collaboratively in small groups provides students with opportunities to work through their thought processes together, setting the stage for powerful learning opportunities.

Third, Just-in-Time Teaching promotes motivation for learning, both in and out of class. Because out-of-class JiTT responses are used to construct in-class activities targeting student-learning difficulties, students see a direct connection between their study efforts out of class and what happens in class; in particular, students see that instructors care about their learning difficulties and directly respond to them during class. Because JiTT is truly student-centered, this approach yields a positive cycle of learning, with students motivated to complete out-of-class JiTT exercises, knowing that their responses will be used to make in-class learning more focused, engaged, and effective. Students are particularly curious to see their own answers projected at the start of class, a typical use of JiTT responses, along with those of other students (all anonymously), and are naturally inquisitive about the "correctness" of their thinking. JiTT promotes intrinsic motivation for engaging in both in-class and out-of-class learning activities. Moreover, student-generated responses provide interpretations of course concepts that often yield compelling examples that are much more engaging (because of their relevance to students) than those constructed by faculty members. When followed up in class with related activities that promote interactive engagement in structured small-group settings, students are able to "try out" their answers in a low-stakes environment and get immediate feedback on their understanding.

Although Just-in-Time Teaching can be used successfully in traditional lecture-based courses, structured in-class small-group activities are a natural complement to the JiTT approach and are likely to increase its educational value. Having students discuss, debate, and practice course concepts using student JiTT responses as a starting point provides opportunities for students to compare and contrast answers, apply concepts, evaluate arguments, challenge preconceptions, and reflect on their own learning. All of these higher-order thinking skills are enhanced through cooperative learning. Moreover, student responses to JiTT questions can often be used to quickly develop more structured cooperative learning activities. For example, the send-a-problem format can require groups to critique JiTT responses, or the cooperative controversy format can use JiTT responses reflecting multiple perspectives on an issue as the basis for debate. We see rich synergies when the JiTT approach is combined with these well-established cooperative learning techniques.

Peer Instruction

Peer Instruction was originally developed by Harvard physicist Eric Mazur (1997) to promote deeper conceptual thinking among his students, even in a

---

[2] For more information about the JiTT approach see Novak, Patterson, Gavrin, & Christian (1999), Patterson (2004), Simkins & Maier (2010) and the "Just-in-Time Teaching" teaching method at *Starting Point: Teaching and Learning Economics* <http://serc.carleton.edu/econ/index.html>.

large-lecture setting. In this model, traditional lectures are stopped every five to seven minutes to present a challenging multiple choice question called a ConcepTest question. Students first consider the question individually and are then polled for their answers using a classroom response system or index cards with answers corresponding to different-colored cards. After polling results are revealed, students consult with classmates and then are re-polled.[3]

Although similar in format to well-known cooperative learning structures, such as think-pair-share and Quick-thinks (Johnston & Cooper, 2009), Peer Instruction often involves the intentional development of in-class questions aimed at uncovering and addressing students' preconceptions or misconceptions regarding discipline-based concepts. Thus, carefully-crafted ConcepTest questions offer cooperative learning practitioners a specific context for this general teaching technique that can increase student learning.

If students are not deliberately guided to confront their misconceptions, they often revert to their pre-instruction, novice understanding. A vivid illustration of this effect occurs in the films *A Private Universe* and *Minds of Our Own* (Harvard-Smithsonian Center for Astrophysics, 1997a and 1997b), in which interviews with just-graduated Harvard students reveal embarrassing lapses in scientific understanding, even after having completed multiple science courses. Failure of his physics-trained Harvard students to correctly answer basic conceptual physics questions prompted Mazur to radically change his instructional practices. He was particularly struck by a student who asked: "Professor Mazur, how should I answer these questions? According to what you taught us, or by the way I *think* about these things?" (Mazur, 1997, p. 4). Combining structured cooperative learning practices with intentionally-designed ConcepTest questions can help to move students toward more expert-like thinking.

Physicists have been quite creative in writing ConcepTest questions used in Peer Instruction, often placing students in non-traditional situations. For example, Mazur (1997) uses the Levi-Straus trademark (in which two horses attempt to pull apart a pair of jeans) as a visual prop and asks if it would matter if a fixed post replaced one of the horses. These unfamiliar contexts provide the opportunity to assess students' ability to apply a newly-learned concept because they must identify the underlying principle to solve the problem, rather than simply apply a formulaic approach to an easily-recognized pattern.[4]

Arguably, cooperative learning practitioners can benefit from the accumulated research on Peer Instruction in the design of think-pair-share and Quick-Think activities. Although physics education scholars are at the forefront of this research, amassing a wealth of understanding about the discipline-specific preconceptions students hold, other educators can build on their work by adopting the practice of designing questions that ask students to transfer understanding to new contexts and use distracters (in these questions) that intentionally target student learning gaps.[5] In addition, cooperative learning researchers can build on the research assessing Peer Instruction by carefully examining the ways in which pedagogical innovations are actually put into practice by instructors with different skills and attitudes (Turpen & Finkelstein, 2009; Chasteen & Pollock, 2009).

How can Peer Instruction benefit from cooperative learning research? In our observations of Peer Instruction, we note that instructors often do not follow recommendations for effective cooperative learning in setting up peer interaction. For example, informal pair work usually is more effective if students are asked to turn to someone they do not know. In this way, friends feel comfortable not selecting one another as partners, a situation likely to lead to off-task conversation. Also, expert cooperative learning practitioners monitor the classroom for students who may be isolated, perhaps because of language barriers, or simply because they are sitting at the end of a row. Instructor intervention or class time given to social skills needed for group work can create a classroom in which all students readily find partners.

---

[3] ConcepTests have their origins in Concept Inventories, another physics education research innovation that has now been adopted in many other disciplines. Concept Inventories are collections of multiple choice questions carefully designed to reveal preconceptions that students bring to the classroom (Richardson, 2004). See <http://mazur-www.harvard.edu/education/educationmenu.php> for more information about Mazur's experience with Peer Instruction and ConcepTest questions at Harvard University and <http://www.colorado.edu/physics/EducationIssues/cts/> for information about ConcepTest use at the University of Colorado-Boulder. Chemistry applications of ConcepTests are discussed at <http://www.flaguide.org/cat/contests/contests1.php>; examples are available at <http://www.chem.wisc.edu/~concept/>.

[4] In recent years, Mazur has begun to use student responses to Just-in-Time Teaching questions to develop relevant "distracters" for his in-class questions, thus illustrating another way to incorporate JiTT in classes (Watkins & Mazur, 2010).

[5] See, for example, the research carried out by Lillian McDermott's University of Washington Physics Education Research Group based on thousands of students at several universities <http://www.phys.washington.edu/groups/peg/peginfo.html>.

Peer Instruction would also benefit from components of cooperative learning shown to enhance learning, such as those that ensure equal participation and individual accountability. As students pair up to discuss their individual answers to a ConcepTest question, more effective learning will occur if students share speaking time evenly, a social skill that may require cooperative learning structures, such as timed periods for each student to present. Randomly choosing students to report their discussions to the larger class ensures that both students are engaged in the exchange and that a dominant student does not take over the process.

In summary, Peer Instruction and cooperative learning practitioners have much to offer one another. The creatively-written ConcepTests used in Peer Instruction are driven by research emphasizing the importance of directly addressing what students bring to the classroom. In turn, Peer Instruction enhances the in-class learning impact of these ConcepTest questions by incorporating small-group teaching practices. We believe that student learning could be even further enhanced through more explicit attention to insights from the cooperative learning literature.

Context-rich Problems

First developed by the University of Minnesota Physics Education Research Group in the early 1990s, context-rich problems are highly-structured problems that put the student at the center of a realistic situation requiring the use of a single core disciplinary concept. Context-rich problems include a short story in which the student is the major character with a plausible motivation for deriving a solution (Heller, Keith, & Anderson (1992); Heller & Hollabaugh (1992). What differentiates context-rich problems from traditional story problems is intentionality in design. In order to engage student interest, link to previous student experiences, and provide guidance about the type of writing needed to answer the question, context-rich problems begin with "You…" and then place the student in a specific situation. For example, *You have been asked by your* [roommate, boss, relative, etc.] *to complete a task* [helping write a novel, explain why something happens in the home, consult with a moviemaking company, etc.]. Through the use of a personal story, often in a non-traditional application, context-rich problems can help students transfer understanding of concepts to new situations, a hallmark of deep learning.

Another key feature of context-rich problems is the intentional crafting of problems to either include excess information that the students must ignore or leave out needed information, such as the target variable. As a result, context-rich problems move students away from simply identifying the appropriate formula or technique and then cranking out a single correct answer. Instead, context-rich problems require students to first determine what must be done, often in the absence of an explicit target variable, and then map out a solution strategy, adding relevant diagrams, omitting unneeded data, and identifying information relevant to the problem, but not explicitly stated. Of course, not all these skills need be included in every problem; instructors can scaffold the context-rich problem approach, building up over time the skills used routinely by expert learners, including: visualizing the problem as a whole before performing any computational steps; incorporating necessary, generally available knowledge not included in the problem; and ignoring, or postponing the use of information not relevant to the problem at hand.

Context-rich problems also help enhance students writing skills. Because the audience and purpose are specified in context-rich problems, the student has a clearer sense of length, detail, and tone to be used. Instead of repeating expressions used in the textbook, students answer context-rich problems with more authentic language revealing whether or not a concept was fully understood. The engaging nature and short length of context-rich problem writing assignments makes them especially appropriate for small group work.

Although students can work independently on context-rich problems, they are easily adaptable to small group work. In a study of context-rich problems used in conjunction with small groups, results indicate that even highly-skilled problem solvers benefited from group work because less-skilled students "provided the monitoring and checking to make sure that conceptual and procedural mistakes were not made" (Heller, Keith & Anderson, 1992, p. 634). Groups of three proved optimal, making fewer conceptual mistakes than pairs and more frequently including all students in the process compared to groups of four. Groups of students with heterogeneous skill levels outperformed homogenous groups, and groups with majority women outperformed majority-men groups (Heller & Hollabaugh, 1992).

In summary, context-rich problems are a valuable addition to the cooperative learning toolkit, offering problems that are especially appropriate for group work because they are non-trivial, inherently engaging, and focused on a specified audience and purpose. In particular, there is rich potential for the use of context-rich problems with jigsaw and send-a-problem structures, as well as with Peer Instruction.

SCALE-UP

Cooperative learning is at the heart of the Student-Centered Active Learning Environment for Undergraduate Programs (SCALE-UP) Project, whose primary goal is "to establish a highly collaborative, hands-on, computer-rich, interactive learning environment for large, introductory college courses" (Beichner, Saul, Abbott, Morse, Deardorff, Allain, Bohhan, Dancy, & Risley, 2007, p. 1). Originally developed at North Carolina State University as a way to replace traditional lecture-oriented instruction in physics with a studio/workshop approach (see Beichner & Saul, 2004 and Beichner, Bernold, Burniston, Dail, Felder, Gastineau, Gjertsen, & Risley, 1999), SCALE-UP combines innovations in pedagogy, classroom structure, and teaching materials to promote hands-on, interactive, collaborative learning, regardless of class size. The SCALE-UP approach has been adapted for use in a variety of disciplines, including physics, chemistry, math, engineering, and literature.[7]

Three basic pedagogical principles underlie the SCALE-UP approach (Beichner, et al, 2007):
- To create a cooperative learning environment that encourages students to collaborate with their peers, questioning and teaching one another.
- To use research-based, interactive learning activities as much as possible and to minimize lecture during class.
- To coach the students during activities by assisting them in answering their own questions and by letting students present their results to the class for review by instructors and peers rather than just telling students the answer.

SCALE-UP relies critically on paying close attention to cooperative learning principles, employing research-based instructional materials and teaching practices that promote interactive engagement, and encouraging reflection and risk-taking in student thinking processes. In terms of cooperative learning, a great deal of attention is placed on group formation (heterogeneous groups based on academic background and avoiding isolation of women and minorities), frequency of group changes (3-4 times per semester), and training in group functioning (including contracts of responsibility and incentives for improved group performance). As noted by Beichner, et al. (2007), "By the nature of how the SCALE-UP classes function, most of [the critical characteristics of successful cooperative learning outlined by Johnson, Johnson, and Smith (1991)] are intrinsically a part of the way students interact in the class" (p. 10).

In practice, the SCALE-UP approach emphasizes the importance of classroom design. In SCALE-UP classrooms students work at round tables in three-person teams, three teams per table (labeled A, B, and C), with each team sharing a laptop computer. This configuration encourages collaborative teamwork within the team and sharing across teams, and allows the instructor to take advantage of a variety of cooperative learning techniques (e.g. Peer Instruction, jigsaw, send-a-problem) and reporting-out methods. In addition to computers, students also have access to lab equipment to conduct experiments. A typical class period might include a variety of teaching modalities, including mini-lectures, hands-on experiments and activities, simulations or data analyses, cooperative learning activities, and demonstrations. In large enrollment sections, multiple instructors (or graduate students) move throughout the classroom to ensure students are focused on the day's activities, answer questions, and encourage reflective thinking. Homework assignments ensure individual accountability and reinforce concepts developed from pre-class readings and in-class activities.

The SCALE-UP approach is amenable to a wide variety of disciplines, even those outside the STEM disciplines where it is most widely used, as the following example illustrates:

> A political science class is in development at one adopting school. The teacher could pick some current event to focus the students' attention, for example a government official's Congressional testimony on some controversial topic. The "A" group at each table would go to the web to see how CNN covered the event. The "B" groups would read the Washington Post coverage, while the "C" groups could find the Fox News website. Then they would compare and see what aspects were covered by all three and which things were missing in some. They might then be sent on a search to find the least biased presentation, perhaps by an international organization like the BBC. Whether the topic is current events or chemistry, the basic idea is the same.

---

[7] The SCALE-UP websites <http://www.ncsu.edu/PER/scaleup.html> and <http://scaleup.ncsu.edu/> include extensive information about the SCALE-UP project, including project history, adaptations across disciplines, assessment results, and references to SCALE-UP-related publications.

Student teams work on interesting tasks while teachers coach. Beichner, 2008, p. 2

The cooperative learning environment in SCALE-UP classrooms is both informed and enhanced by research-based activities intentionally developed to address student learning gaps and provide opportunities for hands-on engagement with course concepts (tangibles) and thought-provoking questions that promote transfer to new learning situations (ponderables). Cooperative learning is intentionally integrated with other research-based pedagogical innovations to create a rich and stimulating learning environment for students. Rigorous and extensive assessment of student learning outcomes from SCALE-UP classes confirms that this pedagogy enhances students' ability to solve problems, increases conceptual understanding, improves students' attitudes toward the discipline, and dramatically reduces course failure rates, especially for women and minority students, relative to traditionally taught classes.[8]

The SCALE-UP approach illustrates what is possible when cooperative learning principles are intentionally integrated with changes in classroom structure and instructional materials developed from learning sciences and discipline-based educational research. It is unlikely that any one of these innovations, by itself, would have produced the results highlighted above. Rather, it is the combination of these three components that leads to a powerful and effective learning environment for students.

Interactive Lecture Demonstration

The Interactive Lecture Demonstration approach was developed by physics educators to help students overcome common, limiting preconceptions about physical laws (Sokoloff & Thorton, 1997).[9] As with Peer Instruction, the Interactive Lecture Demonstration begins by identifying a core concept about which students are confused and then asking students to refine their thinking through guided small group work that includes three steps: predicting the outcome of an interactive demonstration, carrying out the demonstration, and reflecting on the results. Each of the steps is linked to knowledge about how students learn. The demonstration itself can be a classroom experiment, a survey, a simulation or an analysis of secondary data.

1. **Predict.** After a preview of the upcoming demonstration, students make a prediction about the expected result. Research indicates that "students who predict the demonstration outcome before seeing it display significantly greater understanding" (Crouch, Fagen, Callan, & Mazur, 2004, p. 835). These predictions are recorded, shared with a partner, and modified if necessary. At this stage in the process instructors survey the students about their predictions, ask them to explain their thinking, but offer no confirmations or corrections.

2. **Experience.** This demonstration step is implemented as an experiment in the physical sciences, but in the social sciences this could include data analysis, a simulation, or a survey of the class. Ideally, the demonstration is conducted within small groups so that each student can observe the setup and results more readily than if the demonstration is conducted by the instructor in front of the class. However, Interactive Lecture Demonstration developers do not generally offer advice about group composition or group process; rather, Interactive Lecture Demonstrations are designed to encourage student learning even if group work does not proceed in an ideal fashion.

3. **Reflect.** In the final, third step students reflect individually or in small groups on the demonstration results: did they confirm or contradict their original prediction? Why might such results occur? This step has been shown to enhance student achievement and help them develop the ability to learn independently (Bransford, Brown, & Cocking, 2000).

As with the other innovative pedagogies discussed in this chapter, Interactive Lecture Demonstrations belong in the cooperative learning tool kit. The Interactive Lecture Demonstration builds comprehension by directly addressing frequently misunderstood core concepts, follows a three part predict-experience-reflect format grounded in learning sciences research, and provides the opportunity for a wide range of possible demonstrations, all valuable complements to cooperative learning exercises.

At the same time, Interactive Lecture Demonstrations can benefit from more explicit attention to research on small group work. Although it may be true that well-designed worksheets and inherently compelling activi-

---

[8] See <http://www.ncsu.edu/PER/scaleup.html> for evidence of SCALE-UP project impact on student learning.

[9] See also the "Interactive Lecture Demonstrations" teaching method at *Starting Point: Teaching and Learning Economics* <http://serc.carleton.edu/econ/index.html>.

ties may be effective pedagogy, student learning will improve if group work follows well-established cooperative learning best practices. For example, in our observations, Interactive Lecture Demonstration groups would benefit from more attention to group size and composition for which cooperative learning research offers relatively easy-to-follow guidelines.[10] At a minimum, instructors could create groups at random so friends are not working together and marginal students are not relegated to the last-formed group.

Similarly, Interactive Lecture Demonstrations would benefit from attention to equal participation and positive interdependence in what are otherwise carefully designed exercises focused primarily on individual accountability. Equal engagement with the demonstration can be enhanced by assigning roles covering exercise components. In an evaluation of student conversations during Interactive Lecture Demonstrations, researchers found a four-fold increase in "sense-making" discussion, as opposed to logistical or off-task conversation (Redish & Hammer, 2009). Cooperative learning structures that encourage positive interdependence might further increase such discussion if, for example, the Interactive Lecture Demonstration used a jigsaw, cooperative controversy or other format in which student groups interact with one another in formal structures to better understand the concept under study.

Process-Oriented Guided-Inquiry Learning (POGIL)

POGIL is a student-centered, learning process designed to promote deep, lasting learning of core concepts. Students engage in structured group work guiding them to construct discipline-based knowledge while also developing general skills, such as critical thinking, problem solving and communication. These structured activities are anchored in carefully designed materials based on the Socratic method of guided inquiry. Although educators often focus on either enhancing core concepts *or* pedagogic practice, POGIL enhances learning by simultaneously focusing on both disciplinary content *and* the process by which learning occurs, an approach we advocate. Assessment of POGIL outcomes shows positive impacts on content mastery, lower student attrition, and more positive student attitudes about both the course and instructor. (See, for example, Farrell, Moog, & Spencer, 1999; Hanson & Wolfskill, 2000; and Lewis & Lewis, 2005.)

Hanson (2006, p. v) describes the POGIL approach in the following way:

A guided-inquiry format based on the learning cycle of exploration, concept formation or invention, and application is used in these activities. Students work on the activities in teams to acquire knowledge and develop understanding. The teams examine data, models, or examples in response to critical thinking questions. They then demonstrate and apply their knowledge in exercises, and problems are used to develop problem solving skills and higher order thinking, such as analysis, synthesis, transference, and evaluation.

As the description above illustrates, POGIL emphasizes that learning is enhanced when individuals: 1) construct their own understanding; 2) follow a learning cycle of exploration, concept formation and application; 3) connect and visualize concepts; 4) discuss and interact with others; 5) reflect on progress; and 6) assess performance (Hanson, 2006). In the POGIL approach, cooperative learning is but one component in a holistic learning process.

The use of learning teams in the POGIL process is explicitly grounded in cooperative learning best practices.[11] Special attention is given to team composition, addressing both the process of team formation (random or purposeful), team characteristics (size, diversity, short/long term, etc), and processing (responsibilities and collaborative skills). Positive interdependence (demonstrated through goals or rewards) is enhanced by assigning tasks and associated roles to each team member. Given that the ultimate goal is for independent learning, individual accountability is built into the process by rotating roles, including reporting out processes, and conducting follow-up assessment. Finally, learning is further enhanced by allowing time for reflection and metacognition.

By emphasizing a holistic learning cycle that begins with exploration, progresses through concept invention or formation, and ends with application, the process of developing POGIL exercises provides valuable guidance on how to enhance cooperative learning activities that typically focus only on the application phase.

In the exploration phase of the learning cycle,

---

[10] See the "Cooperative Learning" teaching method at *Starting Point: Teaching and Learning Economics* <http://serc.carleton.edu/econ/index.html>.

[11] For an extensive discussion of the role of cooperative learning in POGIL, see Shadle (2010).

"students encounter questions or complexities that they cannot resolve with their accustomed way of thinking" (Hanson, 2006, p. 5). Each POGIL problem is accompanied by a series of critical thinking questions designed to guide students "to the development of a deeper understanding of a concept" (Hanson, 2006, p. 5). The exploration and broadening of learning processes occurs as students seek understanding the problem by proposing, questioning, and testing hypotheses. In the subsequent concept invention or formation phase, the focus is on either identifying (invention) or understanding (formation) the key concept. Finally, the more familiar application phase requires students to use their newly acquired knowledge in a new situation. This can be facilitated through the use of exercises (simple situations and familiar contexts), problems (transferring the use of acquired knowledge to very different situations or combining it with other knowledge), and research questions (extending knowledge by introducing new issues, questions, or hypotheses) (Hanson 2006).

In the context of cooperative learning exercises, more fully incorporating the learning cycle described above suggests that instructors should intentionally develop exercises that emphasize learning during the exploration and concept invention/formation steps of the process prior to application of a model or concept in a new situation. Different cooperative learning techniques can be enhanced with special attention to each of these pre-application POGIL phases. For example, a send-a-problem exercise could be developed in conjunction with the exploration phase, presenting students with a series of problems and rich information sets in which the information required is not clearly identified. Such exercises would provide guiding questions for students to demonstrate their exploration of the problem by evaluating the information for relevance and testing expected outcomes. Repeated phases of the send-a-problem exercise would refine students' skills, leading to an enhanced basis for both concept invention and formation. Concept invention can be facilitated in jigsaw exercises that require expert groups of students to discover patterns and identify consistent outcomes in different situations, which are reinforced when the formal underlying concept is thereafter defined. Concept formation can be developed in the second phase of the jigsaw as students from each expert group come together to engage in the formal identification of the key concepts that will enhance their understanding of the associated patterns and outcomes.

Classroom Experiments[12]

Experiments are activities that guide students through a process of data collection as the basis for inquiry-based learning. Despite this common foundation, the implementation of experiments differs dramatically across disciplines. To demonstrate the potential synergies between cooperative learning and experiments, we ground our discussion in our own discipline of economics and focus on the use of classroom experiments. Classroom experiments in economics are a relatively new phenomenon, with the development of supporting materials and consequent integration into (primarily) introductory courses blossoming in the 1990s. The use of experiments in introductory economics classroom is now supported by an extensive set of resources for economics instructors.[13] As a pedagogic practice, economic experiments increase student learning, interest in the discipline, and course enjoyment (Durham, McKinnon, & Schulman, 2007).

Despite evidence of effectiveness and increasing resources for economic experiments as a pedagogic practice, associated learning research has focused on the development of experiments as methods to introduce traditional economics *concepts* rather than on determining the best pedagogical *processes* for implementation. In short, there is little research on the impact of experimental design on learning.[14] However, learning sciences research [e.g., the results highlighted in Bransford, Brown, & Cocking (2000)] offers insights into ways that classroom experiments can be adapted to improve student learning. In particular, cooperative learning structures that incorporate more opportunities for active student reflection on both the processes involved in the experiment and the expected outcomes are likely to lead to deeper and more durable student learning.

Consider the double oral auction, the most commonly-used economics experiment. The goal of this experiment is to illustrate the interaction of buyers and

---

[12] The section on experimental economics is based on a similar section in Maier, McGoldrick, & Simkins, 2010.

[13] See Bergstrom & Miller (2000), the journal *Experimental Economics*, the teaching method "Classroom Experiments" at *Starting Point: Teaching and Learning Economics* <http://serc.carleton.edu/econ/index.html>, VECONLAB <http://veconlab.econ.virginia.edu/admin.htm>, EconPort <http://www.econport.org/econport/request?page=web_home>, and Aplia <http://www.aplia.com/economics/> for a wide variety of supporting materials.

[14] One notable exception regarding student characteristics is Emerson & Taylor (2007).

sellers, the usual emergence of an equilibrium price, and the impact of various conditions (e.g., price floors or ceilings and asymmetric information) on market equilibria. Although the results are often elegant, few experimental designs require students to interact in other than explicit ways based on predetermined roles. In most cases, once the experiment itself concludes, so does the interaction. Yet results of educational research on experiments in the physical sciences suggest a way to enhance learning through active reflection and serve as a logical point of integration for cooperative learning. This research (Crouch, Fagen, Callan, & Mazur, 2004) suggests that student learning increases when students are forced to make predictions about the experiment's outcome *prior to the experiment* and reflect on how their predictions compared with actual outcomes *after the experiment.*

An instructor might add think-pair-share exercises at various points during an economics experiment, initially asking students to use economic theory to predict what might happen during the experiment and later asking them to interpret experiment outcomes and reflect on why they were generated. When students are expected to participate in a number of related experiments (for example the double oral auction with and without product quality differences), a version of the cooperative learning jigsaw structure can be used by distributing different sample experiment outcomes to each student in a small group and asking each one to match the outcome with the experiment. The jigsaw structure can also be used prior to the experiment as a method of generating predicted outcomes.

In most experiments students must make strategic decisions while assuming the role of, for example, a consumer, a producer, an employer, or an employee. Here, too, student learning could be improved if the activity included the opportunity for students to discuss potential strategies prior to the experiment. Working in pairs enhances student learning since participants would be required to explicitly identify, articulate, and choose between alternative strategies rather than simply putting one into practice. Thoughtful consideration of cooperative learning theory can enhance learning in these situations by ensuring adequate time for students to individually identify a strategy before reflecting on their partner's strategy choice.

Finally, cooperative learning exercises can be employed during the reporting out period of classroom experiments, providing an efficient process for gauging student comprehension. If the experiment is basic, simple techniques, such as think-pair-share may be appropriate. However, in the case of more complicated experiments, cooperative learning groups can be used to sequentially improve on the analysis by employing the send-a-problem structure. Furthermore, when students have different roles in an experiment, groups can be formed to include representatives for each role, creating a jigsaw in which subsequent analysis requires input from each perspective.

Summary

Cooperative learning, along with more recent STEM-based pedagogical innovations grounded in learning sciences research, have been shown to increase student learning in a wide variety of learning environments. Our argument is that student learning is likely to be further enhanced when cooperative learning techniques are intentionally integrated with pedagogical innovations aimed at addressing student pre-conceptions, development of expert-like knowledge, transfer of learning, and metacognition, relative to using any one of these pedagogies alone.

We have provided examples of seven discipline-developed teaching practices, noting the complementarities with cooperative learning and ways in which specific cooperative learning principles or practices might make the highlighted teaching practices more effective at improving student learning. In many cases (Just-in-Time Teaching, Interactive Lecture Demonstrations, and Classroom Experiments), these teaching practices were developed without explicit details about the structure of in-class student interactions; here, the extensive literature on cooperative learning practices provides valuable guidance for instructors. Even for those pedagogical innovations developed with small-group work as a central component (SCALE-UP, Context-Rich Problems, POGIL, and Peer Instruction, in particular), closer attention to cooperative learning principles and use of specific cooperative learning practices (e.g., cooperative controversy, jigsaw, and send-a-problem) are likely to enhance their effectiveness.

For instructors already incorporating cooperative learning practices in their classroom teaching, the pedagogical innovations summarized in this chapter provide specific contexts for the use of cooperative learning. Although cooperative learning is consistent with research on "good practices" in undergraduate education (Chickering & Gamson, 1987), when combined with teaching techniques intentionally designed to integrate more recent research on "how students learn" (Bransford, Brown, & Cocking, 2000), the effectiveness of this widely-used teaching practice is likely to increase. By combining these approaches in an intentional way, instructors can improve both the breadth and depth of student learning, as well as the durability of that learning.

References

Beichner, R. (2008). *SCALE-UP: Student-Centered Active Learning Environment for Undergraduate Programs*. Retrieved May 5, 2010, from http://scaleup.ncsu.edu/

Beichner, R., Bernold, L., Burniston, E., Dail, P., Felder, R., Gastineau, J., Gjertsen, M. & Risley, J. (1999). Case study of the physics component of an integrated curriculum. *American Journal of Physics Supplement 67*(7), S16-S24. Retrieved May 5, 2010 from http://www.ncsu.edu/PER/byAuthorPubs/beichnerpub.html.

Beichner, R. J., & Saul, J. M. (2004). Introduction to the SCALE-UP (student-centered activities for large enrollment undergraduate programs) project. In American Association for the Advancement of Science. *Invention and Impact: Building Excellence in Undergraduate Science, Technology, Engineering, and Mathematics (STEM) Education* (pp. 61-66). Washington, DC: American Association for the Advancement of Science. Retrieved May 5, 2010 from http://www.aaas.org/publications/books_reports/CCLI/.

Beichner, R., Saul, J. M., Abbott, D. S., Morse, J. J., Deardorff, D. L., Allain, R. J., Bohhan, S. W., Dancy, M. H. & Risley, J. S. (2007). The student-centered activities for large rnrollment undergraduate programs (SCALE-UP) project. In E. F. Redish and P. Cooney (Eds.), *Research-based reform of university physics* (1). Retrieved May 6, 2010, from http://www.compadre.org/Repository/document/ServeFile.cfm?ID=4517&DocID=183.

Bergstrom, T. C., & Miller, J. H. (2000). *Experiments with economic principles: Microeconomics*. Boston: McGraw-Hill.

Bransford, J., Brown, A. L., & Cocking, R. R. (2000). *How people learn: Brain, mind, experience, and school*. National Research Council. Washington, DC: National Academy Press.

Chasteen, S., & Pollock, S. (2009, July 29-30). A research-based approach to assessing student learning issues in upper-division electricity & magnetism. Paper presented at Physics Education Research Conference 2009, Ann Arbor, Michigan. Retrieved May 6, 2010, from http://www.compadre.org/Repository/document/ServeFile.cfm?ID=9892&DocID=1524.

Chickering, A. W. & Gamson, Z. F. (1987). Seven principles for good practice in undergraduate education, *American Association for Higher Education Bulletin, 39*(7), 3-7.

Crouch, C. H., Fagen, A. P., Callan, J. P., & Mazur, E. (2004). Classroom demonstrations: Learning tools or entertainment? *American Journal of Physics, 72*(6), 835-838.

Durham, Y., McKinnon, T., & Schulman, C. (2007). Classroom experiments: Not just fun and games. *Economic Inquiry, 45*(1), 162–178.

Emerson, T. L. N., & Taylor, B. A. (2007). Interactions between personality type and the experimental methods. *Journal of Economic Education, 38*(1), 18-35.

Farrell, J. J., Moog, R. S. & Spencer, J. N. (1999). A guided-inquiry general chemistry course. *Journal of Chemical Education, 76*(4), 570-574.

Hanson, D. M. (2006). *Instructor's guide to process-oriented guided-inquiry learning*. Lisle, IL: Pacific Crest Publishing.

Hanson, D. M. & Wolfskill, T. (2000). Process workshops: A new model for instruction. *Journal of Chemistry Education, 77*(1), 120-30.

Havard-Smithsonian Center for Astrophysics. (1997a). *A private universe*. Annenberg Media. Retrieved May 5, 2010 from http://www.learner.org/resources/series28.html.

Harvard-Smithsonian Center for Astrophysics. (1997b). *Lessons from thin air*. Annenberg Media. Retrieved May 5, 2010 from http://www.learner.org/resources/series26.html.

Heller, P. & Hollabaugh, M. (1992). Teaching problem solving through cooperative grouping. Part 2: Designing problems and structuring groups. *American Journal of Physics 60*(7), 637-644.

Heller, P., Keith, R. & Anderson, S. (1992). Teaching problem solving through cooperative grouping. Part 1: Group versus individual problem solving. *American Journal of Physics, 60*(7), 627-636.

Johnson, D. W., Johnson, R. T. & Smith, K. A. (1991). *Cooperative learning: Increasing college faculty instructional productivity*. ASHE-ERIC Higher Education Report No. 4. Washington, D.C.: The George Washington University, School of Education and Human Development.

Johnston, S. & Cooper, J. L. (2009). Quick-thinks: Active-thinking tasks in lecture classes and televised instruction. In J. L. Cooper, P. Robinson, & D. Ball (Eds.) *Small Group Instruction in Higher Education* Stillwater OK: New Forums Press.

Lewis, S. E. & Lewis, J. E. (2005). Departing from lectures: An evaluation of a peer-led guided inquiry alternative. *Journal of Chemical Education, 82*(1), 135-139.

Maier, M., McGoldrick, K. & Simkins, S. (2010). Implementing cooperative learning in introductory economics courses. In B. J. Millis (Ed.), *Cooperative learning in higher education: Across the disciplines, across the academy* (pp. 157-179). Sterling, VA: Stylus Press.

Mazur, E. (1997). *Peer instruction: A user's manual*. Upper Saddle River, N.J: Prentice Hall.

McDermott, L. C. (1991). What we teach and what is learned: Closing the gap. *American Journal of Physics, 59*(4), 301-315.

Millis, B. J. (2010). *Cooperative learning in higher education: Across the disciplines, across the academy*. Sterling, VA: Stylus Press.

Novak, G. & Patterson, E. (2010). An introduction to just-in-time teaching (JiTT). In S. Simkins & M. Maier (Eds.), *Just-in-time teaching: Across the disciplines, across the academy* (pp. 3-24). Sterling, VA: Stylus.

Novak, G. M., Patterson, E., Gavrin, A., & Christian, W. (1999). *Just-in-time teaching: Blending active learning with web technology*. Upper Saddle River NJ: Prentice-Hall.

Patterson, E. T. (2004). Just-in-time teaching: Technology transforming learning: A status report. In American Association for the Advancement of Science. *Invention and Impact: Building Excellence in Undergraduate Science, Technology, Engineering, and Mathematics (STEM) Education* (pp. 49-54). Washington, DC: American Association for the Advancement of Science. Retrieved May 5, 2010 from http://www.aaas.org/publications/books_reports/CCLI/.

Redish, E. F. & Hammer, D. (2009). Reinventing college physics for biologists: Explicating an epistemological curriculum. *American Journal of Physics, 77*(7), 629-642.

Richardson, J. (2004). Concept inventories: Tools for uncovering STEM students' misconceptions. In American Association for the Advancement of Science. *Invention and Impact: Building Excellence in Undergraduate Science, Technology, Engineering, and Mathematics (STEM) Education* (pp. 19-25). Washington, DC: American Association for the Advancement of Science. Retrieved May 5, 2010 from http://www.aaas.org/publications/books_reports/CCLI/.

Shadle, S. (2010). Cooperative learning in general chemistry though process-oriented guided inquiry learning. In B. J. Millis (Ed.), *Cooperative learning in higher education: Across the disciplines, across the academy* (pp. 35-56). Sterling, VA: Stylus.

Simkins, S. P. & Maier, M. (2010) *Just-in-time teaching: Across the disciplines, across the academy.* New pedagogies and practices for teaching in higher education series. Sterling, VA: Stylus.

Sokoloff, D. R., & Thornton, R. K. (1997). Using interactive lecture demonstrations to create an active learning environment. *Physics Teacher, 35*(6), 340-347.

Turpen, C. & Finkelstein, N. D. (2009). Not all interactive engagement is the same: Variations in physics professors' implementation of *Peer Instruction*. Physics Review Special Topics - Physics Education Research, 5, 020101. Retrieved May 5, 2010 from http://prst-per.aps.org/abstract/PRSTPER/v5/i2/e020101.

Watkins, J. & Mazur, E. (2010). Just-in-time teaching and peer instruction. In S. Simkins & M. Maier (Eds.), *Just-in-time teaching: Across the disciplines, across the academy* (pp. 39-62). Sterling, VA: Stylus.

The Value of Interaction Treatments in Distance and Online Learning

Rana M. Tamim, Robert M. Bernard, Eugene Borokhovski and Philip C. Abrami

In a recent meta-analysis, Bernard et al. (2009) explored the relationship between interaction treatments and student learning by synthesizing findings from 74 studies with measures of achievement and 44 studies with attitude measures. After adjustment for methodological quality, the overall weighted average effect size for achievement was 0.38 favoring more interaction treatments over less interactive treatments and was heterogeneous. Overall, the results supported the importance of three types of interaction: among students, between the instructor and students, and between students and course content. This chapter offers an overview of the meta-analysis and its findings followed by an in-depth (qualitative) examination of the research studies that had the strongest effect sizes for each of the three types of interaction. Based on both the quantitative and qualitative findings, particular implications regarding the design and development of learning environments that support student learning in distance education are provided.

The Importance of Interaction in Distance Education

The Bernard et al. (2009) meta-analysis went well beyond the comparison between distance education and in-class or face-to-face instruction to explore the effect of different interaction treatments on students' learning outcomes when various distance education conditions were compared to one another.

The origins of distance education (DE) are humble and first generation DE is often referred to as correspondence education where students received course material and handed in assignments by mail. Even in those somewhat impoverished instructional conditions, interaction was considered an important but missing component of quality DE (Daniel & Marquis, 1979). Later generations of DE took increasing advantage of technology, especially computer technology, to send and receive course material and assignments. Recent advances in technology have increased the power, flexibility, ubiquity, and ease of learning online and at a distance. Likewise, they have provided many of the opportunities for interaction that were unavailable in earlier forms of DE (Moore, 1989). Key features of the latest generation of DE involve greater potential for interaction and so our review sought to understand whether these new developments had any substantial effect on learning and to what extent and under what conditions they functioned as enabling features.

Although interaction was largely absent during so much of the early history of DE, the DE literature is largely unequivocal about its importance (e.g., Anderson, 2003). This is because of the important role that interaction between students, teachers, and content is presumed to play in all of formal education (e.g., Garrison & Shale, 1990).

While interaction is not explicit in all definitions of DE, it is an integral part of some. For example, The United States Distance Learning Association (Holden & Westfall, 2006), states, "distance education refers specifically to learning activities within a K-12, higher education, or professional continuing education environment where interaction is an integral component" (p. 9).

Some of the original thinking about interaction in DE focused mainly on human-human interaction. Daniel and Marquis (1979) defined interaction "in a restrictive manner to cover only those activities where the student is in two-way contact with another person (or persons)" (p. 339). Later, Wagner's (1994) broader and somewhat more abstract and technical definition characterized interaction as "reciprocal events that require at least two objects and two actions. Interactions occur when these objects and events mutually influence one another" (p. 8). Thurmond and Wambach (2004) described the content-driven goal of interaction in DE as "the learner's engagement with the course content, other learners, the instructor, and the technological medium used in the course. ... Ultimately, the goal of interaction is to increase understanding of the course content or mastery of the defined goals" (p. 4). If correct, Thurmond and Wambach are singling out access and engagement with course content as an essential aspect of successful applications of DE.

Some theorists (e.g., Wagner, 1994) have also focused on the social purpose and processes of interaction, particularly in regard to student-student and student-teacher engagement. Gilbert and Moore (1989) distinguish between instructional interaction and social interaction. While it is believed that these social aspects enhance students' performance in DE courses, they probably would not register explicitly on measures of achievement, but most probably would on measures of attitude and course satisfaction.

Holden and Westfall (2006) and a variety of others, make an additional point that is important in a discussion of interaction in DE. It is the difference that exists between asynchronous, mediated synchronous, and blended (i.e., DE plus classroom instruction [CI], also called mixed and hybrid) forms of DE. Mediated synchronous and blended DE contain natural conditions for interaction, especially between the student and teacher and often among students. Although asynchronous DE may or may not contain capacities for text-based and/or voice/video synchronous communication (e.g., MSN, Skype), such facilities could be built into the design of the technology applications available to students and teachers to provide higher levels of interaction.

Responding to the needs of practitioners for better understanding of what components of instructional design and teaching practices have high potential for making learning at distance a more engaging and fulfilling experience, Bernard et al. (2009) undertook a meta-analysis of three types of interactions in DE.

Types of Interaction

An interaction is commonly understood as an active exchange (of actions and information) among individuals, but is extended here to include individual interactions with curricular content. Moore (1989) distinguished among three forms of interaction in DE: 1) student-student interaction, 2) student-teacher interaction; and 3) student-content interaction.

Student-student interaction refers to interaction among individual students or among students working in small groups (Moore, 1989). In correspondence courses, this interaction is often absent; in fact, correspondence students may not even be aware that other students are taking the same course. In later generations of DE, including two-way videoconferencing and Web-based courses, student-student interaction can be synchronous, as in videoconferencing and chatting, or asynchronous, as in discussion boards or e-mail messaging. With DE becoming popular in mainstream education with on-campus students, student-student interaction may also include face-to-face contact. According to social theories of learning and distributed cognition, student-student interaction is desirable both for cognitive purposes and motivational support, and indeed, is at the heart of notions about "constructivist" learning environments in DE. Moreover, properly structured around some key-issues in study materials, student-student interactions may play a vital role in effective learning, as shown in what Mazur (1997) calls "peer-instruction."

Student-teacher interaction traditionally focused on classroom-based dialogue between students and the instructor. According to Moore (1989), during student-teacher interaction, the instructor seeks "to stimulate or at least maintain the student's interest in what is to be taught, to motivate the student to learn, to enhance and maintain the learner's interest, including self-direction and self-motivation" (p. 2). In DE environments, student-instructor interaction may be synchronous through the telephone, videoconferencing, and chats, or asynchronous through correspondence, e-mail, and discussion boards. Face-to-face interaction between student and instructors is also possible in some DE environments and when DE is blended with face-to-face classroom environments. According to Moore (1989) and several other DE theorists (e.g., Anderson, 2003), student-teacher interaction may be directed towards providing motivational and emotional support, outcomes that may register on attitude instruments more than on measures of achievement.

Student-content interaction refers to students interacting with the subject matter under study to construct meaning, relate it to personal knowledge, and apply it to problem solving. Moore (1989) described student-content interaction as "… the process of intellectually interacting with the content that results in changes in the learner's understanding, the learner's perspective, or the cognitive structures of the learner's mind" (p. 2). Presumably, student-content interaction also encompasses the development of mental and physical skills. Student-content interaction may include reading informational texts, using study guides, watching videos, interacting with computer-based multimedia, using simulations, or cognitive support software (e.g., statistical software, graphical organizers, and concept maps), as well as searching for information, completing assignments, and working on projects. All these venues of student-content interaction may be supplemented by specific motivational and guiding support through other forms of interactions, as briefly described above.

Elements of Meta-Analysis Methodology

Meta-analysis is a systematic review technique that was developed by Gene Glass in the 1970's. He first defined it as "analysis of analyses" referring to the examination of a large collection of data presented in different studies with the goal of integrating them to improve the generalizability of the findings (Glass, McGaw, & Smith, 1981).

A *d*-type effect size is a metric that represents the difference between the mean of the experimental group and the control group in standardized units that was first proposed by Glass, McGaw, and Smith (1981). A major advantage of the effect size, as contrasted with a test statistic, is that it is largely independent of sample size. Furthermore, it is possible to aggregate effect sizes and subject them to further statistical analyses in order to explain and understand the variation in a population.

According to Cohen (1988), an effect size in the order of 0.20 is considered to be of small strength, while one in the order of 0.50 is considered medium or moderate strength and finally an effect size in the order of 0.80 is considered to be a large effect size.

Stages in a meta-analysis include: 1) specifying the question, 2) deciding on the inclusion/exclusion criteria, 3) developing and implementing search strategies, 4) reviewing the literature, 5) identifying variables for study, 6) extracting effect sizes, 7) checking homogeneity of effect sizes, 8) running inferential statistics, and 9) interpreting and reporting the findings.

Overview of Bernard et al. (2009) Meta-Analysis

The main purpose of the meta-analysis conducted by Bernard et al. (2009) was to examine evidence of the effects on student achievement of the three types of interaction in DE research studies. The literature search stage of the meta-analysis was aimed at finding as many studies as possible that involved a comparison between two DE treatments. The searches included 20 databases that might contain such studies. In addition to Google searches, we examined bibliographies of previous reviews and meta-analyses and performed branching searches from the references of studies that were located. Finally, manual searches were conducted in 14 professional journals that publish research on DE.

After judging the abstracts of more than 6,000 manuscripts located through searches, 1,034 studies were selected for the full-text retrieval and review. From these, 74 studies were retained for further analyses. Interaction treatments (ITs) were sorted into the three categories based on the type of interaction that was most prevalent. Ten studies contained primarily student-student ITs, 44 contained student-teacher ITs and 20 contained student-content ITs.

A rubric was developed to help determine the treatment and control conditions in these studies. Included studies examined two (or more) DE conditions, making such distinction a challenge. The judgment reviewers exercised had two major elements: a) which condition possessed the greatest potential for active engagement of students, and b) which condition encouraged more interaction. Conditions with greater amounts were designated as the "treatment conditions" and those with lesser amounts were designated as the "control conditions." The decision formed the +/- valence of the effect sizes. Examples of decisions made at this stage of the review are presented in the next section.

Examples of Categorization Decisions

To illustrate how the studies were categorized according to their potential for interaction, three examples have been included here. In each case we describe the two conditions that were compared and explain how the decision was made that designated which was the treatment and which was the control group.

Example 1: Student-Student Interaction Bell, Hudson, and Heinan (2004) provided two methods of online learning to Physician Assistant students in a medical terminology course. Both versions of the course used the same materials, but some students worked independently on the Web (Group B), while others (Group A) received 12 case studies in an online conference setting, which they then discussed through the use of asynchronous messaging. We categorized this comparison as representative of "student-student" interaction, counting the case-based discussion participants (Group A) as the experimental group.

Example 2: Student-Teacher Interaction Rovai (2001) compared fully online instruction in education, delivered via Asynchronous Learning Network (Group A) with blended instruction which included monthly face-to-face meetings with the instructor (Group B). In other words, students in Group B were given extra chances to communicate with their teacher (the means for communication online were equal in both conditions). Naturally, Group B was designated the experimental group for "student–teacher interaction."

Example 3: Student-Content Interaction Bernard and Naidu (1992) offered nursing students two different strategies for studying a course on Community Mental Health, either through creating and exploring concept maps (Group A) or through verifying the knowledge they acquired in post-questioning sessions (Group B). By engaging in constructing concept maps, Group A interacted with the course materials to a greater extent than Group B did and, thus, constituted the experimental condition, whereas students in Group B served as control.

Results of the Meta-Analysis

The results of Bernard et al. (2009) confirmed the importance of each type of interaction on student learning (see Table 1). Each category produced an average effect size that was significantly greater than zero. However, each of the category distributions was significantly heterogeneous, indicating that they contained variation that exceeded what would be expected by random sampling. The results must be interpreted in light of this heterogeneity.

In order to examine more closely what specific conditions were instrumental in fostering students' achievement, studies that resulted in the most positive effect sizes for each type of IT were selected and are described in greater details below.

Effective Experimental Methods Used to Promote Interaction in Distance Education

- Student-teacher interaction

Zhang, K. (2004). Effects of peer-controlled or externally structured and moderated online collaboration on group problem solving processes and related individual attitudes in well-structured and ill-structured small group problem solving in a hybrid course (Doctoral dissertation). Available from ProQuest Dissertations and Theses database. (UMI No. 3141123)

Undergraduate students studied statistics while utilizing a comprehensive web-based courseware (*Cyberstats*). Participants were randomly assigned to experimental and control groups. In both, students worked in self-selected groups of four to complete a team project that included well-structured and ill-structured problems. Higher student-teacher interaction was provided to the participants in the experimental group through teacher structured and moderated online collaboration, while control group members were offered peer controlled online collaboration. Group members in the experimental treatment had access to a private online forum where the instructor provided moderating support as needed after consultation with the researcher. Alternately, group members in the control condition had access to a private online forum where they were the only individuals having access and posting rights. $ES = 1.42$

Huett, J. B. (2006). *The effects of ARCS-based confidence strategies on learner confidence and performance in distance education* (Doctoral dissertation). Available from ProQuest Dissertations and Theses database. (UMI No. 3214480)

Freshmen-level students registered in a computer course that was delivered using *Skill Assessment Manager Software* participated in the study. The participants were randomly assigned to the control and experimental groups. Students in the experimental group received confidence-enhancing emails. An email was sent weekly and examples of issues addressed in the emails included: welcoming notes, reminders about course objectives and deadlines, soliciting participation in blogs and feedback, reassurance for students of continued success, and congratulations for progress. $ES = 1.14$

Annetta, L. A. (2003). A comparative study of three distance education strategies on the learning and attitudes of elementary school teachers participating in a professional development project (Doctoral dissertation). Available from ProQuest Dissertations and Theses database. (UMI No. 3094694)

Elementary teachers from dislocated rural school districts participated in a 40-hour-onsite professional development summer workshop that was

Table 1. Weighted average effect sizes for categories of interaction for achievement.

Categories	K	Mean *ES*	Standard Error	Significant	Heterogeneous
Student-Student	10	0.49	0.08	Yes	Yes
Student-Teacher	44	0.32	0.04	Yes	Yes
Student-Content	20	0.46	0.05	Yes	Yes
Total	74	0.38	0.03	Yes	Yes

followed by "distance education sessions to update and enhance teachers' science knowledge" (p. 47). More than one delivery method was used, and the participants in the experimental group selected for the meta-analysis attended live presentations and discussions with two-way audio video, while the control group was offered scheduled video presentations. Teachers in the experimental group met in media rooms within their rural school district and watched the speaker on a television monitor, in addition to seeing other remote groups when they were talking to the speaker. *ES* = 0.68

- Student-student interaction

Bell, P. D., Hudson, S., & Heinan, M. (2004). Effect of teaching/learning methodology on effectiveness of a Web based medical terminology course. *International Journal of Instructional Technology & Distance Learning*, 1(4), Retrieved from http://www.itdl.org/Journal/Apr_04/article06.htm.

Physician assistant students studied educational terminology with the course being delivered using *Blackboard Learning Content Management System*. In the experimental group, the instructor posted Power Point slides for 12 different case studies along with narration. Case-study questions were also posted and learners needed to respond to at least two case-study questions and reply to at least two of their colleagues' postings. Alternately, students in the control group were offered a tutorial that provided the terminology with the correct pronunciation. *ES* = 0.87

Romanov, K. & Nevgi, A. (2006). Learning outcomes in medical informatics: Comparison of a WebCT course with ordinary web site learning material. *International Journal of Medical Informatics*, 75, 156-162. doi:10.1016/j.ijmedinf.2005.06.004.

Third year medical students studied medical informatics delivered via *WebCT*. Students in both the control and experimental groups had access to the posted course content, however only members of the experimental group were capable of using the virtual learning environment's learning tools. The tools included study material, discussion forums, message system to instructor and other learners, their own notes, and four self-tests. *ES* = 0.37

Brewer, S. A., & Klein, J. D. (2004, October). *Small Group Learning in an Online Asynchronous Environment*. Paper presented at the annual meeting of the Association for Educational Communications and Technology, Chicago, IL. (ERIC Document Reproduction Service No. ED484997).

Undergraduate business students studied business management in small collaborative groups via an asynchronous web-based interactive environment supported by *MS Outlook Express*. The software interface enabled posting messages to the newsgroup visible to the entire class or to the newsgroup dedicated for the small collaborative learning groups. Different treatment conditions were used with two being selected for comparison in the meta-analysis. In the experimental group (role-plus-reward interdependence condition) students were assigned roles in their groups (facilitator, answer drafter, or verifier of the group assignment) with roles being rotated with each unit. Students were awarded bonus points if all group members attained a score of 80% or more. In the control group, (no-structured-interdependence) students were simply asked to discuss the readings and questions in a given assignment and practice to prepare for the test. *ES* = 0.22

- Student-content interaction

Cameron, B. H. (2003). Effectiveness of simulation in a hybrid and online networking course. *Quarterly Review of Distance Education*, 4, 51-55.

Undergraduate students enrolled in an online introductory networking and communications course were taught using two different networks. The experimental group utilized a network simulation package that enabled the "students to build and send data through different network configurations" (p. 52), i.e., interactive in nature. Alternately, the control group utilized Microsoft Visio, which is a "static network diagramming software package" (p. 52), i.e., only featuring illustrations. *ES* = 0.97

Lei, L. W., Winn, W., Scott, C., & Farr, A. (2005). Evaluation of computer-assisted instruction in histology: Effect of interaction on learning outcome. *Anatomical Record Part B, New Anatomist*, 284(1), 28-34. doi:10.1002/ar.b.20062.

First-year medical students were offered a Histology course that utilized different CD-based programs. Each CD was developed by a different faculty member and covered the entire course content. They contained compatible numbers of images, but varied in specific functions (e.g., user manual, digital zoom, interactive [clickable] images and key words and instant feedback in quiz modes). All students had equal access to all three CD's with a different CD being assigned to each treatment group as the primary means of instruction. Students were encouraged, though not required, to use any additional CD and also had on-line access to extra learning resources, including links to relevant references and a Web-based quiz bank. The comparison of the final exam scores included in our meta-analysis was made between students who opted to use the additional CD in their self-learning (experimental group) and those who restricted their study to one recommended CD only (control group). In particular, the experimental group benefited from interactive CD options, clickable images and key words as well as instant feedback in quiz mode. $ES = 0.92$

Bernard, R. M., & Naidu, S. (1992). Post-questioning, concept mapping and feedback: A distance education field experiment. *British Journal of Educational Technology*, 23, 48-60. doi:10.1111/j.1467-8535.1992.tb00309.x

Second year nursing students completed a health course via distance education. All students received a textbook and a study guide. Students in the experimental group received training in concept mapping through a self-study workbook and they had to complete concept maps for different lessons. They received feedback in the form of instructor designed model concept maps. Students in the control group had to complete end of lesson tests to which no feedback was provided. $ES = 0.79$

Discussion

The major conclusion from this review is that designing ITs into DE courses, whether to increase interaction with the material to be learned, with the course instructor, or with student peers impacts positively on student learning. We can only speculate on the internal mental processes that these ITs foster, but we believe that an increase in cognitive engagement and meaningfulness may be the result of different amounts and types of interaction induced through the presence of ITs.

It may be that the presence of ITs functioned in exactly the way they were intended, by activating student interaction, so that our estimates of the effects of interaction are fairly accurate. But just because opportunities for interaction or collaboration were offered to students, does not mean that students availed themselves of them, or if they did interact or collaborate, that they did so effectively. The latter case is the more likely event, so the achievement effects resulting from actual interaction may be underestimated in our review. It is possible that some treatments provided enough tools for interactions of all kinds, but these tools were vastly underused, while in some cases even modest means did not prevent full-scale meaningful interaction or resulted in higher levels of student motivation. For example, Huett (2006) provided students in the experimental group with confidence building tactics and confidence enhancing e-mails in addition to the computer simulations available to both groups. Although the e-mails may have provided minimal interaction with the teacher, they may have had a strong impact on the students' involvement in the course resulting in an ES of 1.14.

Larreamendy-Joerns and Leinhardt (2006) point out another possibility: "Although online learning environments that allow for social interaction constitute a remarkable advance, they should not be construed as inevitably conducive to learning, solely because student-student and student-instructor exchanges take place. Nor should they be understood as obviously consistent with a vision of knowledge as practice or with efforts to nurture communities of practice" (p. 591). According to this, activity itself may not be the active ingredient, particularly when it comes to student-student interaction.

Guided, focused and purposeful activity may be the answer to the question of truly effective interaction. Consider, for example, the Zhang (2004) study where students were involved in teacher structured and moderated online collaboration resulting in the strongest effect size of 1.42. Such purposeful activity may allow learners to set clear goals and develop strategies for achieving those goals, monitor their activity, and reflect on their accomplishments using self, peer and teacher feedback.

Since student-student interaction is largely in the hands of students, it may prove to be the most difficult to design and implement so that it reaches its highest potential. Nonetheless, we believe that when student-student interaction becomes truly collaborative, and learners work together to help each other achieve learning objectives, the benefits of interaction may be major. Webb (1982) found that the most effective learning groups were those where elaborated explanations were present. Using strategies like positive interdependence and individual accountability to create cohesive teams may motivate learners to become purposeful in their activity.

As is quite evident from the examples considered earlier, student-content interaction does not necessarily mean more frequent or more intense access to learning materials, nor does it imply presence of additional sources of information. Rather, increase in effective student-content interactions is associated with what provides cognitive support and promotes deeper understanding of the content. Simulations that allow students to observe consequences of their actions and if necessary, adjust and readjust them as in learning how to design telecommunication networks (Cameron, 2003) or concept maps that help students to examine relations among key constructs to be learned (Bernard & Naidu, 1992) were more effective for learning outcomes than static representations or practice in post-questioning sessions. Moreover, within the included primary studies, whenever meaningful student-student and student-teacher interactions were observed, they were typically structured around some form of interaction with content.

If one considers the main focus of distance education as self paced independent learning, it seems that a designer's first consideration should be to provide strong associations with the content. Although we were not able to examine more refined questions regarding content ITs, it makes sense that those involving more overt student activity would be preferred over more passive forms. However, with the development of technological tools and their impact on accessibility and communication opportunities, a second determination could be made as to the desirability of stronger student-student or student-teacher connections. Since technical capacities for facilitating human-human interaction seem to be constantly improving, it is likely that we can expect noticeable improvements in all forms of interaction that involve collaboration, discussion, and feedback. Strengthening all three forms of interaction seems ideal, but Anderson (2003) points out that this may exceed the availability of human and technical resources needed for cost effectiveness.

Increasing the quantity of interaction may lead to enhanced learning and satisfaction, but increasing the quality of such interactions, especially in terms of cognitive engagement and meaningfulness, is of greater importance. There appears to be at least two ways to foster increases in the quality of interactions: instructional design and software design.

Instructional designs that foster higher quality interactions focus on course features that promote high quality learning activities. For example, cooperative learning structures may help ensure high quality student-to-student interactions by using positive interdependence among the learners as well as individual accountability to ensure cognitive engagement and meaningfulness. This is evident in the Bell, Hudson & Heinan (2004) study, where students worked collaboratively on case studies to achieve common goals using the Blackboard Online Learning Management System. By incorporating such activities into the course design, the designer offers the students the chance to make the best out of communication tools that support collaborative learning while benefiting from the flexibility of DE. Similarly, designing effective course strategies for problem-based learning and guided-discovery forms of DE may promote the quality of student-content interactions. Finally, the quality of student-student-teacher interactions may be increased by ensuring that students focus on comprehension and higher order thinking skills rather than activities that deal with lower-level factual information, procedural details of a course, or assessment issues.

It is arguable that the range of established tools currently available to educators, such as Learning Management Systems (LMS) technologies, has yet to be developed sufficiently or examined systematically by the community of DE developers/researchers for their capacity to activate interactive behavior. We encourage more and better-quality research along these lines, as well as increased research activity in elementary and secondary school applications of DE. From a practical point of view, we suggest that greater attention be given to course design to ensure that students are provided with adequate opportunities for interaction with teachers, peers and content.

Authors' Note: This study was supported by grants from the Social Sciences and Humanities Research Council of Canada and the *Fonds québécois de la recherche sur la société et la culture* to Bernard and Abrami. The authors express appreciation to Anne Wade, Dr. Mike Surkes and Edward Clement Bethel for their contributions to the research and *Review of Educational Research* article upon which this chapter is based. Thanks to David Pickup for help with the manuscript. Contact: Dr. Rana Tamim, Hamdan Bin Mohammed e-University, P.O. Box 71400, Dubai, UAE. E-mail: r.tamim@hbmeu.ac.ae.

References

(References marked with an * are studies from the meta-analysis)

Anderson, T. (2003). Getting the mix right again: An updated and theoretical rationale for interaction. *International Review of Research in Open and Distance Learning*. 4(2), 9-14. Retrieved from http://www.irrodl.org/index.php/irrodl/article/view/148/709

Bernard, R. M., Abrami, P. C., Wade, A., Borokhovski, E., Tamim, R., Surkes, M., & Bethel, E.C. (2009). A meta-analysis of three interaction treatments in distance education. *Review of Educational Research, 79*, 1243-1289.

Bernard, R. M., & Naidu, S. (1992). Post-questioning, concept mapping and feedback: A distance education field experiment. *British Journal of Educational Technology, 23*, 48-60. doi:10.1111/j.1467-8535.1992.tb00309.x

Cohen, J. (1988). Statistical power analysis for the behavioral sciences (2nd ed.). Hillsdale, NJ: Erlbaum.

Daniel, J., & Marquis, C. (1979). Interaction and independence: Getting the mixture right. *Teaching at a Distance, 15,* 25-44.

Garrison, D. R., & Shale, D. (1990). A new framework and perspective. In D. R. Garrison and D. Shale (Eds.), *Education at a distance: From issues to practice* (pp. 123-133). Malabar, FL: Krieger.

Gilbert, L., & Moore, D. R. (1989). Building interactivity in web-courses: Tools for social and instructional interaction. *Educational Technology, 38*(3), 29-35.

Glass, G. V., McGaw, B., & Smith, M. L. (1981). *Meta-analysis in social research.* Beverly Hills, CA: Sage.

Holden, J.T., & Westfall, P. J.-L. (2006). *An instructional media selection guide for distance learning.* Boston, MA: United States Distance Learning Association.

*Huett, J. B. (2006). *The effects of ARCS-based confidence strategies on learner confidence and performance in distance education* (Doctoral dissertation). Available from ProQuest Dissertations and Theses database. (UMI No. 3214480)

Larreamendy-Joerns, J., & Leinhardt, G. (2006). Going the distance with online education. *Review of Educational Research, 76,* 567-605. doi:10.3102/00346543076004567

Mazur, E. (1997). *Peer instruction: A user's manual.* Upper Saddle River, NJ: Prentice Hall.

Moore, M. G. (1989). Three types of interaction. *American Journal of Distance Education, 3*(2), 1-7. doi:10.1080/08923648909526659

*Rovai, A. P. (2001). Classroom community at a distance: A comparative analysis of two ALN-based university programs. *Internet and Higher Education, 4,* 105-118. doi:10.1016/S1096-7516(01)00053-7

Thurmond, V. A. & Wambach, K. (2004). Understanding interactions in distance education: A review of the literature. *International Journal of Instructional Technology and Distance Learning, 1*(1). Retrieved from http://itdl.org/journal/Jan_04/article02.htm

Wagner, E. D. (1994). In support of a functional definition of interaction. *American Journal of Distance Education, 8*(2), 6-29. doi:10.1080/08923649409526852

Webb, N. M. (1982). Student interaction and learning in small groups. *Review of Educational Research, 52,* 421-445. doi:10.3102/00346543052003421

Intellectual Exploration Together

Donald Bligh

The Problem

For over 30 years research has shown the lonely life of graduate students. They are not academic staff. They are somewhere in between undergraduates and professors, on their own. Maybe they meet their supervisor once a week, but what they really need is intellectual stimulus and friends to bounce off half-formed ideas without fear of being judged. This need for stimulus and social support could be true of anyone beginning a project, either graduate student or junior or senior faculty.

Fewer social contacts and fear of judgement by superiors are only two factors inadvertently favouring secrecy. "I don't want someone else to pinch my research idea. I'll keep quiet about it until it's fully formed. Besides my field of investigation is very specialised. Other people I meet don't know enough about my topic to offer sensible comments."

The Paucity of Intellectual Cross-Fertilization at the Planning Stage

I think the last point is a mistake. Intellectuals from totally different disciplines can sometimes comment with insight from a different perspective in a revealing way. There can be analogies between very disparate fields. Moreover, it may need only one sharp observation or suggested method amongst 100 pieces of verbal garbage to make all the difference between a pedestrian and an innovative piece of research, development or scholarship.

And isn't that partly what universities are for? Aren't they supposed to be places where cross-fertilization of ideas can take place precisely because they contain people from varied intellectual backgrounds? To my observation that is not what happens. Universities have long ceased to function in that way because they have gotten bigger, and their departments have gotten bigger. They operate in separate buildings. In the natural course of events what is there to persuade Professor X to visit Y's departmental building to discuss Y's specialism? He will feel like an intruder, not a fellow seeker after the truth. And there are other pressures to stick in your own small group and write your next publication. Physical and organic chemists don't talk to each other. Human geographers are seen as having little in common with the geomorphologists. And none of these people think the Shakespearian specialist in the English Department can contribute anything to their scientific research. Where are today's polymaths comparable with those of yester-years? Where are today's Albert Schweitzers, Maynard Keynes, Bertrand Russells and JBS Haldanes? In those days the Senior Common Room was less crowded and brought together people across the departments so that each mind was more likely to be illuminated by someone from another field. And there was time to talk.

The Curious Delay in Knowledge Integration

There always was a delay in cross-fertilisation and application of new ideas. Curiously it was often 40-60 years. In philosophy, Boolean logic (1845) was "discovered" by Russell and Whitehead (1905) and applied in earnest only in the second half of the 20th Century. R. A. Fisher's developments in statistics in the 1920s did not fully take off in the social sciences until the 1960s. The fruits of Crick and Watson (1953) only ripened in the late 1990s. Quicker applications, such as those from the revolutions in physics in the first quarter of the 20th Century, chiefly occur under the urgency of war or threatened wars.

Why 40-60 years? I could understand if it was one generation not two. The delays are often more than the length of a career. Cross-fertilisation seems slow. Can't we create the circumstances that foster it?

A Solution

The Methods of Intellectual Exploration Together

Discussion is the method to foster the development of ideas and traditionally the way it is used in the class is as follows. The professor is an expert in his field and because of his expertise it is usually expected that he will manage the discussion. He gives his students carefully designed tasks to discuss in groups so they learn to think in ways fitting his expertise. The professor has given them all the facts he sees as relevant to achieve this. He selects students with the right backgrounds and abilities to address issues in his field. He knows when he has succeeded because they will reach the same answers he does. He sees it as a matter of developing the professional's way of thinking about issues in his discipline and getting feedback. He tells them when they get the right answer: They get high grades. Encouraged by their sense of achievement, students give him high ratings and he knows he is a successful teacher.

NO!! Intellectual Exploration Together (IET) turns all that on its head. The person who manages an IET and introduces the topic from the front of the class is not usually a professor or an expert, but a humble seeker after the truth, a novice called the "seeker." He may be a student, a research postgraduate, or anyone contemplating an investigation, some research, or an exploration of an issue. And of course that could be a professor. He could be chairman of a Government enquiry. There could be a duo of seekers agreeing or disagreeing. The essential point is that the seeker, whoever he or she may be, is seeking ideas, suggestions, viewpoints and even advice from friends, colleagues or others from a wide range of disciplines.

The people sitting in the classroom are professors and other recognised experts in their respective fields, but not necessarily in the field where the seeker works. These experts and the seeker taken together are called "explorers" They don't necessarily know any relevant facts about the issue introduced by the seeker, but they have learned to think in ways applicable to their particular expertise. They know about, and practise, intellectual methods appropriate to their field. For example, they might think of analogies from their fields that might be applied to the issues the seeker has placed before them.

Here's the paradox. It is the seeker who manages the event because he is ignorant. He doesn't fully understand the issue he is raising and seeks the advice of his audience. He does not know how to start his research and is open to ideas. It is his openness that manages his own learning. The seeker can explain the faltering journey he has travelled so far and possibly some of the routes so far rejected or now being considered. The job of those who attend (the explorers) will be to explore possible ways forward with, and for, the seeker. The seeker says, *I've been exploring this question. We know XYZ, but what we don't know is this and that, and for various reasons it would be good if we did. These are the lines of enquiry I've travelled along. This is how far I've got. What's good about the journey I've travelled so far? What are its limitations? Have you other suggestions? Can you help me find the way forward? How else could this question be approached?* Another similar approach is, T*his is what we know about this subject so far. What are the next questions we ought to be asking? They could be along this or that line of thinking. We could use this method or that. What do you see as the merits and demerits of each?* Answering questions of this kind are what Intellectual Exploration Togethers are all about. Answers broaden the seeker's outlook and suggest a way forward. They can save months of work, often futile work. IETs are particularly appropriate for establishing new disciplines. For example, consider the experts needed to establish the physiology of social work, the artificial intelligence of literary analysis, and swarm communication technology.

The seeker's problem may be that he does not know how to conceive the issue, or perhaps any method of thinking about it. Clarifying a research problem is often the most difficult and significant step in research. Researchers constantly have to redefine their problems as they find new perspectives. When you change your perspective, to some extent, work up to that point is wasted. Seekers may feel angry and frustrated that they've gone back to the beginning again. IETs attempt to short circuit these circular journeys.

Because of his limited understanding the seeker's introduction is often extremely vague and hesitant and the topic impossibly wide. We have all been there! Other explorers need patience, empathy and constructive ways to seek clarification. Because his problem may be unclear, the seeker does not know what facts he should give his class full of professors and other experts or what might be relevant.

The job of the seeker is to manage the IET. That may be a challenge; but it is his event. The seeker may use any method he wishes, though personally I cannot see how an Exploration can elicit the full potential of every explorer if small group discussions, such as buzz groups, horseshoe groups, cross over groups, brainstorming, or case study and so on, are not used (Bligh, 2000).

What is an Intellectual Exploration Together?

An IET is an occasion at which up to 40 people work hard exploring ways together to help another person with care and empathy, yet also seek solutions to problems with intellectual rigour.

The skill lies in task design and in the management of discussion membership and methods. Instead of the manager having knowledge he wants others to learn; it is he who is saying "Help me learn." That's why all the usual language of teaching methods is inappropriate. It is not a seminar or a tutorial. It is not cooperative learning; still less is it a lecture. It is not even a "conference" in the way those are usually organised. Presentations by the seeker should be kept to an absolute minimum.

His aim is to elicit from the professors and experts the widest variety of possible approaches to the broad issue he has raised. They will conceive of his problem in a multitude of (possibly incompatible) ways. There are no right answers and no one way of thinking. It is a process of discovering options and deciding the best way forward. Far from being encouraged by common agreement, all involved may go through periods of utter frustration and may feel very dissatisfied with the process. That is what real problem solving is like. It is the sweat and agony of creativity, but worth it in the end, a common experience of researchers.

Intellectual Exploration Togethers should be occasions of intellectual excitement. The process involves a risk for the seeker as manager, because he can't know what lines of investigation the explorers will produce and he must be open-minded to let the explorers lead along chains of reasoning wholly unfamiliar to him. He may then need to take up their suggestions and redirect discussions towards topics he had not dreamt of before. That is difficult. He must also find a way of collecting and recording all the suggestions he manages to elicit.

IETs commonly go through the following sequence: (1) brief introduction of puzzlement; (2) elicitation of ideas or options in small groups, followed by a break; (3) pooling of ideas; (4) using cross over groups to sift the ideas, possibly to form recommendations; and (5) drawing conclusions and thanks. This is similar in some ways to a brainstorming sequence because creativity is what is required, but there is none of the pressure or allocation of roles that traditional brainstorming involves. Nonetheless, the seeker should organise the tasks with such intensity that the explorers will leave the IET mentally exhausted, yet exhilarated that they have achieved something, that they helped someone else, and, yes, that they too have learned something in a field not their own.

Groups are more spontaneous, creative and humorous if they are face-to-face. But there is no reason, in principle, why the means of communication cannot be by email, teleconferencing or other distance methods. Indeed the advantage of distance methods is that group membership can be the most acknowledged intellects from all over the world simultaneously exploring together.

IETs are not an everyday method. What can be prepared should be. An event has to be sold. Experience suggests that participants can initially be sceptical, but are enthusiastic afterwards.

IET is Fundamental to the Purpose and Process of a University

IET rediscovers part of what early universities used to be, a place where novices and experts are explorers together in a joint enterprise seeking the truth. The central purpose of higher education is criticism: favourable, constructive, and unfavourable. Accepting, and working upon, criticism is of the essence. It is fundamental to intellectual rigour. Recognition and recording of what we don't know and cannot know is also part of the process.

As an aside, I might say I have always thought that academic journals should have a section that does this. Instead of people building a reputation only by writing about what they have learned and achieved, journals should also have sections or editorials pointing out what we don't know, but perhaps could know, how we might find out, and how the answer would fit into what we know now. We need a new Encyclopaedia of Ignorance.

First example: Educational neuroscience

Let's now look at a couple of examples of IETs. In the first, the seeker introduces her problem as follows: *Neuroscience is advancing rapidly using computerised tomography (CT scans), magnetic resonance imaging (MRI) and functional MRI (fMRI). At first, such technological innovations can only be afforded and applied by the few (e.g., the history of photography). They then become cheaper, more accurate, detailed, reliable, laser guided and widely available. Imagine availability moves down the social strata until every teacher can make diagnoses of where and why each child has individual weaknesses and abilities in particular tasks. Nerve pathways for every task can be intimately studied. Teaching becomes a branch of neuroscience therapy. Scientific certainties encroach upon yet another area that was once an art and a field of speculation for philosophers. In your groups list the key issues that arise.*

In addition to neuroscientists, explorers may include experts in scientific determinism, ethics, politics, sociology, the literature on indoctrination, the history of science, the jurisprudence of civil and criminal law, human rights and so on. The groups record their concerns and perspectives and come together to share them before lunch.

After lunch, groups are reconstituted by the crossover method and are asked to prioritise the issues and describe programmes by which each might be studied. Again these proposals are shared between groups in a plenary session and each is subjected to close, yet supportive critical scrutiny. The seeker acts as chairperson and may record the discussion for more detailed study later because the intellectual level may be higher than she is used to. In addition to severe critical appraisals, discussions include much laughter, ridicule, excitement and enjoyment.

The issues are serious and can be ground breaking. As in this example, IETs can be intended not merely to add some new knowledge, but to take a discipline into totally new areas of study such that the discipline is changed, never to be the same again. Very likely the chief benefits of IETs relate to spin-off issues unrelated to the problem originally raised by the seeker. Professors amongst the explorers may have explored so widely that they have new insights that prove useful on a later unforeseen occasion.

Notice that an IET is particularly useful for imaginative, speculative and creative issues. It can be used by governments to tackle some of the big issues of the day, such as what to do about climate change. In contrast, although originally designed to help new postgraduate researchers, IETs can be used in undergraduate classes to free up rigid thinking by demanding classmates' ideas from outside the usual box.

Second example: The concept and practice of Intellectual Leadership

The Society for Research into Higher Education (SRHE) is funded* to promote IETs, particularly those that might invent and establish totally new areas of human knowledge and enquiry. SRHE, though mostly active in UK, has an international membership, publishes books, journals, abstracts of research, organises conferences and so on. SRHE may choose any topic for exploration and invite anyone to manage it on the basis of her intellectual rigour. They, or the seeker, may choose to invite specific explorers or leave it open for anyone to apply. They have chosen to explore, in 2010, the concept and practice of Intellectual Leadership

---

* Footnote: The Donald Bligh Fund administered by SRHE was established with £50,000 from the author to use IETs to develop new areas of knowledge.

mainly by reference to the individual academic rather than his institution. Professor Bruce Macfarlane, was the principal seeker. He wrote [Explorations]:

> ...will be achieved firstly by commissioning short opinion pieces or triggers (300 – 500 words) from leading thinkers and writers in the world of higher education and beyond. The second part of the event will deploy world café, a participative process which enables participants to identify and then offer to host conversations, ... with participants recording their thoughts using paper tablecloths and with the opportunity to move between tables–and hence conversations. Explorers will write a short reflective piece that they will share in the final plenary.

Part of the challenge lies in reconciling the power of leadership with academic freedom for the intellect. The concept of Intellectual Leadership seems to contain a contradiction. A bridge can be made where there is intellectual consent, but what if there is not? Is leadership the art of building consent? Is consent enough, or is acceptance necessary? Acceptance can be tacit or a mental act. How much of the latter is required for agreement? And what does Intellectual Leadership at the individual level require?

Some of these conceptual distinctions are subtle and have to be teased out. For language to communicate there needs to be some consensus about them. That requires a group activity. IETs provide a forum to do so. There is an analogy with judgement in a Supreme Court. The conflict is presented by lawyers from two sides who are, in effect, humble seekers or suppliants. A group of judges with acknowledged wisdom are experts who explore ramifications of the case to seek consensus through discussion. Theirs is an Intellectual Exploration Together.

Conclusion

A major function of a university is to seek new knowledge. So isn't it curious that nearly all the educational literature on small groups, even by the authors in this book, is about teaching old knowledge? It's almost as if there is an assumption that research is only done by individuals without consulting a collection of known experts. Yes, of course established research teams meet together, but we don't seem to have an established procedure for the humble seeker when she first considers a topic, to meet with experts to clarify her problem and procedure. Nor do we have sufficient regular mechanisms in which experts from widely disparate fields seriously turn their gifted insights towards unfamiliar problems. That is an inefficient practice with wasted opportunities. IETs can remedy this deficiency and foster an academic community.

References

Bligh, D. (2000) What's the Point in Discussion? Intellect Books Bristol, UK

Boole, G. (1848) The Calculus of logic, Cambridge and Dublin Mathematical Journal Vol. III (1848), pp. 183-98.

Macfarlane, B. (2009) Proposal for an intellectual exploration (Donald Bligh Fund), Research and Development Committee of the Society for Research into Higher Education, London.

Watson, J. D., & Crick F. H. C. (1953) A Structure for Deoxyribose Nucleic Acid, Nature vol 171, pp737-738

Whitehead, A. N., & Russell, B. A. W. (1910) Principia Mathematica, 3 vols, CambridgeUniversity Press.

www.ingramcontent.com/pod-product-compliance
Lightning Source LLC
Chambersburg PA
CBHW080546170426
43195CB00016B/2691